Princely Treasures

Princely Treasures

Archduke Géza von Habsburg

Thames and Hudson

First published in Great Britain in 1997
by Thames and Hudson Ltd, London

British Library Cataloguing-in-Publication Data

A catalogue record for this book is available
from the British Library

ISBN 0-500-01809-X

Printed in Italy

CONTENTS

Foreword
and Acknowledgments

Beginning with their appearance on Planet Earth some sixty thousand years ago, human beings have always evinced a spiritual and intellectual need to express themselves by one means or another. And it was from this urge towards self-expression that collecting evolved as an act of connoisseurship. For countless millennia, accumulating amounted to little more than hunting, gathering, and hoarding. Only in Greek and Roman times did aesthetics come into play and transform such activities into something beyond mere necessity. Moreover, it was not until the Late Middle Ages that Europe saw the birth of the true-blood, passionate collector of objects deemed valuable by reason of their form, their materials, and/or their content.

The nomadic hunter and his successor, the sedentary cultivator, painted images on walls, gathered pebbles, and engraved animal bones. The urban dweller, or early historic Man, whose existence dates from the 4th millennium BC, discovered precious metals in the form of alluvial gold and silver, which the clever learned to melt, cast, raise, or forge into beautiful adornments and vessels. Rulers prized such artifacts and wanted to be buried with them, as in the case of the Sumerian Queen Pu-Abi, whose burial chamber at the Royal Cemetery of Ur dates from c. 2600 BC. Far more famous is the tomb of Tutankhamum (c. 1350 BC), the boy-pharaoh of Egypt's 18th Dynasty, whose burial site was discovered almost intact as recently as 1922. It contained some of the most resplendent goldwork ever seen, confirming that by this time items fashioned of precious metals, often embellished with enamel and inset gems, had become primary signs of sovereign status within the realm.

Museums appear to have been first organized in Europe during the 6th century BC, when they functioned as temple treasuries. According to Pausanias, the Greek traveler/geographer of the 2nd-century AD, these sacred repositories held vast numbers of votive offerings in gold and silver, which made them in some sense banks as well as museums. The same writer also cites the *Pinakotheke*, a public painting gallery or hall built alongside the Propylaea, the monumental entry gate at the western end of the Acropolis overlooking Athens.

Private collections are known to have existed not long thereafter, assembled, for example, by the Kings of Pergamon in Asia Minor as well as by the Ptolemaic pharaohs of Egypt. Furthermore, they included both sculpture and painting. At Alexandria, the capital of Egypt founded by Alexander the Great in 332 BC, the building within the palace complex that housed Alexander's library was designated *Museion*, a term which came to mean "place of learning." By the 1st century BC, republican Rome had its first library, thanks to Gaius Asinius Pollio, a friend of the poet Virgil and a discerning collector who built the venue. Pollio is also credited with having been the first private collector to make his holdings accessible to the general public.

Great quantities of treasure excavated in former Roman provinces – at Kaiseraugst near Basel as well as at Hildesheim in Saxony – attest to the exceptionally high quality of the plate made during the hegemony of Imperial Rome. In Roman culture silver plate was primarily functional, serving as tableware, albeit tableware which, in the event of need, could be readily converted into bullion or cash reserves. And the tradition would prevail until the Late Middle Ages.

Meanwhile, precious metals played another role, which was to decorate places of worship. After 313 AD, when the Emperor Constantine declared Christianity a lawful religion throughout the Roman world, the officially favored churches would be richly endowed with gold and silver, as they were to be again under the Byzantine Emperor Justinian (527-565). Such wealth arrived primarily in the form of lavish revetments and major donations. For this kind of treasure, the sanctuary in Hagia Sophia, the great cathedral of Constantinople, surpassed anything to be found elsewhere in the world. As for the host city, the capital of the Eastern or Byzantine Empire founded by Constantine himself, it possessed what was surely the largest open-air sculpture museum ever known. Thereafter, until the end of the Middle Ages, church treasuries, containing both secular and religious artifacts, would reflect the growing temporal power of the Roman Catholic Church. The trend can be traced through Charlemagne's Palatine Chapel at Aachen (792-805) and the Ottonian Church of Saint Michael at Hildesheim (1001-1033).

Medieval treasuries, such as those at Abbot Suger's Saint-Denis northeast of Paris and at Saint-Maurice d'Agaune in the Swiss Valais, were renowned for their rare Roman vessels, venerable relics dating from the Age of Augustus and later encrusted with semiprecious stones. The Tesoro di San Marco in Venice, a storehouse of both Oriental and Western objects, boasted many remarkable antiquities among the rich booty taken in 1204 during the notorious Crusader sack of Constantinople. On high feast days the Serenissima paraded its liturgical treasures in an eye-popping display of wealth and power. Churches also became safe havens for such "magical" or "mysterious" curiosities as ivory tusks, whale skeletons, stuffed reptiles, meteors, and dinosaur bones, these last once thought to be the bones of human giants.

East and West alike, princes considered it imperative that they have jewels, gold, and silver as part of their courtly trappings. The nobility, from the very beginning of feudalism, felt compelled to wear gems, own precious objects, and live surrounded by conspicuous opulence. A show of fine plate and glittering jewels constituted the obligatory proof of a grandee's high standing in the world. To aid in the display there was the *credenza* – a "cupboard of state" – set up in a great dining hall. Tudor England had the Royal Jewel House, and when Henry VIII and Elizabeth I raided its store of plate for New Year presents they were following the ancient custom of *largitio*, inherited from late Roman times when the Emperors offered commemorative gold and/or silver dishes to their loyal field commanders. Such gifts clearly bore political freight, serving to bind giver and receiver together in a mutually beneficial relationship.

The earliest collections, as contemporary inventories reveal, were nothing more than the reigning prince's *guardaroba* or personal belongings. No evidence earlier than the second half of the 14th century has emerged to suggest that exceptional objects were acquired for their own sake. Then around the turn of the 15th century, first in France and soon afterwards in Italy, *études*, *cabinets*, and *studioli* began to appear in palaces, built hard by the seigniorial living quarters. Here the great lord kept prized books and objets d'art for his personal enjoyment or the pleasure of a small circle of initiates. Shortly after 1500 the Medici in Florence revived the ancient vision of a universal, all-encompassing collection, derived from Pliny's classification in *Historia Naturalis*. Traveling Humanists exported it across the Alps, as did the Medici themselves in the course of their numerous dynastic marriages into the Valois and Habsburg families. By the end of the 16th century, *Kunstkammer* collections, the Northern equivalent of the universal museum, had come into being at virtually every major princely court in Austria, Germany, and Scandinavia. Initially sources of delight for a new, exclusive class of collectors, these private museums would soon become fundamental programs for ratifying the fame and glory of the ruling house. Gradually, however, princely collectors acknowledged the interests of scholars and travelers, a step in the process of transforming *Kunstkammern* into the first public museums.

The German word *Kunstkammer*, which means "Art Cabinet," or the earlier *Kunst- und Wunderkammer* ("Cabinet of Art and Curiosities"), both of which originated in the 16th century, stood for a highly miscellaneous kind of collection, encompassing virtuoso objets d'art; oddities of nature enshrined in gold mounts; magnificent artifacts of carved hardstone set upon silver-gilt supports; flamboyant ornaments cast in silver or gold *pièces d'apparat* made for display on dressers; complicated scientific instruments of surprising precision, among them clocks, armillary spheres, and celestial globes; and amusing as well as intricate automata designed to provide raucous fun at gargantuan, bibulous meals. Meanwhile, at the same time that such marvels of craftsmanship were given pride of place in many a princely Kunstkammer, others no less captivating would be diverted to the *Schatzkammer*, an updated version of the medieval treasury which originally included secular as well as sacred works of art. During the Renaissance the Schatzkammer served as a storehouse of valuables, such as family and crown jewels, bullion and important documents. In Munich and Dresden, for example, Schatzkammer and Kunstkammer co-existed, making it natural for their names, at times, to be used interchangeably. Moreover, objects could migrate from one collection to the other, according to the whim of the prince, in defiance of whatever logic might have dictated their classification in one category or another. The high value placed upon some cameos and hardstone vases, whether antique or modern, may also have justified placing certain Kunstkammer items in the more secure environment of a Schatzkammer. As this would suggest, collectibles of great worth were often deemed the legitimate equivalents of gold and silver bullion. The scheme of values explains as well the ease with which monarchs could raise money by pawning their Kunstkammer holdings.

In the present book, therefore, the primary focus will be on the Kunstkammer, but not to the exclusion of Schatzkammer objects, without which the story would be incomplete. Still, we have generally avoided crown jewels and articles of personal adornment in favor of objects of virtue, an old English term meaning the fruits of great virtuosity or excellence. Meanwhile, we have included portraits, paintings, maps, and exteriors as well as interiors in order to create an overall cultural context for the principal subject.

Absolutely central to our story is the generation of collectors who emerged within the Holy Roman Empire between 1560 and 1620, involving senior members of the Habsburg, Wittelsbach, and Wettin families. The precedent, however, had been set by the Valois in France and the Medici in Florence. In their wake came virtually every prince and princeling in Renaissance Europe, vastly swelling the ranks of Kunstkammer collectors, all of whom wanted to own rock-crystal vases engraved in Milan, *pietre dure* works from Florence, bronze figurines by Giambologna and Adriaen de Vries, and elaborate silver pieces fashioned by the goldsmith workshops of Nuremberg and Augsburg. To cover every Kunstkammer collection of the period would be redundant as well as impossible within the confines of a single volume. Notwithstanding, we are sad to have omitted, among others, the Princes of Liechtenstein, the Margraves of Baden, the Dukes of Holstein-Gottorp, and the Dukes of Wurttemberg, not to mention Isabella d'Este and the splendors of her collection in Mantua.

The selective nature of *Princely Treasures* coincides with the book's purpose, which is to introduce a fascinating but little known cultural phenomenon to a wide, international public for the first time. The Kunstkammer collections explored here have been published only in scholarly journals or in a handful of monographs and catalogues, virtually all in languages other than English. One major exception is *The Origin of the Museums* (Clarendon Press, Oxford, 1985) edited by Oliver Impey and Arthur MacGregor, who thus provided a veritable bible for everyone drawn to the "Cabinet of Curiosities in Sixteenth- and Seventeenth-Century Europe." The numerous contributors to this seminal publication laid the groundwork for the study of almost all the premier collections assembled during the Renaissance. The book became an indispensable source for *Princely Treasures*, whose author happily acknowledges a major debt.

Most students of the fine and applied arts know *Kunst- und Wunderkammern der Spätrenaissance* written by the great Viennese art historian Julius von Schlosser and first published in 1908 by Klinkhardt and Biermann, Leipzig. Given the early date of this publication, it is understandable that many of the opinions expressed therein have been revised. Today, the best illustrated German-language publication on our subject is Elisabeth Scheicher's *Die Kunst- und Wunderkammern der Habsburger* (Molden Edition, Vienna, Munich, and Zurich, 1979), a book that reaches far beyond the limits implied by its title. Here, the in-depth analysis of Archduke Ferdinand's collections at Schloss Ambras, which Frau Scheicher curated, remains exemplary.

Princely Treasures, the present contribution to the subject, has been fermenting in the author's mind for many decades, and is now made possible, first of all, by the generous collegial help offered over the years by the directors, curators, and staff at the various Kunstkammer collections: Dr. Manfred Leithe-Jasper, Dr. Rudolf Distelberger, and Frau Ilse Wegscheider, Kunsthistorisches Museum, Vienna; Frau Elisabeth Scheicher and Dr. Auer, Schloss Ambras, Innsbruck; Dr. Eliska Fucikova, Hradschin Castle Museum, Prague; Dr. Reinhold Baumstark and Dr. Lorenz Seelig, Bayerisches Nationalmuseum, Munich; Dr. Dirk Syndram and Herr Albero Bubach, Grünes Gewölbe, Dresden; M. Daniel Alcouffe, Louvre, Paris; Dr. Mogens Bencard, Chronological Collection of the Kings of Denmark, Schloss Rosenborg, Copenhagen; and Dr. Mikail B. Piotrovsky and Mr. Oleg Neverov, State Hermitage Museum, St. Petersburg.

Last, but not least, the author wishes to thank Alexis Gregory, publisher of The Vendome Press, whose shared enthusiasm for collecting Kunstkammer objects and whose vision brought about the birth of *Princely Treasures*. Gratitude is also owing to Daniel Wheeler, Vendome editor-in-chief, who contributed well beyond the call of duty, helping to shape the background material with his vast knowledge of art and history. Finally, I offer a special tribute to my wife Elizabeth, who patiently read and corrected the first typescript draft of each chapter, even while assuming the new responsibilities of being mother to our first daughter Isabella.

GÉZA VON HABSBURG
April 1997

The Valois

After the collapse of the Roman Empire, collectors in the true sense of the word did not re-emerge in Europe until the evolution of nation states and the revival of urban life in the 13th century. Nowhere did this medieval renaissance flower earlier or more abundantly than in France, thanks to the ability of its Capetian monarchs to assert the authority of the crown and thus diminish the warring rivalries of local rule, whether exercised by feudal barons or by wealthy land-owning abbeys. As centralized governments took form, drawing their support from the broad base of national communities, the cities found in the very complexity of social elements allied with them the means to hold their own with both kings and castle lords. In the free atmosphere of towns, the guilds, representing the interests of artisans with like skills, and the middle class, composed of such professionals as doctors, lawyers, and teachers, as well as merchants and craftsmen, joined in an interplay of forces whose dynamic balance yielded profit and protection for people of every condition. Symptomatic of what they could produce were the great Gothic cathedrals, communal efforts in which builders, working with the modular blocks and masses of Romanesque architecture, attained such lightness and clarity, such soaring, harmonious spaces that the only suitable analogy lies in the realm of spiritual exaltation (fig. 2). Gothic was, quite simply, the style of the whole new urbanized realm, the architecture of universities, law courts, and palaces as well as the formal language of chapels and cathedrals.[1] The Romanesque, on the other hand, with its massive walls, low vaults, and few windows, had been the architecture of rural abbeys, monastic enclosures sealed to the violent world outside for the sake of a more vital, serene life within.

Paris had been a capital since Roman times, but the process whereby the tiny settlement would become the nerve center of a major kingdom did not begin in earnest until Philip II (Philippe-Auguste; 1180-1223) had secured most of the territory known as France. With this, he established a court in Paris,

saw the completion of Notre-Dame, paved the narrow, winding streets, built a defensive wall around the entire community (1180-1210), and reinforced it with a stout bastion called the Louvre, located on the right bank of the Seine. With the establishment of the Sorbonne in 1253, Paris could also boast the oldest university north of the Alps, making it an intellectual capital as well as a great seat of political power.

Until the reign of Charles V (1337-1380), however, French monarchs, including Saint Louis (Louis IX; 1214-1270), lived in the royal palace on the île de la Cité near Notre-Dame. Meanwhile, the Louvre served primarily as a safe haven for the royal treasury and a prison for distinguished captives, such as Ferdinand of Portugal, Count of Flanders, defeated at the decisive Battle of Bovines in 1214. The Hundred Years War had broken out in 1337, forcing the French monarchs to defend themselves against the dynastic claims of their English cousins. In 1357, moreover, a citizens' revolt erupted in Paris during the captivity of Jean le Bon in England, forcing the Dauphin Charles to witness the execution of his own marshals in front of the old royal palace. To gain a secure home for himself, as well as a place from which the rebellious populace could be held under military control, Charles, who succeeded to the throne in 1364, commissioned his master mason, Raymond du Temple, to transform the Louvre into a sumptuous royal residence. This meant the installation of new lodgings, grandiose reception halls, large windows, a chapel, pleasure gardens along the river, and even a menagerie. A man of letters, as well as a patron of art and architecture, Charles also had the northwest tower, originally a falconry, converted into the Library Tower, where he housed part of the large royal collection of manuscripts,[2] transferred there from Saint Louis's favorite residence, the Château de Vincennes northeast of Paris. As portrayed in one of the most famous manuscripts of the Middle Ages, the *Très Riches Heures du Duc de Berry*, Charles V's Louvre was a masterpiece of Gothic architecture – white, bristling with crenellations, towers, turrets, and crockets, weathercocks

2

1. Goldene Rössl von Altötting, *1404 (Paris). Detail of fig. 4.*

2. Sainte-Chapelle, Paris, 1241-1248. *Built at the behest of Saint Louis (Louis IX), the Sainte-Chapelle represents the Gothic style in its purest, most rayonnant form. Here, architecture becomes a veritable cage of brilliant stained-glass panels, its slender, attenuated members, soaring ogives, and elegant traceries analogous to the effects achieved by contemporary jewelers and goldsmiths of the Late Middle Ages. The Saint-Chapelle served as a royal chapel but also as a monumental reliquary for the Crown of Thorns brought from the Holy Land at the end of the Seventh Crusade.*

3

and banners – its details as filigreed as the work of goldsmiths (fig. 3). The latter, by this time, had become a significant presence in Paris,[3] especially since 1254 when Saint Louis returned from the Seventh Crusade laden with holy relics. Among these were the Crown of Thorns and fragments of the True Cross, treasures that had to be mounted in precious settings for display in the Saint-Chapelle, itself a glittering reliquary erected on the scale of a radiant Gothic chapel (fig. 2).

Charles formed not only a great library but also a collection of art works, known from an inventory drawn up in 1379-1380 covering various royal residences in and around Paris, including the opulent Hôtel Saint-Pol newly built in the Marais.[4] The inventory runs to 3,906 entries, some of which include dozens of items. The King's plate may have amounted to little more than the usual accoutrements of power, but the justly famous library surpassed all precedent in both wealth and variety. Although not a connoisseur of gems, Charles also owned a number of cameos, a collection he kept at the Château de Melun southeast of Paris. Both the manuscripts and the cameos could be seen as an incipient fascination with antiquity, a focus that would grow into a consuming passion after Charles VIII invaded Italy in 1494 and discovered the Italian Renaissance.

Charles VI
(1368-1422)

Jean le Bon (John the Good), as his name implies, was known less for wisdom than for goodness, not least because he had granted large feudal appanages to the three younger brothers of the Dauphin Charles. In this way he created the powerful Dukes of Anjou, Berry, and Burgundy, each with near total authority over his provinces. In time, the heirs of these grandees would threaten the security and cohesion of the kingdom itself, especially at the height of the Hundred Years War, when Burgundy sided with England for reasons of the lucrative wool trade between Britain and the Netherlands. Two of Charles V's siblings, the Dukes of Anjou and Berry, became important collectors, as we shall see further along. Meanwhile, all three Dukes served as regents during the minority of Charles VI, who was but twelve years old when Charles V died in 1380. At the age of seventeen, young Charles dutifully married Isabeau of Bavaria, the bride chosen by his father. Three years later he rid himself of his uncles, by which time, however, the regents had plundered the royal collections, drained the treasury, and provoked popular uprisings in both France and Flanders. Once in control of

his own government, Charles recalled his father's ministers and elevated his brother, Louis, Duc d'Orléans, to the role of counselor. Unfortunately, this promising start soon foundered on the recurring bouts of madness to which the King fell prey as early as 1392 and continued, with ever greater intensity, to the end of his life. During *les absences du roi*, the uncles, mainly Philip the Bold (Philippe le Hardi) of Burgundy, regained power, and with predictable results, including the invasion of France by Henry V of England.

As for the collections left to Charles VI, losses occurred not only because of seizures by Anjou and Burgundy but also because the young King gave away pieces while having others modified or even melted down to pay for festivals and tournaments. Still, the collections grew, most notably from the New Year's gifts called *étrennes*. An inventory was made in 1391, followed by another in 1400.[5] The latter, with its 2,085 entries, covered items in the Louvre and the other royal châteaux, at Melun, Vincennes, and Saint-Germain-en-Laye. Listed as well were the treasures housed in the recently completed Bastille, the monumental, eight-towered fortress where the King had his greatest valuables deposited for safekeeping near the Hôtel Saint-Pol, his preferred residence. From Melun went a cache of rings and cameos as well as a portion of Isabeau's jewels, stored in ten locked cabinets furnishing the Tour du Coin and the Tour des Joyaux. Miraculously, a few identifiable pieces among the enameled gold items cited in the Bastille inventories exist even today.

The most extravagant of the surviving works is the so-called *Goldene Rössl von Altötting*,[6] a magnificent votive image of Charles VI kneeling at the feet of Mary and the Infant Jesus (figs. 1, 4). Fashioned of gold, enamel, and jewels, it stands 24 1/2 inches high. The title of the piece arises from a vignette below the principal scene, where a groom handles a white horse fitted with a golden harness. According to the royal inventories, this splendid work of art – a rare example of Parisian goldsmithery from the Middle Ages – was the *étrenne* given by Queen Isabeau to her husband in 1405. Only six months later the King pawned the sculpture to his brother-in-law, Duke Ludwig of Bavaria, as partial payment of an enormous dowry (120,000 francs) and an annual allowance (100,000 francs) promised to Anne de Bourbon, Ludwig's first wife. For the same purpose, other valuables – twenty-one in all – would also be taken from the Bastille, a process that went on for several years, until the trains of horses seen carting off treasure destroyed Isabeau's reputation in France. Owing to the terrible cost of defending the nation during the Hundred Years War, the *Goldene Rössl* was never redeemed. It therefore remained in Bavaria, whose reigning

Wittelsbach dukes donated the devotional object to the shrine at Altötting near Munich, where it survives today. Two other similarly crafted groups sent to Ludwig are known from 18th-century renderings in oil on canvas,[7] made before the pieces were melted down in Germany.

In late-14th-century France, the largest and most significant collection of goldsmith work appears to have been the one assembled by Louis I, Duc d'Anjou (1339-1384), the eldest of Charles V's brothers. Louis could afford it, for, quite apart from his rich fiefdom in the Loire Valley, he held the throne of Naples as well as claims to the Kingdom of Sicily. An inventory of about 1366 lists 1,000 objects, a number that grew to 3,600 in a minutely descriptive inventory drawn up around 1380.[8] Sadly, none of this hoard survives, no doubt because of the tendency to consign precious metals to the melting pot, inasmuch as treasures of the sort collected by Louis I were regarded as a variety of tradable currency.

Jean, Duc de Berry (1340-1416)

Arguably the most fascinating personality among these early Valois collectors was Jean, Duc de Berry, son, brother, and uncle of three successive Kings of France. Berry not only received his eponymous duchy, as well as the Duchy of Auvergne, from Jean le Bon; he also served as governor of the Languedoc province, all of which made him the effective ruler of much of central France. Among his vast assets were seventeen or more *hôtels* and châteaux, in all of which the Prince spent time every year, moving from one to the other at regular intervals. Along with him went servants, artists, and a chaplain, as well as cartloads of rich furnishings: huge tapestries, English embroideries, gold brocades from Lucca, and silk wall hangings, all known from surviving inventories. An avid builder, he commissioned the Château de Mehun-sur-Yèvre,[9] the Hôtel de Nesle in Paris, and the palace and chapel in Bourges. To his own personal wealth the Duc de Berry added that of the two rich heiresses he married, Jeanne d'Armagnac in 1360 and Jeanne de Boulogne in 1389. Even so, the whole proved inadequate to the cost of the opulent style of life maintained by this royal Prince and his extraordinary entourage.

Certainly the Duc de Berry spared no expense when it came to collecting richly illuminated manuscripts, a field in which he fully earned the title "Prince of French Bibliophiles." Of the three hundred manuscripts he owned, about one-third of them exist today with the Duke's autograph ownership

inscription still in place.[10] The Duc de Berry was not merely the greatest art patron of his time; he was also medieval Europe's first truly passionate collector. Unlike his predecessors, Berry did not collect simply to accumulate treasure as an instrument of power. Moreover, the Duke had certain endearing weaknesses common to his type, such as the inability to return rare manuscripts once he had borrowed them. There was, for example, the *Chroniques de France* lent to him by the royal abbey at Saint-Denis, only for the borrower to have the treasure entered into his own inventory. Eventually, it would be given up, for as the Duke lay dying, his confessor instructed him to have his executors do the right thing. Tommaso di Saluzzo, in his *Chevalier errant*, tells of the bustle surrounding the Duke's departure to assume his duties as Regent of Languedoc, assigned by King Charles VI. At the very peak of excitement, two Venetian dealers were announced as having arrived with precious stones to sell. Forthwith, the Regent forgot affairs of state and canceled the departure! The insatiable Berry was even known to have claimed back his own presents from the estates of deceased beneficiaries.[11]

In 1414-1416 Robert d'Estampes, the Duc de Berry's Chancellor, established a priced inventory of the ducal possessions.[12] It reveals the Prince to have been a greedy collector of jewels, including twenty rubies regarded as the finest of the day. One stone was the so-called *rubis de la nue*, while another 240-carat gem cost the astronomical sum of 18,000 gold guilders. Berry also had a great hunger for sacred goldsmithery – crosses, chalices, retables, and reliquaries – most of which he would bequeath to the Sainte-Chapelle in Bourges. Two such treasures have survived, one of them the so-called "Royal Gold Cup" (fig. 5), an exquisitely enameled piece displaying scenes from the life of Saint Agnes. Created around 1380, it was given by the Duc de Berry to his nephew, Charles VI, in 1391 and is thus listed in the Bastille inventory of 1400. Originally, the cup may have been intended as an *étrenne* for the Duke's elder brother, King Charles V, who had been born on the Feast of Saint Agnes (21 January).

The inventory cites a *magno jocali auri* ("big golden jewel"), which may be the *Reliquary of the Holy Thorn* emblazoned with the Berry arms and now preserved at the British Museum in London (fig. 7). Made by Renequin de Hallen, using pearls and precious stones gathered from a dismantled crown, the reliquary is decorated with numerous figures enameled in white, rather like those on the *Goldene Rössl*. It may very well have been an *étrenne* for Berry's younger brother, Philippe le Hardi (Philip the Bold), Duc de Bourgogne, passing by descent to Mary of Burgundy who, in 1477, married Archduke

6

5. *Royal Gold Cup, c. 1380 (Paris). Gold, enamel, and pearls; height 9 1/4" (23.5 cm). British Museum, London. Decorated in champlevé enamel with scenes from the life of Saint Agnes, this hanap is described in the 1391 inventory of Charles VI as a gift to the King from his nephew, Jean, Duc de Berry. Originally, it may have been intended as an étrenne for the Duke's brother, King Charles V, who was born on the Feast of Saint Agnes but died in 1380. The treasure was later heightened by the addition of a pearl diadem around the base and two gold bands, one of them decorated with enameled Tudor roses.*

6. *Brothers Limbourg. January: Très Riches Heures du Duc de Berry, c. 1413. Vellum; 11 7/16 x 8 1/2" (29 x 21 cm). Musée Condé, Chantilly. Jean, Duc de Berry, that ultimate ancestor of the royal collectors rediscovered in this book, had himself portrayed here at table on New Year's Day, an occasion for exchanging gifts or étrennes. Clearly prepared to treat his court to a great feast served on fabulous plate, the Duke turns to welcome a host of well-wishers coming from afar. On the table stands a massive nef, or spice boat, part of the silver and gold or silver-gilt service set on the sideboard at the left.*

7. *Renequin de Hallen. Reliquary of the Holy Thorn, c. 1400 (Paris). Gold, enamel, rock crystal, balas rubies, sapphire, and pearls; height 11 3/4" (29.7 cm). British Museum (Waddesdon Bequest), London. Decorated with a Last Judgment surrounded by prophets and angels, this goldsmith's gem of the Late Middle Ages displays the arms of Jean, Duc de Berry, who may have presented it as an étrenne to his younger brother, Duke Philip the Bold of Burgundy. Very likely, it then passed by descent to Mary of Burgundy, the daughter of Charles the Bold, the last Duke of Burgundy, who married Archduke Maximilian of Habsburg, the future Emperor Maximilian I. The reliquary remained in the Habsburg collections until removed for repair and then fraudulently sold to Anselm von Rothschild, who subsequently presented it to the British Museum. Possibly identical to a magno jocali auri cited in the Berry inventory, the jewel is also one of the very few identifiable works surviving from the treasury of Charles V.*

8. *Reliquary of the Holy Blood, c. 1380-1390 (Paris). Gold, enamel, sapphires, spinels, and pearls; height 17 1/2" (44.5 cm). Louvre, Paris. Traceable to the year 1412, when it formed part of the Breton treasury, this sacred object entered the French royal collections after Duchess Anne of Brittany became the wife of Charles VIII of France. Henri III, the last of the Valois monarchs, donated the reliquary to the treasury of the elite Ordre du Saint-Esprit, which he founded in 1578. Formed like a monstrance set with Gothic niches inhabited by figures representing the Holy Trinity, the Virgin Mary, the apostles and saints, the reliquary, like the works seen in figs. 4 and 7, exemplifies the high quality of enamels en ronde bosse ("in-the-round") created for the French court in the early 15th century.*

8

9

9. *Jacques Sourdeau. François I Wing, Château de Blois, 1515-1524. Built after the French discovered the Italian Renaissance, beginning with the invasion of Italy by Charles VIII in 1492, Blois reflected the turn the French had decisively made away from the Gothic Middle Ages. The François I Wing evinces this development not only in double tiers of loggias on the exterior façade but also on the courtyard side, where the famous open staircase is both complicated and simplified enough to suggest that the mathematical/scientific mind of Leonardo da Vinci had something to do with the design.*

10. *Jean and François Clouet. François I, King of France, c. 1530. Oil on panel; 37 3/4 x 29 1/8" (96 x 74 cm). Louvre, Paris. Truly a formal court portrait, this representation of the King shows him splendidly attired in gleaming white, black, and tan, the personal colors adopted by François in 1518. Looped over his chest are the necklace and insignia of the Order of Saint Michael. The painting, with its extraordinary elegance and refinement, was long regarded as the very paradigm of high Mannerist portraiture.*

Maximilian of Austria, the future Emperor Maximilian I. Their grandson, Emperor Charles V, continued to own the piece, according to his inventory, and it reappears in an 18th-century inventory of the Habsburgs' Schatzkammer in Vienna. In 1860 the reliquary was consigned for repair to the dealer Salomon Weininger in preparation for an industrial arts fair. The unscrupulous Weininger proceeded to make several replicas of the treasure.[13] He then returned one of the copies to the Hofburg, while selling the original to Anselm von Rothschild, whose son in turn bequeathed it to the British Museum.

A closely related work, the *Reliquary of the Holy Blood* (fig. 8), survives as a consequence of its having been presented by Henri III, the last of the Valois monarchs, to the treasury of the Ordre du Saint-Esprit.[14] This would be the most elite of France's chivalric orders, founded by Henri in 1578 as a means of binding rebellious nobles to the crown during the worst days of the Wars of Religion. Such treasuries proved safe havens for precious objects, since they possessed enough aura to remain beyond the reach of bankrupt sovereigns.

The Berry collection of cameos was renowned throughout Europe, prompting the Venetian architect Averlino Filarete, almost fifty years after the Duke's death, to write in his *Trattato d'architettura*: "One praises the Duc de Berry because of his uncommon love for these things; if he heard that there was somewhere an object worthy of his collections, he cared not for the money, but had to own it, if humanly possible."[15] Filarete even believed, no doubt incorrectly, that the Valois Prince had also owned the *Gemma Augustea*, the world's most famous cameo (fig. 174). This large onyx cameo was stolen in 1591 from the Saint-Sernin treasury in Toulouse, only to be tracked down in Venice by another determined collector, the Emperor Rudolf II, who acquired it for the colossal sum of 12,000 ducats (see Chapter 7).

Even before the Medici in Florence, the Duc de Berry developed a taste for Roman coins and antiquities, thereby placing himself in the vanguard of the oncoming Renaissance. He even allowed himself to be sold a series of eight jewel-mounted gold portrait medals by Italian dealers who had represented them as "antique." Inventory descriptions and the evidence of bronze casts made of two medals suggest that the dealers had defrauded His Lordship, selling him what were in fact modern pastiches.[16] This may be the first instance of forgeries fabricated with a

particular client in mind, and it would certainly not be the last, especially in the 19th century, when those compulsive collectors, the Rothschilds, proved susceptible to the wares of gifted forgers.

As a collector, the Duc de Berry stood on the threshold between the otherworldly aspirations of the Middle Ages and the Humanism of the Renaissance. On the medieval side were the works of a religious character, such as the reliquaries just cited, "the chalice of the Marriage of Cana," "bones of the massacred Innocent Children," "a milk-tooth of the Virgin," and "the engagement ring of the Virgin with Saint Joseph" (so described in the inventory along with the following cautionary note: "as stated by Mme de St. Just, who gave the ring to Msgr. at New Year 1406"). Meanwhile, in his *estudes*,[17] or private "studies," Berry stored many secular objects, among them mounted porcelains (probably from China), microscopic carvings, and paintings, as well as such *naturalia* as shells, ostrich eggs, coconut cups, wild boars' tusks, mammoth bones, monsters, and crystals. These reflect an open and inquisitive mind, a curiosity about the world and its mysteries that could be seen as an early anticipation of the *Kunst- und Wunderkammern* so prized by later European courts, beginning in the second half of the 15th century and continuing throughout the 16th century. The Duke even maintained a zoo of exotic animals – ostriches, dromedaries, chamois, bears, camels – which again placed him ahead of his time. Zoos, after all, contained the living counterparts of the skeletons and other natural-history specimens deemed essential to all later Wunderkammern.

In the domain of lavish living, the only serious competitor to the Valois appears to have been John, Duke of Bedford (1389-1435), a younger brother of Henry V of England who married Anne, a daughter of Jean sans Peur (John the Fearless), Duke of Burgundy, England's ally at critical moments during the Hundred Years War. Following the death of Henry V in 1422, Bedford became Regent of both England and occupied France during the the minority of Henry VI, who was barely nine months old when his father died. While installed in the Louvre, the Duke appropriated Charles V's library and had it dispatched to England. His inventory abounds in household goods, works of art, goldsmith work, and illustrated manuscripts, most notably the *Bedford Book of Hours*, attesting to a love of splendor and an aesthetic discernment comparable only to those of his Valois relatives.[18]

François I
(1494-1547)

Thanks to the valiant leadership of Joan of Arc, the French finally took the offensive in the Hundred Years War, and by 1453 they had driven the English entirely out of France, except for a foothold in Calais, held until 1558. Already in 1429, the Maid of Orléans had escorted the timorous Dauphin, son of the mad Charles VI, to Rheims and seen him crowned as Charles VII (r. 1422-1461). When the war ended the feudal nobility had been decimated, a tragedy that, ironically, could only benefit the monarchy, leaving it free to unite France more solidly under royal authority and to ally with the lesser nobles, the bourgeoisie, and the lower classes. The process continued under Louis XI (1423-1483), Charles's son and heir, who even managed to reclaim Burgundy, after the Swiss slew Charles the Bold, Duke of Burgundy, at the Battle of Nancy in 1477. Louis XI was succeeded by his son, who would reign as Charles VIII (1470-1498) following the regency of his sister, Anne de Beaujeu. Charles, through his marriage to Anne de Bretagne, secured Brittany for France, and by leading an army down the Italian peninsula, he succeeded briefly in making good on the Angevin claims to the throne of Naples. While in Italy, Charles also discovered the Renaissance, acquiring a love of Classical beauty and refinement, as well as a love of luxury, that would have momentous and lasting consequences for France and the whole of northern Europe.

When Charles VIII died without issue, he was succeeded by his cousin Louis d'Orléans, a grandson of Charles VI's younger brother, who, as Louis XII (r. 1493-1515), could also not resist the siren song of Renaissance Italy. Meanwhile, he further secured the French kingdom by marrying his predecessor's widow, Anne de Bretagne, but with no better luck in producing a male heir. For the sake of dynastic succession, he married his fifteen-year-old daughter Claude to her cousin, François d'Angoulême, who in 1515, at the age of twenty-one, mounted the throne as François I (fig. 10). The royal couple were less than ideally matched, what with Claude described as "a limping girl... white-faced, low-sized and extraordinarily fat"[19] and François as "very tall [and] well featured," despite "a large nose, and, in the opinion of many, legs that are too thin for his body."[20] A Valois to the core, François embraced life with gusto, pursuing his political, intellectual, and artistic interests with the same joyous vigor he mustered when playing the gallant among numerous beautiful and willing ladies. His court may have been corrupt, and his Italian campaigns futile and financially ruinous,

but the thirty-two-year reign could scarcely have been more brilliant, spanning as it did the golden years of the French Renaissance.

In 1515, François followed his two immediate predecessors into Italy, where, after a stunning victory at Marignano, he gained possession of Milan. A year later he returned to France in triumph, bringing with him the aged Leonardo da Vinci, who would remain the King's guest until his death three years later. Having tasted the good life south of the Alps, François now "grew hungry with feeding" as he launched into eager acquisition of jewels and enamels, superb harnesses and heavy gold spurs, precious plate, the finest linen and perfumes. He also launched into building on a grand scale, first at Amboise, where he had grown up, and then at Blois (fig. 9). On the edge of the game-rich Forest of Blois, François built from scratch the most romantic of all French castles, the Château de Chambord (fig. 11).

Also in 1519, following the death of Emperor Maximilian I, François lobbied hard, mainly with large bribes, to win election as Holy Roman Emperor. The effort was to no avail, since the German Electors, despite promises to the contrary, voted for Archduke Charles, the grandson of Maximilian I and Mary of Burgundy. The outraged François proposed an alliance with Henry VIII of England, hoping for a balance of power in Europe, the better to contend with the Habsburg Empire, on which, it was now said, "the sun never set." In 1520, the two monarchs, accompanied by large retinues,

10

11

12

11. *Château de Chambord, 1519-1550. Designed and built for François I, the great hunting lodge in the Loire Valley has long been attributed to an Italian architect – sometimes even to Leonardo da Vinci – because of its symmetrical plan, a Greek cross within a square with a double-helix staircase at the center. Be that as it may, the Renaissance rationality of the main mass melds into the wild romance of the upper reaches, where dormers, chimneystalks, and lanterns sprout almost as thick as the game-rich forest lying all about. By 1539 the building was sufficiently advanced for François I to play host there to Emperor Charles V.*

12. *Rosso Fiorentino. Galerie François I, Château de Fontainebleau, 1533-1540. A masterpiece of the French Renaissance, the Galerie François I gave the great Italian Mannerist painter/decorator Rosso Fiorentino his finest opportunity, which he seized to create a handsome ensemble of dark-wood paneling, paintings ripe with shot colors, and rich stucco enframements. Characteristic of the pictorial or sculptural style are coiling strapwork, languidly attenuated nudes, and arcane though clearly erotic content.*

13

13. *Raphael. The Holy Family, 1518. Oil on panel; 81 ¹/₂ x 55" (207 x 140 cm). Louvre, Paris. The Holy Family, together with another work by Raphael, served as a gift from Pope Leo X Medici to François I and Queen Claude to mark the wedding of Lorenzo di Piero de' Medici, Duke of Urbino, and the King's cousin, Madeleine de la Tour d'Auvergne. The masterpiece was sent from Rome by road for presentation to the French royals in Nantes in 1518. Raphael's most celebrated picture in France, The Holy Family remained at Amboise until about 1530, after which it was transferred to Fontainebleau, where the King had it cleaned by Primaticcio.*

14. *Lo Spinario (Thorn Puller), 1540 (Rome). Bronze; height 28 ³/₈" (72 cm). Louvre, Paris. The Roman bronze, one of the most copied works of antiquity, has stood in the Capitoline Museum in Rome since 1471. The Louvre example, cast from the original, was commissioned in 1540 by Cardinal Ippolito d'Este from two Florentine sculptors, Giovanni and Giacomo, through the mediation of Benvenuto Cellini for a cost of 50 scudi. It arrived at Fontainebleau the following year and is first mentioned in the Cour des Fontaines in 1608.*

met on the northern coast of France near Calais, creating a scene of such unexampled splendor that it was called the "Field of the Cloth of Gold." According to one contemporary writer, the tents "were draped with gold cloth inside and out, as many rooms as halls and galleries, all full of satin cloth and gold and silver drapery. And above the said tents were many devices and gold apples, which were beautiful to see when the sun struck them."[21] Needless to say, François spread before the English King the full panoply of his regal collection: tapestries, Oriental carpets, silks, and brocades, porcelains and vessels of gold and silver-gilt.

Thwarted in his expansionist ambitions, François at various times during his reign sought closer ties with the Papacy. In 1516, for instance, he signed the Concordat of Bologna with Pope Leo X Medici, thereby gaining a certain control over Church appointments in France. Two years later, François and Leo arranged the marriage of the King's cousin, Madeleine de la Tour d'Auvergne, to a nephew of the Pope, Lorenzo di Piero de' Medici, the newly created Duke of Urbino. The fête celebrating this political match was designed by none other than Leonardo da Vinci. Pope Leo, the maecenas par excellence during that cultural climax known as the High Renaissance, presented François with a number of superb paintings, among them Raphael's *Holy Family* and *Saint Michael*, both of which now hang in the Louvre (fig. 13).[22] A year later the young Duchess of Urbino died

14

while giving birth to Catherine de' Medici, François's future daughter-in-law, who in 1547 would become Queen of France.

At the Battle of Pavia in 1525, François lost everything he had won in Italy at Marignano eight years earlier; moreover, he found himself a prisoner of the victorious Charles V. In Madrid, where the Emperor held him, François was even obliged to surrender Burgundy. After a war of revenge against Charles, François fared better only to the degree that he recovered Burgundy. Still, the bellicose rivalry between the two sovereigns continued at various intervals for many years to come. To advance his cause, François, known as *le roi très chrétien*, even forged relationships with "infidels" and "heretics" – Suleiman the Magnificent and the Princes of Protestant Germany.

Meanwhile, the King's ambitious building plans continued apace, now at the Louvre, where the new and grander Cour Carrée had been initiated in 1527 with the dismantling of the medieval keep. Much closer to the royal heart was the reconstruction of Fontainebleau, a magnificent hunting lodge forty miles southwest of Paris.

Neither project advanced very rapidly, owing in part to the Treaty of Cambrai (1530), which obliged François to pay a ransom of 1.2 million ducats for the recovery of his two sons, still captive in Madrid. To raise the necessary funds, François had little choice but to sell virtually all his jewels, save for a few historical pieces left to him by the Queen, who had died in 1524. The treaty also required that he marry Eleonora, the Emperor's younger sister. In preparation for the new alliance, François classified eight exceptional family pieces as "jewels of the crown," inalienable patrimony to be held in trust by each successive monarch. With this began the collection known as the "French crown jewels." It included a necklace of eleven large diamonds and the celebrated "Côte-de-Bretagne," a balas ruby, or spinel, of 212.44 carats, which survives, in modified form, among what remains of the crown gems.[23] Altogether, the collection was estimated to be worth 304,240 *écus d'or au soleil*, meaning the value of 1,035 kilos of pure gold. In a gesture designed to impress the Imperial party, these *bagues de la couronne* (*bagues* signifying not "rings" but "jewels") were entrusted to Queen Eleonora for personal use as she made her festive entry into Bordeaux.

Having momentarily settled his differences with the Emperor, François began the second phase of construction at Fontainebleau in 1531. The château was now meant to rival Charles V's palace at Granada and Henry VIII's St. James's and Whitehall palaces in London (fig. 12). François I appears to have conceived an interest in art at an early age, a tendency encouraged by his mother, Louise de Savoie. Barely ten years old, the Prince is recorded as having requested certain paintings from the Florentine intermediary Niccolò Alamanni. François had before him the example of Louis XII, who had returned from his Italian campaign with such masterpieces as Leonardo's *Virgin of the Rocks*[24] and *Belle Ferronnière* (Musée des Beaux-Arts, Nancy),[25] and, very likely, Raphael's *Belle Jardinière* (Louvre).[26] Having inherited such a collection of masterpieces, François, once crowned, quite naturally focused on Italian art. Leonardo, Rosso, Primaticcio, and Serlio all worked for the King, as duly noted, but so too did Andrea del Sarto and Benvenuto Cellini. Moreover, both Titian and Michelangelo would have joined their company if François had had his way. In all, fifty-three Italian School paintings have been identified as once present in the royal collection.

At Fontainebleau, François made the Chambre des Bains a repository for his collection of paintings. Here, as part of the decorative ensemble, were installed religious as well as secular masterpieces by Raphael, Giulio Romano, and Girolamo da Carpi, all mutilated to fit within established stucco frames and exposed to steam from the baths!

The King's collection of marble and bronze sculptures, based upon antique models, stood for the most part in gardens, fully exposed to the elements, although some of the antiquities were probably housed in the Pavillion des Antiquités. In 1515, the year of his accession and the victory at Marignano, François asked Pope Leo X to make him a gift of the *Laocoön Group*, a splendid Hellenistic marble unearthed only in 1506. Much later, in 1540, Cardinal Ippolito d'Este presented the Valois monarch with a bronze cast of the famous *Spinario*, or *Thorn Puller*, a Roman bronze of the 1st century BC (fig. 14). It had been specially commissioned through Benvenuto Cellini. In 1536 the same prelate had given François his hoard of antique bronzes as well as his collection of some 250 antique silver medals.

Benvenuto Cellini (1500-1571), the brilliant Florentine goldsmith/sculptor who achieved as much fame for the amorous revelations of his *Autobiography* as for his masterpieces, was given to all manner of daredevil exploits, sometimes criminal or violent. During the sack of Rome in 1527, Cellini, according to his own account, played a heroic role in defense of the city and even killed Charles de Bourbon, one of the Imperial commanders. Even so, he ended up imprisoned at Castel Sant'Angelo for having allegedly stolen jewels from Pope Clement VII Medici. Rescued by François, he entered the King's service, spending the years 1537 and 1540-1545 in

15

France, where he arrived with the help of his patron, Cardinal Ippolito d'Este. While at Fontainebleau, Cellini undertook a number of major commissions, which mostly remained unfinished at the time of his departure. Of the twelve life-size silvered bronze figures of Olympian gods and goddesses he initiated, only *Jupiter* was actually cast, and it has not survived. Two other monumental projects, the *Porte Dorée* and the *Fontaine de Mars*, also perished, but from the first there still exists a model for a satyr and the magnificent lunette relief known as the *Nymph of Fontainebleau* (fig. 15).

François, although barely literate in Latin and not at all in Greek, evinced a keen appetite for Classical manuscripts and books, as well as for texts in Hebrew and Arabic. Having inherited Louis XII's considerable library at Blois, he added to it while also gathering his own library at Fontainebleau. In 1544 the King integrated the two collections, by transferring the 1,890 volumes at Blois to Fontainebleau. The whole was housed on the upper floor above the long Galerie. By the end of the reign, the library contained 3,000 volumes, which would later form the core of the Bibliothèque Royale (today Bibliothèque Nationale) in Paris. Some seventy of the books have been identified, the leather bindings of many tooled with the King's device: an F combined with a *salamandre ardent*.

François I adored the luxurious effect created by tapestries, those eminently portable works of art and craft which could bring a near Oriental splendor to almost any environment, from a campaign tent to the Louvre. A royal inventory of 1542 lists 408 tapestries, some of the entries consisting of extensive sets. Alas, virtually all of this Renaissance patrimony fell victim of the French Revolution, when financial stress made the fungible value of the silver and gold thread appear more important than the artistic or historical worth of the finished pieces. Only a precious few of François's tapestries survive, all of them outside France. As elements fundamental to the *fastes*, or pomp, with which the Valois had always to surround themselves, tapestries went everywhere the King did, particularly on such prestigious occasions

15. *Benvenuto Cellini.* Nymph of Fontainebleau, *1541-1545. Bronze; 80 1/2 x 160" (205 x 409 cm). Louvre, Paris. This fragment from the destroyed* Porte Dorée *is the only surviving example of the large-scale sculpture created by Cellini while in service to François I at Fontainebleau. The nymph personifies the great forest and hunting lodge embracing the royal stag, a stand-in for the King. Cellini, thanks to his skill as a jeweler and goldsmith, could readily translate the School of Fontainebleau style, with its elegantly attenuated nudes, into high relief.*

16. Matched pricket candlesticks, *c. 1530 (Paris), nozzles 1581-1582. Silver-gilt, rock crystal, pearls, and garnets; height 12 ¹/₂" (32 cm). Louvre, Paris. These articles from the Cabinet du Roi at Fontainebleau appear in a 1561 inventory prepared at the outset of the reign of Charles IX. His successor, Henri III, presented them to the treasury of the Ordre du Saint-Esprit in 1578.*

17. Coupe de Saint-Michel (Saint Michael's Cup), *c. 1530-1540 (Antwerp). Gold, enamels, diamonds, emeralds, rubies, and pearls; height 20 ³/₈" (51.7 cm). Kunsthistorisches Museum, Vienna. This magnificent Flemish cup and cover, surmounted by a figure of Saint Michael vanquishing the Devil, was acquired by François I from the Antwerp merchant Josse Vezeler in 1532. In 1570 Charles IX de-accessioned the jewel from the French royal treasury and presented it, along with three other superlative works of art (figs. 24, 29, 129), to Archduke Ferdinand II, Governor of Tyrol, when the latter served as proxy for Charles at the Austrian nuptial Mass binding him to the Archduke's niece Elizabeth in 1570.*

18. Ciborium, *c. 1530. Silver-gilt, rock crystal, enamel, garnets, pearls, agate, and shell cameos; height 13" (33 cm). Louvre, Paris. Also once present in the Cabinet du Roi at Fontainebleau, this rare example of French Renaissance goldsmith work probably belonged to François I. The ciborium, which first appears in an inventory of 1561, was presented by Henri III to the treasury of the Ordre du Saint-Esprit in 1578, together with twelve other "ancient" pieces.*

17

18

as the Field of the Cloth of Gold. Another event requiring maximum display of royal wealth and power came in 1533, when François I met Clement VII at Marseilles for the wedding of the King's second son, Henri, Duc d'Anjou, and the Pope's cousin, Catherine de' Medici, the orphaned daughter of Madeleine de la Tour d'Auvergne, whom the King, fifteen years earlier, had married to the Medici Duke of Urbino. On this occasion alone, the cost of moving furniture, tapestries, and silver came to the astounding sum of 4,623 livres.

The Marseilles summit would not have been complete without an exchange of lavish gifts. To Clement VII, François I offered a Flemish tapestry reproducing Leonardo's *Last Supper* (Vatican Museums)[27] and a rare book of miniatures, while to Cardinal Ippolito d'Este he presented a caged lion! The Pope countered with a rare horn, supposedly from a unicorn, elaborately mounted in gold, the entire jewel valued at 17,000 ducats. François also received from Pope Clement a gold-mounted casket paneled in rock crystal and decorated with the papal arms. It had been commissioned in 1530 from Valerio Belli of Vicenza, who received 2,000 scudi for his work, which took two years to complete and involved engraving scenes from the Life of Christ. The resulting panels are considered Belli's lapidary masterpiece (fig. 19). François bequeathed the treasure to his daughter-in-law Catherine, who in turn left it to her favorite granddaughter, Christine de Lorraine. When the latter married Grand Duke Ferdinando de' Medici, she took along the casket as one of the most glittering items in her dowry. Having passed into the famous grand-ducal collections in Florence, it was spared the destruction that befell so many royal treasures during the French Revolution of 1789-1795.

Benvenuto Cellini, during his service at the Valois court, worked not only as a sculptor but also as a goldsmith, a profession for which he had been originally trained. From his hand, a silver ewer and basin, presented to François I by Cardinal Ippolito d'Este in 1541, three silver vases, several gold figures, and a jeweled hat badge have all disappeared. Gone as well are the "numberless designs that Rosso [Fiorentino] made for saltcellars, vases, bowls, and other fanciful things, all of which the King afterwards [had] made in silver... Let it suffice to say that [Cellini] made designs for all the vessels of a sideboard for the King..."[28] What does survive, miraculously, is the celebrated *Saliera* or *Saltcellar* which Cellini created for François I, only for it to be presented by Charles IX, the King's grandson, to Archduke Ferdinand II of Tyrol in 1570, when the latter served as proxy for Charles at the Austrian nuptial Mass binding him to Archduchess Elizabeth (fig. 29). Having escaped the melting pot in 1562, this resplendent and virtuosic showpiece comes down to us as the sole surviving example of goldsmithery from the hand of Cellini, probably the most inspired goldsmith of his day. Cellini had modeled the work for Cardinal Ippolito d'Este but then executed it in 1540-1543 for the French sovereign, at a cost of 1,000 scudi. Fundamental to the wit of such an object is the artist's playful miniaturization of the monumental marble figures carved by Michelangelo for the Medici tombs in Florence. They represent Neptune, because salt, after all, comes from the sea, and Tellus, the personification of earth, the source of pepper. Once again, they display the languid, attenuated elegance characteristic of Fontainebleau Mannerism, already seen on a monumental scale in Cellini's *Nymph* tympanum (fig. 15).

A work only recently identified as having belonged to François I is the *Coupe de Saint-Michel*, or *Saint Michael's Cup*, a magnificent lidded cup fashioned in the Netherlands of silver-gilt and jewels (fig. 17).[29] Dating from around 1530, it was sold to the King in 1532 by the Antwerp dealer Josse Vezeler and taken as part of the "display plate" assembled for another encounter between François and Henry VIII of England, this time at Boulogne-sur-Mer. The chronicler Florange writes of "a big buffet... loaded on six steps, with gold and silver plate, and gold cups enriched with jewels."[30] The Flemish cup was also de-accessioned from the royal treasury by Charles IX and presented to Archduke Ferdinand in 1570. Thus, it too survives in the Habsburg Imperial collections at the Kunsthistorisches Museum in Vienna.

Now come to light are documents which not only reveal where François I kept his valuables but also describe their nature.[31] In 1537 the King ordered his Treasurer, Charles de Pierrevive, to take charge of

19. *Valerio Belli. Casket with scenes from the Life of Christ, 1532 (Vicenza). Rock crystal, silver-gilt, and enamel; length 10 5/8" (27 cm). Museo degli Argenti, Florence. The panels, considered Belli's masterpiece, were commissioned in 1530 by Pope Clement VII Medici at a cost of 2,000 scudi. In 1533 the Pope presented the casket to François I at Marseilles on the occasion of the marriage of the King's son, the future Henri II, to Catherine de' Medici. A Fontainebleau inventory of 1561 describes it as "a crystal coffer engraved and decorated with silver-gilt and enameled figures, weighing XV marcs II ounces." Queen Catherine bequeathed the treasure to her favorite granddaughter, Christine de Lorraine, who repatriated it to Florence in 1589 when she became the wife of Grand Duke Ferdinando I de' Medici.*

19

the collection housed in a *cabynet en l'estage qui est sur la chapelle* ("cabinet on the floor above the chapel") in the Louvre. It consisted of 167 items, *vaiselle d'or et d'argent, reliquaires et joyaulx,* inventoried by Jean Briconnet, Président des Comptes, and Philibert Babon, Trésorier de France. Apart from "modern" plate, the cache included several well-known historic treasures inherited from Anne de Bretagne, among them the *Nef de Sainte-Ursule,* now in the treasury at Rheims Cathedral,[32] and the *Reliquary of the Holy Blood* (fig. 8).[33] In 1540 the first was logged out and the second in 1543, probably for transfer to Fontainebleau.

At Fontainebleau, François I had the Cabinet du Trésor du Roi installed above his apartments on the top floor of the *donjon.* Sadly, the earliest inventory of its contents dates back only to 1560-1561. Very likely, however, the items listed as contemporary with the reign of François once belonged to this monarch. Two such pieces are an Italianate rock-crystal and silver-gilt ciborium[34] and a pair of traditionally formed pricket candlesticks, again made of rock crystal and silver-gilt (figs. 16, 18). Both the ciborium and the candlesticks figured among the gifts made by François's grandson, Henri III, to the treasury of the Ordre du Saint-Esprit in 1578. A much later description characterizes François's Cabinet du Trésor as the "Cabinet des Curiositez," a place filled with "odd little pieces, such as ancient medals, silverware, vases, figurines, animals, clothing, and works from the Indies and foreign countries, and a huge number of little trinkets... vases and dishes of porcelain and very oddly decorated crystal."[35]

Matteo dal Nassaro, a lapidary and hardstone engraver from Verona, worked for François I for over thirty years, from 1515 to 1547. His atelier, shared with goldsmiths and jewelers, was located on a barge anchored near the Louvre on the right bank of the Seine, whose flowing waters drove the wheels for cutting and polishing. By this time the Hôtel de Nesle, the Duc de Berry's onetime Paris residence, was also used to house the activities of artists and craftsmen in service to the court.

In his mastery of *la politique culturelle,* François I virtually set the standard for the great Renaissance prince, ostentatiously displaying wealth, luxury, and good taste in order to overawe and thus to overpower. Despite his military and foreign-policy failures, or the prodigality and licentiousness of his court, François achieved an illustrious reign, if for no other reason than the spectacular resurgence of the arts in contemporary France. Jean Goujon in sculpture and the Clouets, *père et fils,* in painting rivaled the Italians without imitating them. The poets Rabelais, Marot, and Budé came to the fore thanks to the patronage of the King and his sister, Marguerite de Navarre. The great Flemish composer Josquin Desprez died in France during the period, while the poets of the Pléiade were born. François also laid the foundations of the Collège de France. Such was the cultural efflorescence during the first half of the 16th century that it would not be surpassed until the reign of Louis XIV.

Henri II
(1519-1559)

The only son of François I and Claude de France to survive the King was the Duc d'Anjou, who would reign as Henri II from 1547 to 1559 (fig. 20). More robust in physique than in disposition, Henri long ignored his plain but intelligent wife, Catherine de' Medici, in favor of such strong-willed courtiers as Diane de Poitiers, the King's aging but still ravishing mistress, and the Guise brothers, Charles and François.

In the cultural realm, Henri supported many of his father's projects, including the reconstruction of the Louvre under the direction of the architect Pierre Lescot. Indeed, he, more than any other French monarch, made the Louvre his principal residence, even while regularly moving the court from one château to another, or stopping at the elegant Hôtel des Tournelles in the Marais. Jean Goujon decorated not only the attic story on the façade of the new wing but also the principal hall within, the vast Salle des Cariatides, with its famous musicians' gallery supported by monumental caryatids in Classical drapery, clinging as if wet. On a smaller scale, the period marked the revival of Limoges as a flourishing center of the enameler's art. Most striking were the wares of a few established workshops specializing in grisaille or polychrome mythological subjects set forth on black grounds. Limoges pieces initialed by such artists as Pierre Reymond, Pierre Courtois or Courteys, Jean de Court, or Léonard Limousin found a large export market, making their way into many a Renaissance Kunstkammer, where they survive, as in the Dresden Green Vaults (figs. 21, 239).

The reign saw, in addition, the advent of the Saint-Porchaire potteries, which turned out purely decorative earthenware objects notable for their clear lead-glaze finish. The pieces are intricately decorated in the Mannerist style, including punched strapwork patterns and cavities filled with clays of contrasting colors. Because of the royal insignia, such as the interlaced crescents of Diane de Poitiers and the monogram of Henri II, on many Saint-Porchaire works, it is thought they may have originated in a court workshop. The Louvre owns the largest single group of these rare treasures, thirteen in all (fig. 23).

20

20. *François Clouet. Henri II, c. 1550. Oil on panel. Louvre, Paris. More than any other monarch, Henri II made the Louvre his principal residence, to which he brought the glory of Jean Goujon's sculpture, found in the Salle des Caryatides as well as on the façade of the new Renaissance wing, now doubled in length at the King's command. The period also saw the revival of Limoges enamel ware and the flowering of Saint-Porchaire pottery. Most of all, Henri II gave France Catherine de' Medici, his Queen Consort and a great collector in the tradition of her Florentine family.*

21

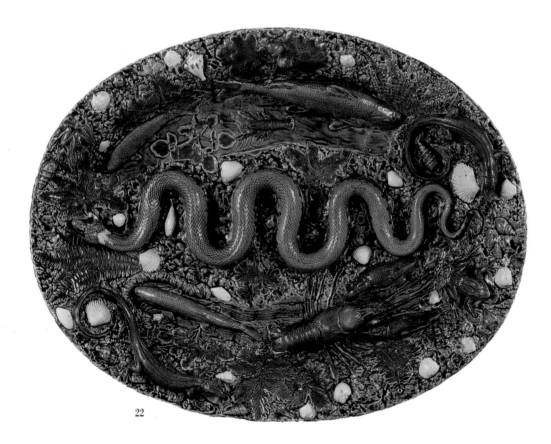

22

21. *Léonard Limousin. Connétable de Montmorency, 1556 (Limoges). Enameled copper and gilded wood; height 2 ⅞" (7.2 cm). Louvre, Paris. In this master, the Limoges art of enameling on copper found one of its most original and prolific exponents. His subject here was the all-powerful Connétable or Constable of France, as well as a notable patron of the arts, during the eventful reigns of François I and Henri II. The frame is set with eight different enamels, four bearing the Montmorency cipher and two inspired by Rosso Fiorentino's satyrs in the Galerie François I at Fontainebleau.*

22. *Bernard Palissy (attrib). Earthenware dish, 2nd half 16th century. Glazed terra-cotta. Louvre, Paris. Palissy achieved fame and royal patronage for his glazed potteries, conceived as small ponds crawling with reptiles and insects, mostly cast from dead specimens and rendered in naturalistic colors. The stil or style rustique he practiced was shared by the great Nuremberg goldsmith Wenzel Jamnitzer (figs. 43, 134, 217).*

23. *Saint-Porchaire cup and cover, c. 1550. Lead-glazed earthenware; height 14 ⅝" (37.2 cm). Louvre, Paris. Although the work seen here appears not to be of royal provenance, many rare works from Saint-Porchaire were made for Henri II and the Connétable de Montmorency. They are notable for their fine-grained, whitish paste, unusual shapes, and Mannerist decorations, including strapwork, dense interlaces of brown lines, and metal-punched cavities filled with clays of contrasting colors.*

24. *Richard Toutain the Younger. Onyx ewer, c. 1560-1570 (Paris). Onyx, gold, enamel, diamonds, emeralds, and rubies; height 10 $^{11}/_{16}$" (27.1 cm). Kunsthistorisches Museum, Vienna. This ingenious work of French goldsmithery can be broken down into a cup and a separate flat-bottomed ewer. A contemporary inventory description has only recently made it possible to attribute the piece to the court jeweler cited here. The attribution is further supported by the style of the mounts and their white strapwork on a black-enamel ground. Like the priceless treasure seen in fig. 17, Toutain's ewer was taken from the French royal treasury by Charles IX and presented to his uncle-in-law, Archduke Ferdinand II of Tyrol.*

25. *Rock-crystal ewer, c. 1560 (Paris). Rock crystal, silver parcel-gilt, enamel, and rubies; height 16 $^{1}/_{8}$" (41 cm). Prado, Madrid. First mentioned in the 1561 inventory of Jeanne d'Albret, Queen of Navarre, this ewer, with its handle formed as Narcissus contemplating himself in the vessel's contents, would be owned by her son, Henri IV, the first of France's Bourbon monarchs. It subsequently passed into the collection of the Grand Dauphin, eldest son of Louis XIV. At his death the ewer was part of the patrimony left to the Grand Dauphin's second son, Philip V of Spain, whose collection thus became known in Madrid as Las Alhajas del Delfin ("the Treasure of the Dauphin"). The two objects illustrated on these facing pages are rare examples of 16th-century French lapidary and goldsmith work, dating from a period when Milan and Florence were the pre-eminent centers of such production.*

25

26

26. *Corneille de Lyon. Catherine de' Medici (detail), c. 1533. Oil on panel. Musée Condé, Chantilly. Catherine de' Medici emerged from her role as the ignored wife of the Duc d'Anjou (future Henri II) to become Queen Regent of France, at a time when religious division was evolving into civil war. She also brought to France the love of art and culture so instinctive to her Florentine family.*

27. *Benvenuto Cellini. Saliera, 1540-1543. Detail of fig. 29.*

Catherine de' Medici
(1519-1589)

On the last day of June 1559, Henri II staged a great tournament at the Hôtel des Tournelles to celebrate the marriage of his daughter Elisabeth to Philip II of Spain. While tilting with Captain Montgomery of the Royal Scottish Guards the King suffered a wound in the eye and died ten days later. Only the year before, the Dauphin had married Mary Stuart, who, for the purpose, had been reared at the French court. The young, and probably syphilitic, heir would reign as François II (1544-1560) but only until December of the following year, when suddenly he died at the age of sixteen, leaving the throne to his younger brother, who succeeded as Charles IX (1550-1574). With her ten-year-old child now on the throne, Catherine de' Medici became Regent of France, soon exercising power as if she had been truly royal-born (fig. 26). First she ordered the Hôtel des Tournelles demolished in revenge for its having been the site of her beloved husband's accidental death. Unwilling to remain in the Louvre during the ongoing reconstruction, Catherine commissioned Philibert Delorme to design and build the Tuileries Palace, so called for the tile potteries formerly on the site. This splendid new residence was to rise west of the Louvre just outside Charles V's defensive rampart. Typically Medici, Catherine ordered an immense Renaissance garden laid out beyond the western façade, where it remains today, although redesigned in the 17th century by André Le Nôtre. Here she recruited the great ceramist Bernard Palissy to create a grotto lined with his distinctive repertoire of glazed and naturalistically colored terra-cottas crawling with snails, frogs, and other denizens of the damp, all cast from dead specimens. His fame, however, rests upon his

27

"rustic wares" – dishes treated as if they were small ponds playing host to a population of slimy-surfaced snakes, lizards, and insects (fig. 22). The Queen, who had inherited Palissy from the Connétable Anne de Montmorency, awarded the potter with the title *Inventeur des rustiques figulines du Roi*. The *stil rustique*[36] he practiced had another great exponent, Wenzel Jamnitzer, a Nuremberg goldsmith whose works could be found in almost every important 16th-century Kunstkammer (fig. 134). The Louvre owns a magnificent silver-gilt dish by Jamnitzer, who decorated it with creatures cast from dead specimens (fig. 43). The piece was acquired by Louis XIV in the 17th century.

Catherine de' Medici must be credited with the arrival in Paris of some of the engraved rock-crystal and other hardstone vessels now in the Louvre's Galerie d'Apollon and in the Prado collection known as *Las Alhajas del Delfin*. Still, the provenance of no more than a few pieces can be traced as far back as the 16th century, and so they will all be discussed in a later passage dealing with the treasures of Louis XIV and his son, the Grand Dauphin. For the moment, only those objects bequeathed by Catherine to her granddaughter, Christine de Lorraine, can be securely traced to the Queen Mother, who may have taken them to Paris in 1533 as part of her dowry. After Christine married Ferdinando I, Grand Duke of Tuscany, in 1589, the treasures passed back into the Medici collections in Florence. They include a rock-crystal cup decorated with delicately engraved foliage and attributed to the great Milanese lapidary Gasparo Miseroni (fig. 84).[37] The cover, added in France, is richly embellished with a pierced openwork design composed of a gilded and enameled interlace of tendrils, scallops, triangles, and the monogram HC. The initials could stand for Henri and Catherine, but they are so conjoined as to cause suspicion that they also incorporate a D, for Diane de Poitiers. From the Queen's dowry as well are two other important items: an elegant heliotrope cup with French mounts in enameled gold, and a superb rock-crystal charger boldly engraved with Noah's Ark by Giovanni dei Bernardi di Castelbolognese (fig. 85).

In 1560-1561 the treasures at Fontainebleau were inventoried for the first time.[38] The list includes Cellini's *Saliera* (figs. 27-29) and a Burgundian jeweled and gold-mounted rock-crystal beaker once owned by Philip the Bold (Philippe le Hardi), Duc de Bourgogne. These two pieces, along with the *Saint Michael's Cup* (fig. 17) and a rare gold-mounted ewer by Richard Toutain (fig. 24), were presented by Charles IX to Archduke Ferdinand of Tyrol in 1570 when, as noted earlier, the latter stood in for the King at the time of his marriage by proxy to Archduchess Elizabeth of Austria (see also Chapter 6). Other items

28

28. *Benvenuto Cellini. Saliera, 1540-1543. Detail of fig. 29.*

29. *Benvenuto Cellini, Saliera (Saltcellar), 1540-1543 (Paris). Gold, enamel, and ebony; height 10 ¼ x 13 ³/₁₆" (26 x 33.5 cm). Kunsthistorisches Museum, Vienna. This exceptional salt and pepper dispenser is the only surviving example of goldsmithery from the hand of Cellini, arguably the most inspired goldsmith of his day. A virtuoso allegory, it presents Neptune,*

god of the sea and source of salt, interlocked with Tellus, goddess of earth, the source of pepper. The figures represent not only witty miniaturizations of Michelangelo's heroic sculptures but also Fontainebleau Mannerism at its most languid and elegant. After modeling the piece for Cardinal Ippolito d'Este, Cellini finally cast it in gold for François I. It too formed part of Louis IX's rich gift to Archduke Ferdinand II of Tyrol. See also figs. 17, 24, and 129.

29

30

described in the tantalizing inventory are the horn of a unicorn ("a large unicorn mounted on one side in gold, standing on three unicorn's heads") and the rock-crystal casket ("a crystal coffer engraved and decorated with gilded silver and enameled figures"), both offered to François I by Pope Clement VII (fig. 19). The finest Kunstkammer works made for King Charles were a gold-plated and enameled repoussé shield, dating from 1572, and a magnificent helmet of enameled gold,[39] both of them acquired by the Louvre at auction in 1793, at the height of the French Revolution.

Another fine creation of the period is a rock-crystal ewer with a parcel-gilt handle designed as Narcissus contemplating his own image in the vessel's liquid content (fig. 25). It can be identified in a 1561 inventory of property belonging to Jeanne d'Albret, Queen of Navarre and mother of Henri de Navarre, the son-in-law of Henri II and Catherine de' Medici who would become Henri IV, King of France. As a result of this dynastic reconfiguration, a number of Navarre treasures would enter the French royal collection in 1601. The ewer seen here was inherited by Louis XIV, Henri IV's grandson, who passed it on to his son, the Grand Dauphin, and through his son, Philip, into the Spanish royal collections (see Chapter 2).

During the reign of Charles IX, Catherine de' Medici found herself alternately in and out of favor, generally counseling pragmatic tolerance even as the bloody Wars of Religion erupted. Finally, however, the Queen Mother and her vacillating son managed to set off, or at least failed to prevent, the infamous Saint Bartholomew's Day Massacre on 24 August 1572, which cost the lives of hundreds of Protestants gathered in Paris for the wedding of Catherine's youngest daughter, Marguerite, to Henri de Navarre, himself a Huguenot leader.

Henri III
(1551-1589)

Among the hands bloodied by the Saint Bartholomew's Day Massacre were those of the famously effeminate Duc d'Anjou, the third son of Henri II and Catherine de' Medici (fig. 30). Elected King of Poland in 1573, Henri returned to France a year later, following the premature death of Louis IX, whom he succeeded as Henri III, a ruthless oppor-

tunist in the conflict between Catholics and Protestants. His fifteen-year reign would unfold in virtually nonstop religious turmoil. In the hope of binding the French nobility to his person, Henri established the Ordre du Saint-Esprit in 1578. And, indeed, it would become the most prestigious of France's chivalric orders. To mark the event, he established a special treasury and presented it with twelve historic articles taken from the Cabinet du Roi at Fontainebleau, all listed in the inventory of 1561. He then added ten silver-gilt items of "modern" manufacture.[40] The first group comprised objects dating from the 15th century through the first half of the 16th, including sacred pieces inherited from Anne de Bretagne as well as two works probably acquired by François I – the silver-gilt ciborium and the pricket candlesticks mentioned earlier (figs. 16, 18). These were consigned to Richard Toutain, the self-styled "goldsmith to the Queen, mother of the King," for restoration, regilding, and fitted cases. Hallmarked, or *poinçonnés*, for the years 1579-1582, the "modern" pieces[41] include several items with traditional "secular" shapes, among them two "pilgrim flasks"[42] and a pair of ewers and basins.[43] The collection evidently came from eight different silversmiths through the retailer and goldsmith Pierre Hotman. As for the order's rather austere plate, it constitutes the largest single group of precious objects to survive from the period. Far more sophisticated is a silver-gilt ceremonial mace with four delicately chased reliefs[44] created for the order only a few years later (fig. 31). Delivered by a member of the Dujardin family in 1585, it may be the most representative example of French goldsmithery made during the reign of Henri III.

Although married to Louise de Lorraine, Henri III produced no heirs, which doomed him to become the last male member of the ancient Valois dynasty. He therefore recognized Henri de Bourbon, his brother-in-law and the King of Navarre, as the next in line of succession. The heir designate, being famously Protestant, was bitterly opposed by the powerful Duc de Guise and the Catholic League. In the resulting struggle (the "War of the Three Henris"), both the Duke and the King succumbed to assassins' daggers. Henri de Navarre, however, did not gain the throne, or even access to the French capital, until after 1593, when finally he abjured Protestantism, allegedly declaring that "Paris was well worth a Mass."

II

The Bourbons

Henri IV (1553-1610), the son of Antoine de Bourbon and Jeanne d'Albret, could trace his claim to the throne of France through his descent from Louis, Duc d'Orléans, a younger brother of King Charles VI (fig. 33). With his accession came a dynastic shift, from the Valois to the Bourbons. For Henri, it also brought a shift in religious confession, from the Calvinism of his upbringing to the Catholicism required of a French monarch. If this revealed him to be a shrewd and pragmatic politician, so did the rest of his resolute yet conciliatory reign. In 1598, Henri proclaimed the Edict of Nantes, which, by tolerating Protestantism, brought the Wars of Religion to a close. In this he reflected the wise and moderating spirit of his contemporary, Michel de Montaigne. With the able Duc de Sully as his chief minister, the King restored the nation to solvency, encouraged agriculture, new industries, and foreign trade, built roads and canals, and fostered colonization of Canada. He also endowed Paris with a still greater Louvre as well as the beautiful Place Royale, today known as the Place des Vosges, in the heart of the Marais. This elegant and serene monument alone would signify the transition France was then making from the Renaissance to the Baroque Classicism of its *Grand Siècle*.

In 1599, Henri IV had his childless marriage to Marguerite de Valois ("La Reine Margot") annulled, shortly after which his beloved mistress, Gabrielle d'Estrées, died in childbirth before he could marry her. The following year the King entered into a dynastic match with Maria de' Medici, the "terribly robust and healthy" daughter of Grand Duke Francesco I of Tuscany (fig. 35). Still, he continued to earn his reputation for gallantry (*le vert galant*), which, together with his legendary Gallic wit and common touch, has made him, among Frenchmen, the most popular of Kings. Concerned for prosperity at all levels of society, Henri is reputed to have said "there should be a chicken in every peasant's pot every Sunday."

To advance both industry and the arts, Henri IV banned the importation of Flemish tapestries, while inviting Flemish weavers to settle in France. Indeed, he made room for them in the arcaded spaces under the new 500-meter Grande Galerie built along the Seine embankment to connect the Louvre to the Tuileries Palace. The art of the bronze also came in for revival, a development owing in part to the sculptor and founder Barthélemy Prieur.

According to contemporary biographies, Maria de' Medici arrived in France with a dowry of 600,000 écus, an immense sum even in the eyes of the jaded French court. Moreover, the ship transporting her to Marseilles is said to have been laden with gold, jewels, and tapestries of unparalleled splendor. For the ratification of her marriage in Lyons, the bride wore a brilliant supposedly valued at 150,000 lire.[1] An imperious and blundering intriguer, Marie de' Medici was also a sumptuary addict who spent fortunes bedecking her bovine person in shimmering satins, rustling silks, and gems by the kilo. Portraits by Scipio Pulzone and Franz Pourbus the Younge show the Queen literally covered in pearls and diamonds. Her private collection, inventoried in 1610, included 11,538 larger diamonds and 5,878 pearls. The biggest of the diamonds was the 35-carat Petit Sancy, which the King had acquired on her behalf for 25,000 écus in 1604. To Marie's great annoyance, Henri failed to acquire the 55.232-carat Grand Sancy, a stone bought instead by Mary Stuart's son, King James I of England, for 60,000 écus. It would, nevertheless, enter the French crown jewels in 1657, after Cardinal Mazarin purchased it from Marie de' Medici's daughter, Queen Henrietta Maria, widow of Charles I of England.

Louis XIII
(1601-1643)

In 1610, when the tolerant Henri IV perished of dagger wounds inflicted by a crazed Catholic, his heir was but ten years old. As Regent, Marie de' Medici cultivated the favor of Spain by marrying young Louis XIII to the Infanta Anna (Anne of Austria) and his sister, Elisabeth, to King Philip IV. Two years later, in 1617, Louis threw off his mother's domination, banished her to Blois, and caused the assassination of her favorite, the despised Florentine Concino Concini, at the very entrance to the Louvre.

33

32. Wall sconce, *c. 1630 (Paris). Gold, enamel, agates, and cameos; height 17 ³/₄" (45 cm). Louvre, Paris. For this sumptuously Baroque treasure, erroneously titled* Chandelier *or* Plaque de lumière de Marie de Médicis, *the anonymous goldsmith from the reign of Louis XIII re-utilized older cameos, possibly from the French royal collection. This explains the misidentification with Marie de' Medici and Henri IV, whose portraits appear in a cameo on the left. Louis XIV paid heavily to acquire the sconce from the Parisian dealer Lebrun.*

33. *Franz Pourbus the Younger.* Henri IV, *c. 1600. Oil on canvas. Louvre, Paris.*

34

35

34. *Philippe de Champaigne. Cardinal de Richelieu, 1635. Oil on canvas; 222 x 155 cm. Louvre, Paris.*

35. *Peter Paul Rubens. The Queen Triumphant: Marie de' Medici as Minerva Victrix, 1625. Oil on canvas; 9' x 10 ⅝' (2.764 x 1.49 mm). Louvre, Paris. Although a political blunderer, Marie de' Medici proved worthy of her Medici and Habsburg heritage in her commitment to the arts, especially the work of jewelers and goldsmiths as well as the painting of Peter Paul Rubens.*

After a reconciliation in 1622, Louis learned to trust one of her protégés, Armand du Plessis, the future Cardinal Richelieu, who, though unpopular, soon emerged as possibly the most astute statesman in French history (fig. 34). In 1630, the ever jealous Queen Mother attempted to have Richelieu dismissed, whereupon Louis sent her once more into exile, this time in the Spanish Netherlands. Marie de' Medici, despite years of pleading, would never again be allowed to set foot on French soil. Her personal jewelry, which the Queen had taken with her, did not revert to the French crown; instead, it was sold, after she died in Cologne, to pay her colossal debts.

Marie de' Medici had a true Florentine's eye for art and love of building. After the murder of Henri IV, she asked Salomon de Brosse to build her a palace on Paris's Left Bank reminiscent of the Palazzo Pitti in Florence. The magnificent pile is known today as the Palais du Luxembourg. To decorate its principal gallery, the Queen commissioned Peter Paul Rubens to paint a cycle of twenty-one monumental paintings glorifying the reign of Henri IV and the regency of Marie de' Medici (fig. 35). Arguably the cycle is the single most admired of the artistic achievements distinguishing the Louis XIII period. And these were considerable, for Richelieu was a dedicated advocate of cultural progress. Not only did the Prime Minister found the French Academy; he and the King lent their support to such creative individuals as the playwright Pierre Corneille, the architect Jacques Lemercier, and the painters Philippe de Champaigne, Simon Vouet, and Nicolas Poussin. René Descartes, the preeminent French philosopher, also came to the fore during the reign of Louis XIII, albeit from a base in

Holland. Goldsmithery flourished as well, salient examples of which are the so-called "Chandelier" and Pierre Delabarre's sardonyx ewer of 1630, shaped like a Roman helmet and mounted in gold (figs. 32, 39). The rarest piece of French goldsmith work from the mid-17th century is "Anne of Austria's Casket," a large paw-footed wooden box clad in a gold fretwork of swirling acanthus foliage and flowers (fig. 36).

Louis XIII, never in strong health, died prematurely in 1643, leaving France to be governed once more by a female regency, that of his Queen, Anne of Austria, the daughter of Philip II of Spain and his fourth wife, Archduchess Anna of Austria. The heir, Louis XIV, was four years old. Again, there was a wily prelate, Cardinal Mazarin, to guide the affairs of state, which he continued doing until his death in 1661 (fig. 37). His policies were essentially those of Richelieu, reinforcing the royal power by quelling the restive aristocracy and challenging the Habsburgs on every front. Thanks to the leadership of two excellent generals, the Prince de Condé and the Vicomte de Turenne, the greatest threat to the new regime came from within. This was the Fronde, or uprising by such vested interests as Parlement or disaffected nobles, that twice erupted during the minority of Louis XIV, forcing the royal family to flee Paris and then to remain in the Louvre, safely ensconced beyond the protective moats. Meanwhile, Cardinal Mazarin, another Louvre resident, lived in great estate. There, as well as in the Hôtel Tubeuf (now part of the Bibliothèque Nationale), he formed a splendid collection of objets d'art,[2] which, once bequeathed to the King, became the nucleus of the French royal collection.

36

Louis XIV
(1638-1715)

At the death of Cardinal Mazarin in 1661, Louis XIV, aged twenty-three and married to another Spanish Princess, Marie-Thérèse of Austria, took control of his own government and held it firmly until the end of his long reign (fig. 40). He succeeded in large part because of the centralizing policies of both Richelieu and Mazarin, which had so transformed the state into a divine-right, absolute monarchy that Louis could, as legend has it, declare: *L'État, c'est moi.* It also helped that he had ministers as able as Jean-Baptiste Colbert and the Marquis de Louvois, the first making France economically supreme in Europe and the latter laying the foundations of French military greatness. By war and by treaty, Louis expanded the frontiers to embrace bits of Flanders, Franche-Comté, and the Alsatian city of Strasbourg. Thanks to his patronage, the Comédie-Française came into being, as did the Gobelins tapestry works and the Savonnerie carpet manufacture. The entire period was extraordinary for the brilliance of its talents, including the painters Claude Lorrain and Nicolas Poussin, the sculptor François Girardon, the playwrights Jean-Baptiste Molière and Jean Racine, the writers Jean de La Fontaine, Jacques Bossuet, and François Fénélon, and the composers Jean-Baptiste Lully and François Couperin. Louis XIV proved to be a compulsive builder, starting with the Louvre, where he finished the Cour Carrée by quadrupling it, as Henri IV had planned. The magnificent eastern façade – La Colonnade – by Claude Perrault canonized Classicism as the French national style, which would come into its full glory at Versailles, Louis XIII's hunting lodge some twelve miles west of Paris. Here, Louis XIV, with a team composed of the architects Louis Le Vau and Jules Hardouin-Mansart, the painter/decorator Charles Le Brun, the sculptor Antoine Coysevox, and the gardener André Le Nôtre, expanded the château and its vast park until the royal enclave became the grandest and most coveted symbol of royalty ever created. At Versailles the politics of luxury and prestige had been realized with a vengeance, all to the greater *gloire* of France and its Sun King, who moved there for good in 1674.

For the great formal interiors at Versailles – the *grands appartements* and the Galerie des Glaces – the court silversmiths Claude Ballin I and Nicolas Delaunay created an enormous range of silver furnishings: chairs, tables, mirror frames, guéridons, massive orange-tree tubs, and *torchères* or candelabra standing over eight feet tall. Today one of the few pictorial witnesses to this wealth of art and craft is a tapestry depicting Louis XIV's visit to the Manu-

facture des Gobelins on 15 October 1667.[3] The *tenture* is one of a series woven from cartoons prepared by the court painter Charles Le Brun and now exhibited at the Musée National du Château de Versailles. At the center of the scene, of course, is the King surrounded by court artisans – *ébénistes*, weavers, goldsmiths – who take turns displaying their wares for royal approval. Tragically, the silver furniture, along with the royal plate, disappeared into the melting pot in 1689-1690 and 1709 to pay for the wars waged to gain the throne of Spain for Louis's grandson Philippe. One of the few important pieces of French silver furniture to survive is a four-foot baptismal font executed by the silversmith Jean-François Cousinet and the sculptor Bernard Fouquet between 1696 and 1707 for the Swedish Royal Chapel.[4]

Louis XIV was an enthusiastic collector of precious stones. Unlike his predecessors, he never pawned or sold any of the royal family's diamonds or colored stones, even under the most difficult circumstances. Quite the contrary, the King steadily augmented the crown jewels throughout his reign. His greatest single acquisition, at a cost of 898,731 livres, was the eye-popping assemblage of diamonds brought back from India by Jean-Baptiste Tavernier, a French traveler, in 1668. Among these fabulous stones was a 115.28-carat blue diamond valued at 220,000 livres. When cut down, it yielded the famously "cursed" Hope Diamond, among numerous other extraordinary gems.

Complete and consecutive inventories, dated 1669, 1681, 1684, 1701, and 1729, exist for the works of art collected by Louis XIV. Two sections of the lists are dedicated to the King's hardstone vessels or *gemmes*, as they were called at the time. One concerns agates and the other colored hardstones, while the second records only rock crystals.[5] Later inventories, dated 1775 and 1791, as well as accounts and appraisals drawn up by court jewelers in 1775-1782 and 1784-1789, make it possible to identify many of the items now preserved at the Louvre in the Galerie d'Apollon. It appears that, despite revolution, theft, and auction, a fair number of the most important gems acquired by Louis XIV have actually survived. Recently identified as well are a number of hardstone treasures today owned by other institutions.[6]

Louis XIV collected on a grand scale, with semiprecious stones holding a particular fascination for him. In this he fell into the tradition established by François I and Henri IV. The superb collection amassed by Cardinal Mazarin, which the King inherited, was rich in such objets d'art.[7] Louis, moreover, instructed his agents to acquire specific types of hardstones for him abroad. Thus, in 1686-1687, the Parisian retailer and jeweler Sylvestre Bosc received

37

36. Casket, *mid-17th century (Paris). Gold, wood, and blue silk; length 17 ¾" (45 cm). Louvre. According to tradition, this lavish casket, mounted in a gold fretwort of scrolling acanthus flowers and foliage, was presented by Cardinal Mazarin to Anne of Austria, Queen Regent of France during the minority of her son, Louis XIV.*

37. *Philippe de Champaigne.* Cardinal Mazarin, *c. 1650. Oil on canvas, 1.40 x 1.16 m. Musée de Versailles. Sent to France as Papal Nuncio, Mazarin joined the French court, serving under Richelieu, at whose death he became chief minister throughout the regency of Anne of Austria and the minority of Louis XIV. At his death, the mass of books and art he had assembled would pass into the crown collections.*

38. *Pierre Delabarre (attrib). Ewer, c. 1630 (Paris). Sardonyx, gold, enamel, and precious stones; height 11" (28 cm). Louvre, Paris. Louis XIV, who loved goldsmith and lapidary art, owned this fluted ewer, a work attributed to the outstanding Parisian goldsmith of his time. Characteristic of Delabarre is the bizarre angular handle with its fanciful dragon.*

39. *Pierre Delabarre. Sardonyx ewer, c. 1630 (Paris). Sardonyx, gold, and enamel; height 11" (28 cm). Louvre, Paris. This remarkable treasure, one of the finest objets d'art in the collection of Louis XIV, boasts an antique - possibly Roman - hardstone body and a contemporary mount fashioned of gold and enamel. Crowning the vessel is the helmeted head of Athena, backed by a dragon handle. This vessel and the one in fig. 38 demonstrate the high quality of Parisian craftsmanship at the end of Louis XIII's reign.*

39

40

40. *Hyacinthe Rigaud. Louis XIV, 1701.
Oil on canvas; 9'1 ⁷/₈" x 5'10 ⁷/₈"
(3.3 x 1.7 m). Louvre, Paris. A
collector as avid as the Duc de Berry,
Louis XIV had a great appetite for
richly mounted hardstone and rock-
crystal vessels, a taste that would be
matched by his son, the Grand
Dauphin.*

41. *Adriaen de Vries (attrib). Rape of
Deïaneira, early 16th century. Bronze;
height 32 ¹/₄" (82 cm). Louvre, Paris.
After Giovanni da Bologna, his master,
Adriaen de Vries (c. 1550-1626), also
from the Netherlands, was the most
sought-after sculptor in Mannerist
Europe. He worked for the Duke of
Savoy but also for Emperor Rudolf II,
in whose service he remained the
longest, beginning in 1603. The three-
figure group seen here once belonged to
Louis XIV.*

payment for a crate sent from Istanbul containing jade vases. Also paid was a certain Galand for acquisitions made in the Levant. The same Galand, in turn, would continue buying medals, agate vases, and other curiosities for the Cabinet des Médailles and the King's library. In 1685, one Dalence in Augsburg was commissioned to purchase "rarities" for the French sovereign, after which he would be paid for three agate and jade vases.

According to an inventory of 1713, Louis XIV owned 377 hardstone vases, including 142 made of agate, 65 of jasper, 32 of jade, and 14 of lapis-lazuli. As this would suggest, the list excluded items in rock crystal. A few of the colored hardstone works were Roman or Byzantine in origin, some dating only from the 16th century, while the large majority were "modern" or contemporary. Many have characteristic mounts, making them likely candidates for attribution to 17th-century Parisian ateliers, run by such jewelers as Laurent le Tessier de Montarsy or Josias Belle, both installed under the Louvre's Grande Galerie.

At Versailles, Louis XIV's collections were displayed on brackets in the mirror-lined Cabinet du Conseil, the Cabinet des Coquilles, the Petite Galerie or Galerie des Bijoux, and the Cabinet des Raretés or Cabinet des Agates. At the Louvre, it was the Galerie d'Apollon that housed the royal collections, set within what was the first true manifestation of the Louis XIV style, a sumptuous ensemble of classicized boiseries, gilded stucco reliefs, and painted, trompe-l'oeil ceiling, created in 1662 by Le Brun, Girardon, and Le Vau. Today the vitrines filled with royal treasures glitter under a central ceiling composition, *The Triumph of Apollo*, painted in 1849 by the great Romantic master Eugène Delacroix.

The Galerie d'Apollon

The present installation of the Galerie d'Apollon dates from 1946. It preserves in one showcase what remains of the crown jewels following an auction in 1887 and costly repurchases, by the French state, of certain key pieces. At the infamous auction Tiffany's of New York bought twenty-two of the most important lots. Several vitrines in the center of the Galerie and along one side contain a large number of hardstone vessels, the remnants of the royal family's much-loved *gemmes* still in France. The collection continued to grow throughout the first half of the 18th century, after which it began to contract. In 1752 Louis XV ordered the sale of a number of hardstone pieces. The *gemmes*, no longer appreciated, disappeared into the garde-meuble, the royal warehouse located after 1774 behind the eastern range of

Gabriel's beautiful colonnaded façade overlooking the Place Louis XV (today Place de la Concorde). Here the crown jewels and the *gemmes* were exhibited to the public during a few days each year. In 1791 the revolutionary government had a new inventory drawn up. Five years later the Directory used a selection of objects from the garde-meuble to pay off a pair of its creditors. Others were transferred to the Musée d'Histoire Naturelle, while the remainder entered the Louvre in 1796. One major theft occurred in 1830. Since then, the number of *gemmes* has remained essentially unchanged.

The collection includes a large number of glorious rock-crystal, jasper, and agate vases, generally dating from the second half of the 16th century or the early 17th century. They are displayed in two oversized cabinets, in a smaller one between them, and in four wall cabinets. Although numerous hardstone vessels dating from the reigns of Louis XIII and Louis XIV – outstanding works in sardonyx and lapis-lazuli – can be identified in the royal archives, the origin of many other pieces lies shrouded in mystery. And this is true even of Cardinal Mazarin's splendid collection, which Louis XIV inherited and then incorporated into his own hoard of art and jewels. For the most part, however, the majority of the Kunstkammer articles in the Galerie d'Apollon were acquired by Louis XIV or by his son, the Grand Dauphin, both of whom were voracious collectors of such art. At royal command, their agents sedulously sought out important objects from earlier periods. This explains why the French royal holdings appear to include more than a few hardstone vases associated with Emperor Rudolf II, who from 1575 to 1612 had reigned over a veritable art-making factory at Hradschin Castle in Prague (see Chapter 7). The Rudolfine pieces would have come on the market following the dispersal of the collections of Queen Christina in Rome, collections rich in Rudolfine works thanks to the Swedish army's sack of Prague in 1648 at the climax of the Thirty Years War.

Among the earlier treasures in the Galerie d'Apollon are a moss-agate saltcellar in a 15th-century mount fashioned of crenellated gold; a rare enameled and silver-gilt *baiser de paix* or *pax* ("kiss of peace") made, very likely, in Siena around 1500; and the so-called "chess set of Saint Louis," a 15th-century gaming board much admired for its delightful border of relief-carved figures and scenes sealed in glazed compartments (fig. 44). A "curiosity" typical of Schatzkammer collections is the *coui des Indes*, a coconut mounted like a Russian kovsh and fitted with an intricate gold handle. Perhaps the finest Kunstkammer work in the Louvre is the unique silver-gilt parade dish created by the great Nuremberg goldsmith Wenzel Jamnitzer in the 1560s

42. *Saracchi workshop.* Vase and cover, 1570s-1580s *(Milan). Rock crystal, gold, and enamel; height: 15 ³/₈"* (39 cm). *Louvre, Paris. The Saracchi, a celebrated family of Milanese lapidarists, were best known for their carved rock-crystal vases. The object seen here, which formed part of the French royal collections, is decorated with Old Testament scenes involving Judith and Holofernes and Susannah with the Elders. Even the dragon handles are of carved and engraved rock-crystal.*

43. *Wenzel Jamnitzer.* Parade basin, *c. 1560 (Nuremberg). Silver-gilt and enamel; diameter 17 ³/₄" (45 cm). Louvre, Paris. This showpiece dish from the French royal collections originated in the atelier of one of the truly great Renaissance goldsmiths. Works by Jamnitzer grace virtually every major European Kunstkammer collection. The basin seen here exemplifies the stil or style rustique, already encountered in the art of Bernard Palissy (fig. 22). Like the French master, Wenzel Jamnitzer favored a decorative repertoire of reptiles, crayfish, and other creatures cast from dead specimens.*

44. *"Chess Set of Saint Louis", late 15th century with 17th-century and later additions. Rock crystal, silver-gilt, gilded bronze, and cedarwood; 17" square (43 cm). Louvre, Paris. An intriguing feature of this rare Late Gothic chess set is the border of small wood-carved scenes housed in sunken compartments under rock-crystal glazing. The set, before it entered the French royal collections, had once been owned by Gabrielle d'Estrées, the mistress of Henri IV.*

43

44

45. Saracchi workshop. Agate cup and cover, 1560s/1570s (Milan). Agate, gold, enamel, and pearls; height 10 5/8" (27 cm). Louvre, Paris. Even today there exist scores of known rock-crystal vessels from the prolific Saracchi ateliers in Milan. The gifted family also worked in other hardstones, especially agate, as here in a lion-capped cup from the French crown collection. The Munich Schatzkammer owns a similar piece.

46. Miseroni workshop. Oval jade cup, late 16th century (Milan). Jade, gold, and enamel; height 7 7/8" (20 cm). Louvre, Paris. Like the Saracchi, the Miseroni were a family of outstanding Milanese lapidarists whose creations

45

were sought by every royal collector in Europe. The boat-shaped cup reproduced here is notable for the beauty of the jade and the décor of carved masks and foliage.

47. Sardonyx cup, late 16th century (Paris?). Agate, gold, and cameos; height 11 1/8" (28.3 cm). Louvre, Paris. Very likely made by a Parisian workshop, this handsome cup and cover culminates in a finial with a single cameo portraying a Roman Emperor. All twelve Caesars are represented in a diadem of cameos ringed about the lip. Such a subject would have appealed to the French court, where the present work formed part of the crown collection.

46

or 1570s (fig. 43). With its throng of enameled crayfish and frogs, interspersed with coiling snakes cast from nature in "white" silver, this magnificent dish constitutes the most extravagant example of *style rustique* in France.

No 16th- or 17th-century *cabinet d'amateur* would have been complete without a clutch of bronzes, and the French royal collection can still boast many remarkable examples, among them a two-figure Deïaneira/Nessos group from the hand of the celebrated Flemish master Jean de Boulogne, better known as Giovanni da Bologna because of his long service at the court of the Medici Grand Dukes in Florence. Also present in the Galerie d'Apollon is a three-figure composition representing Deïaneira, Nessos, and Hercules by Giambologna's gifted pupil Adriaen de Vries, court sculptor to Emperor Rudolf II in Prague (fig. 41).

Many of the Louvre's hardstone vessels originated in Milan during the 16th century. The prolific Saracchi workshop seems to have been the source of an agate cup with a lion-shaped cover (fig. 45), which finds a close stylistic relative in a piece long owned by the Munich Schatzkammer. From the same lapidary atelier came a rock-crystal vase and cover engraved with scenes from the Lives of Judith and Susanna (fig. 42) and a splendid vase carved with the story of Noah. It was virtually imperative that ambitious Kunstkammer collections include outstanding examples of rock-crystal wares created by the Saracchi family.

The Miseroni, another dynasty of Milanese lapidarists, competed with the Saracchi for the same aristocratic clientele. Several works in the Galerie vitrines bear the Miseroni stamp, a so-called "auricular" style notable for the melting fluency of its forms, usually shown off by lavish jeweled mounts. One of their lobed jade cups and covers was formerly thought worthy of attribution to Benvenuto Cellini. A clearly related work is the boat-shaped vessel seen in fig. 46. However, the most admired of the Miseroni pieces is a marvelously carved heliotrope or blood-stone cup from the collection of Rudolf II (fig. 49). Dated 1608, this masterpiece was made by Ottavio Miseroni, then in his twentieth year of service to the Prague court.

In a class by itself is the agate cup set with cameos representing the twelve Caesars (fig. 47), a rare work by reason of its having perhaps been made in a 16th-century French workshop. Mid-17th-century Paris may be the proper attribution for an exceptional group of lapis-lazuli and sardonyx vases with ornate, colorfully enameled mounts. Well worth singling out is the boat-shaped lapis-lazuli cup with a dragon spout, a Neptune figure, a mask-like figurehead, and a décor of contrasting white and pink enamel (fig. 48).

It appears that French goldsmiths were occasionally required to create grandiose mounts for vases of earlier periods, as in a medieval sardonyx cup and a sardonyx ewer possibly of antique origin, both with cameos set in borders of green, white, and pink enamel (figs. 51, 52). Elsewhere, a deeply fluted vase of dark-brown sardonyx and indeterminate age was given an eagle-head spout and a mermaid handle (fig. 50). The most spectacular of these vases is a variegated white and brown sardonyx ewer, possibly Roman, with a dragon handle, a crowning bust of a helmeted Athena, and mounts decorated in white enamel and precious stones (fig. 39). A richly fluted sardonyx ewer with an angular handle conceived as a fantastic bird is reminiscent of those in the surreal paintings of Hieronymus Bosch (fig. 38).

Finally, the *Ancienne Collection de la Couronne* comprises two extraordinary works of art wrongly associated with Marie de' Medici: the so-called *Chandelier* and *Miroir*, both acquired by Louis XIV at astronomic prices. The first is a wall sconce set with a profusion of small brown and white sardonyx plaques and seventeen cameos, a truly Baroque ensemble of decorative elements (fig. 32). The second treasure is a handsome, classically proportioned Renaissance-style mirror ornamented with enamels, jewels, and numerous cameos (fig. 53).

48. Lapis-lazuli cup, *16th century (Italy), mount mid-17th century (Paris). Lapis-lazuli, gold, and enamel; height 16 ½" (42 cm). Louvre, Paris. Resting on four sphinx feet, this colorful boat-shaped vessel from the French crown collection terminates in a dragon spout ready to pour liquid sent rushing forward by Neptune enthroned upon the upper edge above a large mask figurehead. The elaborate polychrome enamel mount dates from the reign of Louis XIII.*

49. Ottavio Miseroni. Bloodstone cup, *1608 (Prague). Heliotrope (bloodstone) and silver-gilt; length 22 ¾" (57.5 cm). Louvre, Paris. Emblazoned with the arms of Emperor Rudolf II, this bloodstone cup was crafted by the leading lapidary in Prague, whom the Emperor ennobled in gratitude for twenty years of service. Miseroni introduced the "auricular" style, with its melting lines and forms, to hardstone carving.*

49

50

52

51

50. Sardonyx ewer, *mount mid-17th century (Paris). Sardonyx, gold, and enamel; height 9 ¹/₂" (24 cm). Louvre, Paris. The large-fluted vessel of antique Roman origin has been set in a jeweled mount with an eagle-head spout and a mermaid handle. The treasure formed part of the French crown collection.*

51. Sardonyx cup, *vessel c. 10th century (Iraq), mounts mid-17th century (Paris). Sardonyx, gold, enamel, and cameos; height 5 ³/₄" (14.5 cm). Louvre, Paris. Another gem from the French crown collection, this two-handled cup, possibly of Middle Eastern origin, became a Kunstkammer treasure thanks to the Louis XIII mount and cover, the latter, like the base, encrusted with cameos.*

52. Sardonyx ewer, *vessel possibly antique, mount mid-17th century (Paris). Sardonyx, gold, enamel, and cameos; height 8 ¹/₁₆" (20.4 cm).*

Louvre, Paris. Here too an old vase has been transformed into a gem by means of an enameled-gold mount featuring an eagle spout and cameos set into the cover. All three vessels on this page, with their antique bodies and aged cameos, were collected as priceless antiquities, worthy of the rich mounts provided by a single Parisian atelier. The goldsmith work is very similar to that found on a number of hardstone vessels in the Alhajas del Delfin.

53. "Miroir de Marie de Médicis", *c. 1630 (Paris). Gold, cornelians, agates and other semiprecious stones, cameos, and enamel. Louvre, Paris. This mistitled work, like the so-called "Chandelier" seen in fig. 32, was acquired by Louis XIV, at a very steep price, from the Parisian dealer Lebrun. The craftsman who made the sumptuous frame incorporated a number of older elements.*

53

54

54. *Hyacinthe Rigaud. Louis de France, Grand Dauphin, c. 1700. Oil on canvas. Château de Versailles. Although no match for his father in longevity, the Grand Dauphin, who died in 1711 before he could ever inherit the French crown, surpassed even Louis XIV in his passion for such Kunstkammer objects as lavishly mounted vessels made of rock-crystal or colored hardstone. Many of those which survive can today be seen in the Louvre's Grande Galerie or at the Prado in Madrid.*

55. Casket with cameos, late 16th century (France). Silver-gilt, enamel, chalcedony, cornelian, agate, lapis-lazuli, amethyst, sardonyx, onyx, and velvet; 5 x 6 ³/₁₆ x 4 ⁷/₈" (12.5 x 15.7 x 12.3 cm). Prado, Madrid. Part of the collection known as Las Alhajas del Delfin, *this edicula-shaped casket is encrusted with 113 hardstones, cameos, and intaglios, all surrounded by polychrome enamel foliage against a ground of black velvet. The relief-carved gems, many of which imitate antique originals, date mostly from the 16th century but include a number of Roman examples. The author of this casket, as well as of a slightly larger, octagonal one, created a handsome vehicle for displaying a large collection of unmounted gems.*

The Gemmes of the Dauphin

Today the Prado in Madrid owns a collection of 120 hardstone vessels, many of them strikingly similar to those in the Louvre's Galerie d'Apollon. The pieces in Spain and many of those in Paris once belonged to the Grand Dauphin, Louis XIV's eldest son, who died in 1711 before he could succeed to the throne (fig. 54). The objects in the Spanish collection are known as *Las Alhajas del Delfin*, meaning the *gemmes* of the Grand Dauphin, the subject of two recent monographs.[8] Like father, like son, the Grand Dauphin Louis was a passionate collector who could easily match the Grand Monarch in his love of hardstones. Indeed, his collection surpassed in size even that of Louis XIV, as witnessed by the 1713 inventory of his estate,[9] which includes two entire sections dedicated to *gemmes*. One consists of 455 entries, all of them for agates, while the other section accounts only for rock crystals. Among the colored hardstone vessels, there are 185 in agate, 69 in jasper, 50 in jade, 30 in cornelian, 27 in lapis-lazuli, 21 in garnet, and 20 in *prime d'émeraude*. According to the inventory, three-quarters of the *gemmes* were displayed at Versailles in the Cabinet des Glaces and the Cabinet Doré, both located in the Grand Dauphin's apartments on the ground floor of the south wing. Here they stood on brackets against mirror-faced walls, an arrangement similar to that for Louis XIV's treasures on an upper story of the palace. The overflow from the collection was kept at Meudon, the Grand Dauphin's château northwest of Paris, where, according to an inventory of 1703, 118 agates were stored in a cupboard on the mezzanine.

Following the death of the Grand Dauphin, his furnishings and hardstones as well as his properties at Meudon and Chaville were appraised at 1.5 million livres, more than enough to cover debts of 300,000 livres. By order of the King, the real estate went to the Grand Dauphin's eldest son, Louis, Duc de Bourgogne, known as the Petit Dauphin, who, unfortunately, died in the following year. As for the furnishings and hardstones, they passed to the Grand Dauphin's second son, Philippe, Duc d'Anjou, who since 1700 had been Philip V, King of Spain, the first of the Spanish Bourbons (fig. 56). The diamonds were inherited by the third son, Charles, Duc de Berry, who survived only until 1714, he too predeceasing Louis XIV. The still-avid King must have reserved some of the rarest hardstone vessels for the crown, inasmuch as 38 of the Grand Dauphin's vases in semiprecious stones entered the French royal collections in 1723. The substantial remainder of the furnishings and hardstones went to settle the Grand Dauphin's debts.

That part of the Grand Dauphin's estate inherited by Philip, or Felipe, V (1683-1746) must have

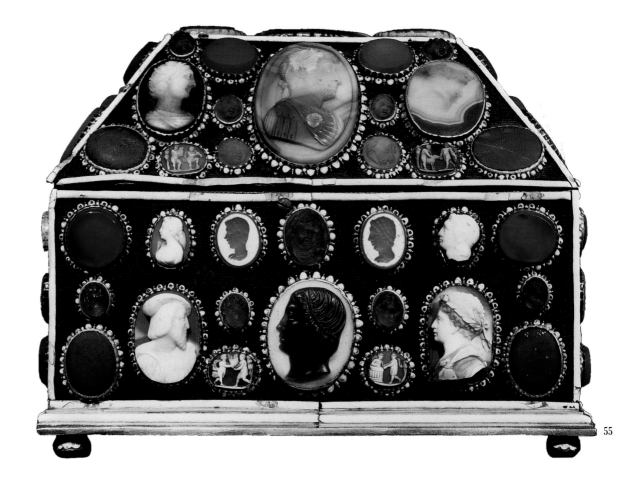

55

remained in France until 1724, the year during which the hardstones finally appeared in La Granja de San Ildefonso. A first inventory, however, was not prepared until after the King's death in 1746, at which time the collection was described as fitted in 137 cases and stored in three crates. The inventory includes 135 entries for hardstone vessels. In 1776, King Carlos III, a keen lover of the sciences, had the *alhajas* incorporated into the Cabinet of Natural History, a development that called for a new inventory. During the Peninsular War of 1808-1814, when Napoleon invaded Iberia and made his brother Joseph King of Spain, the Grand Dauphin's collection was "repatriated" to Paris, haphazardly packed by the military, who left the fitted cases behind. After the collapse of the Napoleonic Empire in 1815, the collection was returned to Spain, albeit considerably worse for wear and minus twelve of the vases. In 1839 the *alhajas* entered the Prado, where, beginning in 1867, they would be exhibited in the main gallery in two octagonal cabinets, one containing hardstones and the other rock crystals. Eleven hardstone pieces were stolen and 35 others seriously damaged in 1918. In 1937, at the height of the Spanish Civil War, the hardstones were again sent to Paris, whence they would be returned to Madrid in 1939. Over the years, the *alhajas* have been restored many times.

Most of the Dauphin's hardstones were acquired by the Prince himself, although nine vessels had been gifts from his wife, Maria Anna of Bavaria, four from his father, Louis XIV, one from his mother, Marie-Thérèse of Austria, five from the Siamese ambassadors who visited Versailles in 1686, and still other pieces from various friends. In many instances the mounts are styled very much like those in the Louvre. Some of the vessels date from the late 16th century, which made them "antiquities" by the time the treasures entered the Dauphin's collection, but for the most part they would have been viewed as "modern," meaning 17th-century work. The earlier history of the *alhajas* has yet to be researched, and so too the art-historical context from which they emerged. In general, the hardstone vessels retain their fitted leather cases, bound in tooled and gilded red morocco decorated with dolphins and the Bourbons' fleur-de-lis. Today the cases are installed at the Museo de Artes Decorativas.

The most exquisite of the *alhajas* may be a stunning mid-16th-century Cellinesque saltcellar held aloft by a bejeweled and enameled gold siren kneeling on a domed chalcedony base (fig. 62). Another dazzling piece is a 17th-century lapis-lazuli vase with a golden base alive with dolphins, dragons, and a putto finished in polychrome enamel.[10] The vessel lost a second putto and its original dragon-shaped

handles during the dislocations of the Napoleonic era. The workshop responsible for this treasure may also have created the chalcedony cup surmounted by a fantastic dolphin/dragon ridden by a white putto.[11] The collection includes two exceptional edicula-shaped caskets covered with a profusion of cameos and intaglios (fig. 55). One of the pieces, octagonal in plan,[12] has iron walls encased in gold mounts and a fretwork of foliage in polychrome enamel worked about 152 engraved or carved stones, most of them intaglios. These are primarily Renaissance in origin, although a fair number date back to antiquity. The octagonal work and its slightly smaller mate seen here served as vehicles for exhibiting a large collection of gems with safety.

One of the most intriguing of the hardstone *alhajas* is a shell with entwining floral branches carved from what appears to be Chinese white jade. It rests on a Louis XIV silver-gilt base of Neoclassical design. A similar piece is made of green jade. Such Oriental hardstones, much appreciated at the time, made their way into other 16th-century collections.[13] Only one object among the Dauphin's *gemmes* is not a hardstone, and this a Turkish cup made of silver-gilt encrusted with turquoise and numerous cabochon rubies.[14] In a Kunstkammer it would have appeared among the exotica, objects generally described at the time as "Indian."

Of the 120 objects that form *Las Alhajas del Delfin*, slightly more than half – 68 in all – are rock crystals. One unusual piece within this group – a Gothic cylindrical jug engraved with florettes and quadrilobes – would have been classified as an antiquity in early collections.[15] Of a later date, however, may be the silver-gilt mount with a bird-shaped spout[16]. A rock-crystal jug with enameled gold mounts, one of a pair, appears to be a French work made in the 1560s (fig. 59). The somewhat heavy spiraled fluting is distinctly reminiscent of works issuing from the Toutain workshop.[17] Another rock-crystal jug with identical fluting originally had jeweled mounts of still greater lavishness. Toutain seems even more present on the foot of this piece, where the white linear decoration has been worked on a black ground.[18] Cited earlier is a jug with a parcel-gilt Narcissus handle that has been identified in a 1561 inventory of assets in the estate of Jeanne d'Albret, Queen of Navarre and mother of Henri IV (fig. 25). This exceptional work of art, which must be counted among the finest of its kind, can also be associated stylistically with the Toutain atelier.

More than fifteen rock-crystal *alhajas* originated in Milan during the 1560-1580 period. In the first half of the 16th century the greatest hardstone engravers were Valerio Belli of Vicenza and Giovanni Bernardi of Castelbolognese. The second half of the

56

56. *Hyacinthe Rigaud. Felipe V, King of Spain, c. 1700. Oil on canvas. Louvre, Paris. Philippe, Duc d'Anjou, might have become the King of France had his grandfather, Louis XIV, not won the Spanish crown for him, assuming that the French throne would have passed first to his son, the Grand Dauphin, and then to Philippe's elder brother, both of whom died before the Grand Monarch himself. From the Dauphin, Philippe, as Felipe V of Spain, inherited a vast collection of gemmes – jeweled and goldsmith-mounted hardstone vessels – which in Spanish became known as* Las Alhajas del Delphin.

57. *Saracchi workshop. Moses Vase,
1570s/1580s (Milan). Rock crystal,
gold, enamel, and rubies; height
6 13/16" (22.5 cm). Prado, Madrid. The
Alhajas del Delfin at the Prado and
the gemmes in the Louvre Galerie
d'Apollon include a wealth of rock-
crystal vessels from the Saracchi
atelier in Milan. The Moses Vase, as
the title suggests, is decorated with
scenes featuring the Old Testament
Prophet.*

58. *Miseroni workshop. Topaz vase, late
16th century (Milan), mounts 17th
century (France). Smoky topaz, gold,
enamel, emeralds, and diamonds;
height 10 7/16" (26.5 cm). Prado,
Madrid. The style of the Miseroni is
fully evident in this monumental vase,
with its relief-carved flutes, scrolls,
and masks. The gemme seen here is
one of the finest in the Alhajas del
Delfin.*

59. *Rock-crystal ewer, 1560s? (Paris).
Rock crystal, gold, silver-gilt, enamel,
and rubies; height 5 1/2" (14 cm).
Prado, Madrid. One of a pair of
aguamaniles, or burettes, this vessel is
remarkable not only for its spiraling
flutes or gadroons but also for its
handle, the latter formed as the infant
Hercules with two entwined snakes
and another infant supporting the
spout.*

60. *Citrine oil lamp, late 16th century
(Italy). Citrine, gold, and enamel;
height 5 1/2" (14 cm). Prado, Madrid.
While Spanish inventories describe this
vessel as an olla ("oil lamp"), such
items can be found characterized
elsewhere as dos cazones por
bebederos ("two spouts for drinking").
Both the carving and the black-
enameled mount would seem to
indicate Milanese craftsmanship.*

57

58

59

60

century saw the emergence of Milan as the important center of hardstone carving. The Milanese workshops of Annibale Fontana and both the Saracchi[19] and Miseroni[20] families supplied all the major courts in Europe – Florence, Paris, Munich, Madrid, Prague, Vienna – with vessels made of rock crystal and colored hardstones. It is clear that, in this period, no self-esteeming Prince would have dreamt of assembling a Kunstkammer without carved rock crystals from Milan.

Milan's first major lapidary was Annibale Fontana, some of whose finest vases grace the collections of the Louvre and the Munich Schatzkammer (fig. 205). However, the most prolific of the Milanese lapidary workshops was that of the Saracchi family, whose members – Simone, Ambrogio, Michele, Stefano, and Rafaele – were active from around 1570 until well into the 17th century. Italian craftsmen, many of them Milanese, also entered the service of foreign courts, examples being Jacopo da Trezzo in Madrid from 1559, the brothers Caroni in Florence from 1572, and Giorgio Caffuri, who was at the Medici court beginning in 1575. Gasparo Miseroni, one of the most sought-after hardstone artists, worked for both the Medici in Florence and the Habsburgs in Vienna, while Girolamo and Giulio Miseroni departed for Madrid. Ottavio Miseroni, together with his brothers Alessandro and Giovanni Ambrogio and even his son Dionysio, heeded the call of Emperor Rudolf II in Prague.

Charles-Émanuel I, Duc de Savoie, is known to have sent examples of rock-crystal work from the Saracchi ateliers to Dresden and Spain. The most important piece of carved rock crystal in Spain is the casket forwarded around 1590 by Catarina, daughter of Philip II of Spain and the wife of the Duc de Savoie, to her sister, Isabella Clara Eugenia, at the Escorial, where the piece remains today. What sounds like a life-size *gallo d'India*, or peacock, made of rock crystal was also dispatched by the Duc de Savoie to the Spanish court, where it would be listed in the inventory of Philip II's estate compiled in 1602. The *alhajas* collection includes large vases in all shapes, dishes, cups and covers, birds and basilisks, a fountain in the form of a dolphin, and two magnificent boat-shaped receptacles.

A typical work of the Saracchi is the splendid rock-crystal vase engraved with scenes representing the Life of Moses (fig. 57). Comparable works can be found at the Kunsthistorisches Museum in Vienna and the Schatzkammer in Munich. The *alhajas* collection boasts an elaborately shaped cup formed as a galley with three wheels, a dragon spout, enameled embellishments, and mounts in silver and gold (fig. 61). Similar objects are cited in the 1602 inventory of Philip II's collections. Of the known works by the Saracchi, the masterpiece may be the galley sent to Duke Albrecht V in Munich in 1579, a vessel once equipped with miniature cannon, soldiers, galley slaves, and a throng of other figures (see Chapter 9). Analogous works are owned by the Louvre, the Museo degli Argenti, and the Green Vaults.

The *alhajas* include as well a double-spouted citrine vase (fig. 60) and a monumental vase of smoky topaz carved with masks, scrolls, and flutes, its enameled gold mounts set with diamonds and cabochon emeralds (fig. 58). The latter has been attributed to the Miseroni workshop in Milan. Works of similar design lend glory to both the Louvre and the Munich Schatzkammer.

61

III

Cosimo, Piero, and Lorenzo de' Medici

Florence, that jewel of the Italian Renaissance, glittered as it did in considerable part because of the Medici and their compulsion to amass treasure in every form of the fine and decorative arts.[1] For three hundred years, beginning in the early 15th century, this remarkable family, who emerged from the bourgeois world of apothecaries and merchant bankers to reign as sovereign Grand Dukes, never ceased to collect on an opulent scale, everything from coins, cameos, and jewels to bronzes, mosaics, etched crystal, and colorful hardstone vessels mounted in gold or silver. As the world knows, the Medici also patronized some of the greatest artists and architects who ever lived, among them Ghiberti, Brunelleschi, Donatello, Uccello, and Masaccio, Fra Angelico, Ghirlandaio, and Botticelli, Raphael, Michelangelo, and Cellini, Pontormo, Bronzino, Giambologna, and Pietro da Cortona. As brilliant in culture as they were in banking and politics, the Medici grasped the spirit of the Renaissance at the very dawn of the new age, eagerly participating in the urge to rediscover and emulate the civilization of Classical antiquity. This meant a new interest in nature and humanity, as well as an urgent desire to reconcile it with the otherworldly, Christian aspirations inherited from the Middle Ages.

At the very center of the effort to redefine life in more humanistic terms were the Medici, particularly those 15th-century giants Cosimo the Elder and his grandson Lorenzo the Magnificent. Both played munificent host to the circle of intellectuals known as the Neoplatonic Academy, the leading lights of which were Marsilio Ficino, Angelo Poliziano, Luigi Pulci, and Pico della Mirandola. Encouraged by Cosimo, Ficino translated many of the Greek classics into Latin, including Plato's *Dialogues*, while the aristocratic Pico dedicated his speculative philosophic-religious *Conclusions* to Lorenzo. Part and parcel of the new ideology of Classical rebirth was the Medici collecting, inasmuch as it began in emulation of the

Roman Emperors, who understood that lavish displays of wealth and culture could invest power with lustre, even with an air of invincibility. Meanwhile, the Medici also collected out of the Humanist or Neoplatonic conviction that art and the rare curiosities of nature were magical things, essences yielding clues to the divine order underlying the world's disorder and thus perhaps to a means of escaping or reforming it.

In Renaissance Florence, the ideal product of Humanist culture was the man, trained in the classics, who possessed both *sapientia* and *eloquentia* – the "wisdom" to know the right path to follow in any situation and the "eloquence" needed to persuade his fellowmen to take it. The very form of his presentation – in words, images, general demeanor, even the works of art and architecture he sponsored or collected – should, through the beauty of its appropriateness, give such pleasure that the ideas and values conveyed would be certain of acceptance. The more beautiful and seductive the form, the greater the responsibility for investing it with valid content. The Humanist sought to possess *virtù*, the quality of being a true "man" (Latin: *vir*) in that he had been true to himself in the virtuosity – the imagination and boldness – with which he met the challenges and opportunities that make for greatness, whether in commerce, statesmanship, or artistic endeavor. The spirit of Humanism called upon its followers to adopt the concept of *l'uomo universale* ("the universal man"), a motivated and gifted individual fully capable of both the active and the contemplative occupations believed essential to a well-balanced and harmonious existence. For such, life was best lived when the human personality showed its versatility in many forms: improvement of the mind, refinement of the spirit, perfection of the body, development of social graces, leadership in public affairs, and appreciation and creativity in the arts. The "scientific" proof of the individual's success in his achievement would be

64

63. Jeweled cup and cover, *mid-15th century (Burgundy), silver base c. 1700. Rock crystal, gold, enamel, sapphires, and balas rubies (spinels); height of cup 3/4" (9.5 cm). San Lorenzo, Florence. One of 33 hardstone vases owned by Lorenzo the Magnificent, whose proud initials it bears, this jeweled cup is a rare treasure surviving from the court of the rich and powerful Dukes of Burgundy. The goldsmith Cosimo Merlini added the base with its silver angels around the turn of the 18th century.*

64. Jacopo Pontormo. Cosimo il Vecchio de' Medici, *c. 1518-1520. Oil on panel; 33 3/4 x 25 1/8 "(86 x 65 cm). Uffizi, Florence. The great Medici banker Cosimo the Elder held the reins of power in mid-15th-century Florence as a kind of benevolent despot acting behind the scenes. He also proved to be an active and sophisticated patron of scientists, theologians, philosophers, and artists, especially the sculptor Donatello.*

65. *Benozzo Gozzoli.* Procession of the Magi, *1459-1460. Fresco. Palazzo Medici-Riccardi, Florence. The Medici had the chapel in their family palace frescoed with a panorama depicting the journey of the Magi, a commission executed by a onetime pupil of Fra Angelico, whose sweetness and charm are fully evident in the detail seen here. The Medici and their retinue participate in the procession winding its way across a Tuscan landscape dotted with the family's numerous castles and villas. One figure whose identity seems clearly signaled is the crowned youth behind whom rises a laurel plant, the Latin name of which is Laurentius, or "laurel-growing." Hence, Lorenzo, who would grow up to be Lorenzo the Magnificent, perhaps the greatest of all the Medici, as we shall see later in this chapter. The almost medieval attention to line and detail in what is otherwise a fully Renaissance painting contributes to the overall sense of enchantment, at the same time that it reflects a Medici love of jeweled refinement, especially in precious collectibles.*

65

fame, proclaimed by Petrarch, following Cicero, to be granted only to the most worthy performance.

In the realm of art patronage and collecting, no one gave a more worthy performance or garnered more attendant fame than the Medici. By the volume, breadth, and range of their holdings, they remained steadfastly consistent with the Humanist search for universality, for a microcosm of choice items whose purpose was to mirror the macrocosm at its most wondrous – thus the wisdom and eloquence of those who had assembled such stunning evidence. By their collecting, the Medici demonstrated their "virtue" and declared their right to lead, rule, and dominate. For the Medici, collecting represented a major and centrally important enterprise, an undertaking for which they could claim to have possessed true Renaissance genius.

Giovanni di Bicci de' Medici (1360-1429) founded the family fortune when he became banker to the papacy, receiving papal revenues on deposit and lending them abroad at fantastic rates of interest to finance the new national governments, their wars, and their overseas expansions. He also recruited Filippo Brunelleschi, the great Italian architect of the Early Renaissance, to design the Ospedale degli Innocenti and both the apse and the sacristy at San Lorenzo, the Medici family church in Florence. He

then paid for their construction. Frugal and taciturn, he was popular with the people of Florence, whose cause he frequently defended against the *grandi*, meaning the old feudal nobility. As a leading citizen, Giovanni di Bicci sat on the committee judging the entries in the competition for the first set of bronze door panels commissioned for the Baptistery. The winning entry, a relief created by Lorenzo Ghiberti and representing the Sacrifice of Isaac, has often been cited as the work that ushered in the Renaissance. Giovanni collected, although none of the objects in semiprecious stone – jewels, cameos, and vases – which survive from the early Medici collections can be specifically associated with the founder.

Cosimo de' Medici, Pater Patriae (1389-1464)

It was Giovanni di Bicci's son Cosimo who established Medici political power (fig. 64). Yet, fully aware of his fellow townsmen's passion for equality, the shrewd Cosimo never assumed any outward sign of authority. Instead, he ruled discreetly from behind a façade of civic benevolence, spending incalculable sums to support art and culture and to endow the first public library since antiquity. Acutely intelligent, literate in

Latin and to some degree in Greek, Cosimo sought the company of artists, poets, and musicians, Humanists and scientists, theologians and philosophers. For Cosimo, the architect Michelozzo designed and began building the Palazzo Medici on Via Larga (today Palazzo Medici-Riccardi on Via Cavour) with its private chapel frescoed by Benozzo Gozzoli. Taking the Magi and their journey to Bethlehem as his subject, Benozzo transformed it into a brightly colored, panoramic landscape filled with the Medici villas and castles as well as with the Medici themselves, attended by their retinue (fig. 65). A lively scene of infinite charm, the pictorial narrative contains many figures that are early portraits, including one of young Lorenzo, the future Magnificent. Michelozzo's vast fortress-like building was the first great Renaissance palace in Florence, a proud statement of the family's newly acquired importance (fig. 66). For the interior courtyard, Cosimo commissioned Donatello, his favorite sculptor, to execute a pair of life-size bronzes, *David* and *Judith Slaying Holofernes*, both now regarded as key monuments in the history of art. Having refused all honors during his lifetime, Cosimo received the posthumous title of *pater patriae* ("Father of His Country"), voted by grateful Florentines.

When it comes to jewelry or precious objects, however, scarcely more is known about Cosimo as a collector than has been discovered for his father.[2] One Kunstkammer item Cosimo did possess was a narwhal tusk, thought at the time to be a horn of the mythical unicorn. Mounted in gold, it was acquired by the great banker as security for a loan. Documents also suggest that Cosimo took an active interest in gems – glyptics – a possibility confirmed by Ciriaco d'Ancona, a contemporary collector of antiquities, who cites certain *prectiosa multa supellectilia* among Cosimo's holdings. Lorenzo Ghiberti, in his *Commentari*, mentions having mounted in gold a magnificent cornelian intaglio "the size of a nut, on the surface of which had been engraved three figures most exquisitely done by the hand of an excellent master of old."[3] According to Giorgio Vasari in his *Vite*, written a century later, it was Cosimo's son Giovanni, then only eight years old, who had purchased the "large cornelian engraved in intaglio with a scene showing the flaying of Marsyas at Apollo's command."[4] A masterpiece generally known as *Nero's Seal*, the gem is now attributed to Dioskurides, an engraver known to have worked for Augustus, the first of the Roman Emperors. Artists as different as Gerard David and Sandro Botticelli drew inspiration from the cornelian, and none other than Raphael turned to it for his version of the theme in the Vatican. In 1456 Piero de' Medici, Cosimo's elder son, had an inventory drawn up of his possessions, among which are listed some twenty cameos and intaglios transferred to him by his father.

Piero Il Gottoso
(1416-1469)

As the inventory would suggest, Piero de' Medici, nicknamed Piero Il Gottoso because of his crippling gout, emerged as the first major collector in the Medici family. An eminent bibliophile and builder as well, Piero proved so relentless in his pursuit of gems that his compatriot Averlino Filarete compared him to the legendary Duc de Berry.[5] The inventory of 1456 includes a category labeled "Jewels and Similar Objects" under which are listed seven vases, twenty-one jewels and rings, and numerous diamonds, sapphires, pearls, and other precious stones, mounted as well as unmounted. Under the same heading appear such princely curiosities as the narwhal tusk acquired by Cosimo, hundreds of silver and gold medals, "the loose tongue of a serpent," "a purse worked in gold containing razor, comb, and scissors," "Damascus ware," porcelain, antique glass, "chiming clocks," and "a chessboard in jasper."[6] A second inventory, this one drawn up in 1465, provides not only brief descriptions but also estimated values in gold florins, or ducats, the proud currency of Florence since 1252. A collection of thirty cameos is valued at 2,580 florins, fifteen vases carved from semiprecious hardstone (*pietra dura*) at 4,580 florins, silver at 6,702, and a quantity of jewelry at 17,689. Among the vases the most valuable appears to have been a "crystal cup with cover mounted in gold, with enameled figures and pearls and balas rubies, and sapphires and rubies," its worth placed at 700 florins. This item, a rare lidded vessel from Burgundy used as a reliquary, survives today in the treasury of San Lorenzo (fig. 63). Listed with the jewelry, a category accounting for the bulk of the collections' value, is a single "shoulder pin of a pound of gold with a large, flat balas ruby and three large pearls and a diamond with many facets," its worth set at 5,000 florins. To understand just how princely these sums were, it is helpful to know that a house in 15th-century Florence could be had for 1,000 florins and the bronzes of Donatello as well as the paintings of Botticelli for less than 100 florins each![7]

Perhaps because of his disability, Piero had a small, private room built near his bedchamber where he could house and study his collections – books and objects alike – with all the quiet deliberation necessary to appreciate their special qualities. The windowless *studiolo*,[8] the prototype for many such dedicated "studies," measured about 12 by 16 feet and boasted walls reveted in intarsia paneling, cabinets decorated with trompe-l'oeil painting, and a floor glazed with terra-cotta tiles by Luca della Robbia. Luca had also designed the ceramics on the barrel-

66

66. *Michelozzo. Palazzo Medici-Riccardi. Begun 1444. Florence. Built by Cosimo the Elder to look as solid as a bank, complete with heavily rusticated masonry on the ground-floor façade, the Palazzo Medici remained the primary residence of the great banking family until they became Grand Dukes and moved into the Palazzo della Signoria. Typically, Cosimo rejected a first design, by Brunelleschi, as too ostentatious. It was here that the Medici fostered the Renaissance, playing host to artists, writers, and intellectuals, among them the Humanists, Donatello, and Michelangelo, who studied the collection of Classical sculpture in the central courtyard.*

68. *Giusto da Firenze (attrib).* Red-jasper cup, early 15th century (Venice/ Florence). Red jasper, silver-gilt, and enamel; height 10 ¹/₂" (26.7 cm). Museo degli Argenti, Florence. Only the mount, now deprived of its finial, is attributed to Giusto da Firenze, while the carved hardstone has been labeled "Fatimid, 11/12th century" and "Venetian 10/13th century." In reality the vessel dates from the early 15th century. The initials LAU.R.MED engraved upon the jasper identify the proud owner: Lorenzo de' Medici.

69. *Sardonyx cup,* early 1st century (Rome), mount c. 1570. Sardonyx and silver-gilt; height 17 ³/₄" (45 cm). Museo degli Argenti, Florence. This magnificent hardstone cup, with its spectacular veining, dates back to Augustan Rome. It too belonged to Lorenzo de' Medici and thus bears his mark - LAU.R.MED. - but the arms on the base are those of Francesco de' Medici, elevated to Grand Duke of Tuscany in 1570. In 1532 this vase, like the one reproduced opposite, was presented by Pope Clement VII Medici to the Church of San Lorenzo in Florence. Both treasures were part of the collection of 33 antique and medieval vessels owned by Lorenzo the Magnificent, a keen collector of hardstone vases, most of them mounted in Florence in the 15th and 16th centuries.

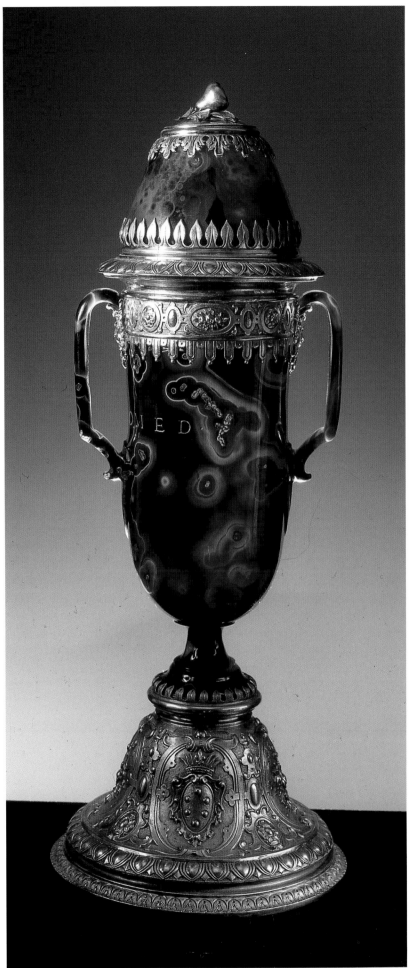

69

70

70. *Giorgio Vasari. Lorenzo the
Magnificent, c. 1578. Oil on panel;
23 x 18" (90 x 72 cm). Uffizi, Florence.
The epitome of the Renaissance man of
virtù, Lorenzo de' Medici not only
supported Humanist intellectuals and
the young Michelangelo; he also
collected every kind of precious object,
from antique cameos to the most
scientifically advanced automata.*

71. *The Tazza Farnese (detail), early 1st
century (Rome). Sardonyx agate;
diameter 8" (20.3 cm). Museo
Nazionale, Naples. This historic cameo
depicts a personification of the Nile on
one side and a Medusa head on the
other. After young Lorenzo de' Medici
acquired the gem in Rome in 1471, the
Medici rated it their most precious
work of art. Following the murder of
tyrannical Alessandro de' Medici, his
wife, Margaret of Austria, took the
cameo into her marriage with Ottavio
Farnese, from whose family it would
pass to the Neapolitan Bourbons.*

vaulted ceiling, which featured twelve tondos representing the months of the year, complete with the length of days and nights, the number of hours, the relevant signs of the Zodiac, the phases of the moon, and the human occupations affected by all such factors.[9] The tondos, now preserved at the Victoria and Albert Museum in London, are the first known attempt at an encyclopedic compendium of the world.[10]

Filarete, who visited the *studiolo* in 1456, wrote in his *Trattato dell'Architettura* (c. 1463) that the books, because of their gilded bindings, looked like a "mass of gold." Also present in the little room were "effigies and images of all the Emperors and Worthies of the past, some made of gold, some of silver, some of bronze, of precious stones or of marble and of other materials which are wonderful to behold." As for Piero, "he will look at his precious stones, of which he has a marvelous quantity of great value, some engraved, others not. He takes great pleasure and delight in looking at these and in discussing their various excellencies. Another day he will inspect his vases of gold and silver and other precious materials and praise their noble worth and the skill of the masters who wrought them. Then at other times he will look at various other praiseworthy objects from all parts of the world, and at various strange suits of armor."[11]

In 1457 the *studiolo* had another visitor, the poet Piero Parenti, who commemorated this occasion with these verses:

> *Gran numer v'è di libri molto ornatj
> et vasi d'alabastro et chalcidoni
> che son d'oro e d'argiento proffilati.*[12]

Cosimo's second son, Giovanni de' Medici (1421-1463), was known for his patronage of living artists as well as for his interest in antiquities, a field in which he competed with such major collectors as the Venetian Pietro Barbo, who became Pope Paul II in 1464. An inventory of the Barbo collection, made in 1457, itemizes a great number of precious objects, including jewels, antique coins, and silver vases, in addition to 821 incised hardstones, 243 cameos, and 578 intaglios.[13] Some of this hoard may have ended up in the hands of a twenty-two-year-old Lorenzo de' Medici, thanks to Pope Sixtus IV, Pope Paul's heir, who distributed gifts to dignitaries, such as Lorenzo, sent to Rome as ambassadors representing their governments at the Pope's coronation.

Lorenzo the Magnificent (1449-1492)

Lorenzo de' Medici was Piero's elder son (fig. 70), the crowned and exquisitely dressed young man portrayed as the third Magus in Benozzo Gozzoli's *Procession of the Magi* (fig. 65). He would mature into one of the most powerful magnates in 15th-century Italy, presiding over Florence during the climax of its Renaissance achievements. Indeed, he fairly enchanted the city with his lavish patronage of pageants, festive tournaments, and resplendent buildings. A gifted poet, Lorenzo, like Dante before him, chose to compose not in the Humanists' Latin but in the vernacular Italian of his day. Gathering about him talented individuals from every field, Lorenzo maintained a veritable court of the creative and the intellectual. "When my mind is disturbed," he said, "with the tumults of public business, and my ears are stunned with the clamors of turbulent citizens, how would it be possible for me to support such contentions unless I found relaxation in Learning?" Lorenzo collected antique sculptures and invited the young Michelangelo to study and work among them. The epitome of the cultivated Humanist grandee, a veritable Renaissance man of *virtù*, Lorenzo was known to his bedazzled compatriots quite simply as *Il Magnifico* ("the Magnificent"). Nowhere is his triumphant spirit better captured than in one of his own poems:

> *Quant'è bella giovinezza
> Che si fugge tuttavia!
> Chi vuol esser lieto, sia:
> Di doman non c'è certezza.*[14]

Lorenzo collected not only antiquities but also cameos, intaglios, and hardstone vessels, the best of which came in the Pope's coronation gift. In his autobiography, Lorenzo described his Roman experience: "In September 1471 I was elected Ambassador to

71

72. Portable altar, *1320-1330 (Venice).*
Jasper, mother-of-pearl, and wood;
13 ³/₄ x 13" (35 x 33 cm). Museo degli
Argenti, Florence. The miniature
paintings on this altar represent the
Crucifixion, the Virgin and Child, the
Evangelists, and various saints.
Overall, the altar bears stylistic
kinship with the diptych altar of King
András III of Hungary taken by Queen
Agnes to the Königsfelden abbey in
Switzerland (fig. 98). It too originated
in Venice, where the love of color,
mosaics, rich marbles, gilding, and
hieratic imagery reflected the
Serenissima's proud identification with
Byzantium. The Habsburgs' deep
involvement with Venice began at a
very early date, as did their sense of
themselves as heirs to the Byzantine
and Roman Emperors. All the more
reason why Rudolf II would exploit
every means to obtain from Venice the
great altarpiece painted in 1506 by
Albrecht Dürer for the Fondaco dei
Tedeschi on the Grand Canal (fig. 154).

72

Rome for the coronation of Pope Sixtus, where I was shown much honor, and thence did bring back the two antique marble heads portraying Augustus and Agrippa, which the aforementioned Pope Sixtus had given me, and furthermore I brought back our insignia in engraved chalcedony, along with many other cameos and medals, which were purchased there, among others the chalcedony one."[15] The "insignia in engraved chalcedony" is the so-called *Farnese Cup (Tazza Farnese)*, which Lorenzo regarded as the most valuable treasure in his collection, worth some 10,000 florins (fig. 71). An ancient cameo, the Farnese Cup is relief-carved on one side with an elaborate allegory of the fertile Nile and on the obverse side with a Medusa head, subjects suggesting, as does the craftsmanship itself, that the jewel originated in the Near East sometime during the Roman Empire.

Not content merely to buy antique gems, Lorenzo vigorously encouraged modern work, inviting such engravers as Giovanni delle Corniole and Pietro di Neri Razzanti to Florence, where employment was conditional upon their willingness to accept Florentine pupils. He further expanded the Medici treasure by purchasing whole collections, from, for example, the estate of Cardinal Francesco Gonzaga. Lorenzo also hired experts and agents, the better to be wise about his expenditures. More than once he declined to overpay for a coveted object, as in 1490 when he wrote in response to an offer of an antique bust: "I would happily buy it from the owner, in the event he may wish to sell it at its proper value."[16]

Lorenzo also had a taste for automata, especially mechanical clocks, seven of which are listed in the final inventory of 1492. One clock, "which runs without counterbalance," was "to be placed in a niche with hearts and perforations in gilt copper,... [and] with arms and sprites enameled on the face where the hours are shown."[17]

Of the several hundred cameos known to have been owned by Lorenzo the Magnificent, some fifty survive.[18] It is interesting to note that in the original collection, the cameos outnumbered the intaglios five to one, whereas in most contemporary collections

73. Mottled-jasper cup and cover, *1st half 15th century (Burgundy or France). Jasper and gold; height 7 1/3" (18.7 cm). Museo degli Argenti, Florence.* The origin of this exquisite cup, fluted to simulate drapery, has been tentatively placed in Bohemia, France, or Burgundy, all centers of refined courtly life in the early 1500s. That it was considered an art work of great rarity is attested to by the unusually lavish gold mount. Lorenzo de' Medici thought the treasure worthy of his collector mark, and Pope Clement VII Medici included it among the vases he returned to Florence as reliquaries for display in the tribuna of San Lorenzo.

74. Rock-crystal ewer, *early 11th century (Fatimid Egypt). Rock crystal and gold; height 16" (40.5 cm). Museo degli Argenti, Florence.* This ewer is one of three similar works dating from the Early Middle Ages, the others being found in the Louvre (from the Saint-Denis treasury) and the treasury of San Marco in Venice. The Arabic inscription reads: "For the personal use of the Commander of the Commanders." The Commander cited was Sultan Hussein, son of Gawhar, founder of the Fatimid dynasty of Egypt. The piece entered the Medici inventories in 1704 and would later be installed in Florence's Museum of National History.

there was one cameo for every ten intaglios. What this reflects is the sheer wealth of the Medici holdings, since rare antique cameos enjoyed the status of art works or luxury items, unlike the intaglios, which were plentiful enough to be worn as rings.

After Lorenzo died in April 1492 the inventory of his property listed some 4,000 items valued at over 75,000 florins.[19] The contents of the *Scrittoio*, the "office" or *studiolo* where most of the treasure was displayed, were estimated to be worth 53,413 florins. This sum accounted for thirty-three hardstone vases appraised at 21,318 florins, or almost a third of the total value of the inventoried estate. Ten of the vases were fashioned of rock crystal, ten of jasper, and the remainder of chalcedony, amethyst, sardonyx, or porphyry. Four of the pieces can be identified, and a total of twenty-one vessels survive with Lorenzo's mark engraved upon them in fine Roman capitals: LAU.R.MED. The letters have been interpreted as signifying LAV. R[RENTIUS]. MED.[ICES], LAV. R.[ENTII] MED.[ICEI], or LAU.[RENTIUS] R.[EX] MED[ICI], the latter perhaps a private reference to the princely aspirations the next generation of Medici would actually realize (fig. 69).[20]

Of the sixty-one known hardstone vases identified with the Medici family, thirty are preserved today in Florence's Museo degli Argenti, sixteen in the sacristy of the Florentine church of San Lorenzo, and eight in the Museo di Mineralogia, again in Florence. Five additional vases are known from drawings,[21] and two others can be found in the Louvre. Ten of the vases are probably antique, dating back to Hellenistic or Roman times, while another nine may very well be of Byzantine or Sassanian provenance. Three of the rock-crystal vessels are clearly Fatimid (fig. 74). The remaining thirty-eight are European works made in the period ranging from the 13th century to the 17th (figs. 68, 73). What remains of the silver-gilt mounts dates mainly from the 15th and 16th centuries.

73

IV

The Grand Dukes
of Tuscany

Only two years after the death of Lorenzo the Magnificent in 1492, Florence, always a turbulent city, underwent its worst political upheaval since the Black Plague in the mid-14th century. In 1494 King Charles VIII of France arrived in the course of his campaign to assure the Angevin claims to Naples, an event which so destabilized the Italian city-states that the peninsula would never again be free of foreign domination until the mid-19th century *Risorgimento*. It caused a revolution in Florence, the collapse of the Medici bank, the expulsion of its owners, and the puritanical interregnum of the fiery Dominican monk Savonarola. By 1512 the Medici were back and once more in power, this time governed from Rome by Pope Leo X, Lorenzo the Magnificent's second son Giovanni (fig. 76), and then by his first cousin Giulio de' Medici, who reigned as Pope Clement VII from 1523 to 1534. In 1527, however, a new revolt erupted in Florence, restoring the Republic until 1530, when Pope Clement, with the military backing of Emperor Charles V, reclaimed Florence and the whole of Tuscany for the Medici. This time the state would be administered by Alessandro de' Medici, a gifted but notoriously amoral young man generally believed to have been the Pontiff's own "mule" (illegitimate son). Invested with the hereditary title of Duke of Florence but universally loathed as a despot, Alessandro married Margaret of Austria, an illegitimate daughter of Charles V, and then died without issue in 1537, the victim of assassins' daggers, one of them wielded by his bitter cousin Lorenzino.

Blamed for the crisis of 1494, Piero de' Medici, Lorenzo the Magnificent's elder son, fled to Venice, taking with him three of the family's most precious gems, including *Nero's Seal*. Prior to his departure, Piero had arranged for most of the Medici treasures to be hidden with trusted parties, among them Baccio Bandinelli and Lorenzo Tornabuoni. The con-

tents of the *Scrittoio* went to the Dominican monks at San Marco Convent, long a beneficiary of Medici patronage. Even in exile, however, Piero managed to recover a number of pieces; still, others were lost, especially the valuables belonging to Cardinal Giovanni de' Medici, the future Pope Leo X, all requisitioned to compensate for damages resulting from the French incursion. An accounting of 1496 reveals that Piero had offered part of his collection as security to the Roman banker Agostino di Mariano Chigi. It lists 167 cameos and engravings preserved in "twenty silver boxes and in a mirrored box," as well as "two other small cameos and a large chalcedony head of a bearded old man and six other engraved stones of various types."[1] Piero's silverware was probably melted down to pay reparations, but the gems and vases pledged to Agostino Chigi would be reassembled in Rome by Cardinal Giovanni de' Medici, which left only forty-six vases in Florence.

Cardinal Giovanni, Florence's envoy to the Vatican, reclaimed his father's precious library from the San Marco Convent and had it installed at Palazzo Madama in Rome. As Pope Leo X, Giovanni presided over that golden age known as the High Renaissance, during which he surpassed all other Medici in his patronage of art, commissioning Raphael to paint the *stanze* in the Vatican Palace and Michelangelo to design the Medici chapel at San Lorenzo in Florence. Characteristic of his munificence is a silver-gilt rock-crystal charger engraved by Valerio Belli of Vicenza, described by Vasari as "a craftsman of such skill that there was never another to equal him."[2] It may have been a gift from Pope Leo to Duke Wilhelm IV of Bavaria, where it remains today at the Residenz in Munich (fig. 199). To San Lorenzo in Florence the Pope donated four vases filled with Christian relics obtained in the Holy Land, thereby continuing the Medici tradition of enriching the family church.

76

75. *Bernardo Buontalenti and Jacques Bylivelt. Lapis-lazuli vase, 1583 (Florence). Lapis-lazuli, gold, enamel, and gilded copper; height 16" (40.6 cm). Museo degli Argenti, Florence. Buontalenti, designer, architect, and hardstone carver at the Medici court, fashioned this gloriously chromatic vessel from five pieces of pyriferous hardstone, after which Jacques, or Jacopo, Bylivelt, the Medici's Flemish court jeweler, mounted it in enameled gold. Engraved on the base are the date 1583, the initials FM, and the arms of Grand Duke Francesco I. Some of the original goldsmith work was later replaced with gilded copper.*

76. *Raphael. Pope Leo X (Giovanni de' Medici) with Cardinals Giulio de' Medici (future Pope Clement VII) and Luigi de' Rossi. 1518-1519. Oil on panel, 60 1/2 x 47" (2.36 x 1.85 m). Uffizi, Florence.*

77. *Valerio Belli. Casket with scenes from the Life of Christ, 1532 (Vicenza). Rock crystal, silver-gilt, and enamel; length 10 5/8" (27 cm). Museo degli Argenti, Florence. Already seen in fig. 19, the casket with its narrative panels of rock crystal, figured among the treasures taken to France by Catherine de' Medici and then returned to Florence by Christine de Lorraine at the time of her marriage to Grand Duke Ferdinando I in 1589.*

78. *Giovanni Antonio de' Rossi. Cameo Portrait of Cosimo I and His Family, 1557-1562 (Florence/Rome). Onyx; 7 1/4 x 6 1/2" (18.4 x 16.5 cm). Museo degli Argenti, Florence. Here the Grand Duke is portrayed in profile along with his wife, the famously aristocratic and beautiful Eleonora of Toledo, and five of their seven children. This virtuoso example of the lapidarist's art was long thought to be the finest cameo carved during the Renaissance. Rossi spent five years on it, a campaign of work that began with a payment of 200 ducats. A preparatory drawing is owned by Christ Church Library, Oxford. Originally the carving was larger and had a personification of Florence at the center.*

By the time of the new troubles in 1527, Giulio de' Medici, the bastard son of Lorenzo the Magnificent's younger brother Giuliano, had been elected Pope Clement VII. Meanwhile, Rome itself had been sacked by Charles V's army, once more scattering the Medici collections, after which they were again reassembled. Clement thereupon decided to secure forty-one of the family's vases by following Pope Leo's precedent and converting them into reliquaries for placement at San Lorenzo. To house and display the vessels, he even had a tribune designed, and to protect them from further assault, he decreed that they should be exposed to the public only once a year on Holy Saturday and Eastern Sunday. Moreover, excommunication would be the fate of anyone who dared to seize or vandalize the treasures.

Pope Clement also commissioned from Valerio Belli a silver-gilt and rock-crystal casket inscribed with scenes from the Life of Christ (figs. 77, 19). A masterpiece of the engraver's art, it cost the extraordinary sum of 2,000 florins and was taken as a gift to François I in 1533 on the occasion of a royal marriage the Pope had negotiated. The wedding bound the French King's second son, the future Henri II, to Caterina de' Medici, Clement's orphaned cousin born to the Duke of Urbino, Piero's son, and Madeleine de la Tour d'Auvergne. The bride would enter history as Queen and even Regent of France during the worst days of the Religious Wars, including the horrific Saint Bartholomew's Day Massacre. Her fabulous dowry comprised not only 100,000 gold écus but also quantities of jewels, precious objects, and the cities of Pisa, Livorno, Reggio, and Modena. She makes several other appearances in this book (see Chapter 1), as the mother of Charles IX, who married Archduchess Elizabeth, the daughter of Emperor Maximilian II; as one of the Valois dynasty's major collectors; and finally as the grandmother of Christine de Lorraine. who returned Pope

Clement's casket to Florence as part of her dowry when she married Grand Duke Ferdinando I of Tuscany. Sadly, other Medici treasures would leave Florence and never return, such as the prized objects from the *Scrittoio* taken by Margaret of Austria as she fled following the murder of her husband, Duke Alessandro. In lieu of her lost dowry, Duchess Margaret seized as many treasures as she could lay hands on, even the *Farnese Cup*. This piece, in fact, gained its name as a consequence of the theft, for Margaret went on to marry Ottavio Farnese, the scion of one of the great dynasties of Renaissance Italy. When the family became extinct in 1743, the heir to its treasures was the son of Philip V of Spain and Elisabetta Farnese, a prince who would become King Carlo III of Naples. As a result, thirty-one of the finest Medici cameos and intaglios have ended up at the Museo di Capodimonte in Naples.[3]

Cosimo I, Grand Duke of Tuscany (1519-1574)

After the death of Alessandro de' Medici in 1537, the Tuscan government passed into the hands of the cadet branch of the family, to which, ironically, Lorenzino had belonged. The first in the new line was Cosimo I, who, supported by Emperor Charles V, assumed the title of Duke in 1539, at the age of twenty. Despite promises to the contrary, he would soon thereafter claim absolute authority, complete with the lavish life-style always associated with royal power (fig. 78). By 1569 he had even persuaded Pope Pius V to make him Grand Duke of Tuscany. Meanwhile, Cosimo set about rebuilding the Medici fortunes, a process nicely advanced by his marriage to Eleonora of Toledo, the elegant, richly dowered daughter of the Spanish Viceroy in Naples. In 1540 he and his bride moved into the ancient Palazzo della Signoria, its battlemented façade overlooking the piazza where Savonarola had been burned at the stake in 1498. In this medieval bastion had once sat the elected officials of the proud Republic of Florence. At its very entrance stood Michelangelo's *David*, placed there in 1504 as a triumphant symbol of republican defiance of the Medici, then in exile.

Cosimo had the interior of the Signoria remodeled in a grandiose, regal manner by Giorgio Vasari, the Mannerist adolator of Michelangelo and author of the famous *Le Vite de' più eccellenti Architetti, Pittori, et Scultori Italiani* (*Lives of the Artists*), dedicated to Cosimo and sometimes called the most important book on the history of art ever written. Deep in the heart of the colossal pile Vasari carved

77

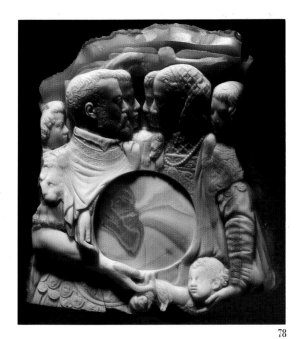

78

79

80

out a chapel for Duchess Eleonora, who then had it frescoed by the great Mannerist painter Agnolo Bronzino. He also installed a *tesoretto*, described by the architect as "the cabinet of Duke Cosimo, where he has assembled small antique bronzes, coins, and miniatures, held to be rarities by his Illustrious Excellency."[4] Equally important, he innovated the *guardaroba*, a large, carefully guarded room serving as "wardrobe" or warehouse in which the family could store their treasures, with a curatorial staff assigned to maintain a complete and detailed record of every item deposited or retrieved. Thus, despite the massive dispersal of the Medici collections, which began in earnest after the dynasty expired in 1743, the *guardaroba* inventories provide a complete record of the wealth of art and precious objects amassed, maintained, given, and received by the Medici. An inventory exists for the collections of Cosimo I as they stood in 1553.[5]

For Duchess Eleonora, Cosimo bought the Palazzo Pitti, a splendid garden residence on the opposite side of the Arno. It had been embellished with an arcaded and heavily rusticated courtyard by Bartolommeo Ammanati, a Mannerist pupil of Michelangelo known as much for his sculpture as for his architecture. The Pitti would soon be connected by a covered passage to the Uffizi across the river. Built from scratch by Vasari, the Uffizi provided "offices" for the city's administration, courts, and archives, displaced from the Signoria when Cosimo and his family moved in. With its two parallel wings stretching from the Signoria to the Arno, there joined by a four-story loggia overlooking the river, the Uffizi would figure large in the history of art, not least because of its exemplary Mannerist styling, characterized by exaggerated proportions and a "weightless," willfully eccentric use of the Classical orders.

Cosimo took great pride in his generous and involved patronage of the arts, which indeed flourished throughout his reign. He founded a tapestry manufactury as well as a court workshop dedicated to hardstone carving. Vasari and Bronzino not only worked tirelessly for the court; they also served as the Duke's agents seeking out both works of art and talents to create them. None of the latter exceeded the achievements of Bronzino himself, a uniquely brilliant portaitist who, under commission from Cosimo, painted an entire gallery of all the Medici, beginning with Giovanni di Bicci (figs. 79, 82). This collection became the prototype for many an ancestral gallery assembled in the castles and palaces of Northern Europe.

Another Medici court artist on a par with Bronzino was the sculptor/goldsmith Benvenuto Cellini (1500-1571), today famous for the amorous revelations of his *Autobiography* as much as for his surviving masterpieces. He also left detailed accounts of how he created certain works, principally the monumental bronze *Perseus and Medusa*, commissioned by Cosimo for the Loggia dei Lanzi directly opposite the entrance to the Signoria (fig. 80). Cellini knew only too well that his sculpture would have to compete head on with two other masterpieces already in the piazza, Michelangelo's *David* and Donatello's *Judith and Holofernes*, the latter commissioned a century earlier by Cosimo the Elder for the courtyard of Palazzo Medici. He succeeded in meeting the challenge, for the *Perseus* is as remarkable a sculpture as ever emerged from the Mannerist school, its stylistic qualities most evident in the lithe and almost perverse elegance of the nude male figure, not to mention the jeweled, inventive perfection of the rich locks of hair, the serpents writhing over the head of the Medusa, and the torrents of blood gushing from the gorgon's truncated neck. Even so, the real drama lay in the casting of the huge work as a single piece, a process that took years to prepare and lives forever in the breathtaking account, fraught with fear, fury, and a roof on fire, given by the artist in his *Autobiography*. For Cosimo and Duchess Eleonora, Cellini also produced numerous Schatzkammer works: gold and silver vases, enameled jewels, and designs for hardstone vases. His celebrated *Saltcellar*, created for François I of France, was seen earlier here, in the Valois chapter, and will be cited again in the chapter on Archduke Ferdinand of Tyrol (figs. 27-29).

Other artists and craftsmen in the service of Cosimo I included the Florentine goldsmiths Domenico and Giovanni Paolo Poggini, the Milanese hardstone carvers Giovanni Antonio de' Rossi and Jacopo da Trezzo, and the Florentine sculptor Pier Maria Serbaldi, famous for his porphyry figures (fig.

79. *Agnolo Bronzino.* Grand Duke Cosimo I, *1546. Oil on canvas. Museo Mediceo, Florence.*

80. *Benvenuto Cellini.* Perseus and Medusa, *1545-1554. Bronze; height 18' (5.49 m). Loggia dei Lanzi, Florence. In this virtuoso sculpture, a monumental bronze commissioned by Grand Duke Cosimo I, to symbolize his triumph over republican rebellion, Cellini successfully competed with two masterpieces already in the Piazza della Signoria: Dontello's* Judith and Holofernes *and Michelangelo's* David. *He also defined on a grand scale the Mannerist style most esteemed by Late Renaissance collectors of Kunstkammer objects.*

81. *Pier Maria Serbaldi.* Venus and Cupid, *early 16th century (Florence or Venice). Porphyry; height 10 ¹/₄" (26 cm). Museo degli Argenti, Florence. Material, theme, style, and even the engraved signature in Greek letters all exemplify the revived interest of the Medici court in Classical antiquity. Stylistically, the sculpture reflects influence from the Lombardi family of Venice, in whose atelier Serbaldi worked. The artist earned the nickname* Tagliacarne *("Meat-cutter"), conceivably because of his taste for cutting stone as red and white-flecked as meat. For all that, the piece radiates an almost Rococo charm, not least because Venus holds a protesting Eros by the hand as if to restrain the naughty infant from shooting an arrow at the bird she holds in her other hand. The abandoned quiver lies at the goddess's feet.*

81

81). Rossi spent five years creating a white onyx cameo portraying Cosimo and his family, a work often cited as a masterpiece of Renaissance gem-carving (fig. 78). Between 1550 and 1574 the Duke ordered a series of rock-crystal and hardstone vases from the Saracchi, Fontana, and Miseroni work-shops in Milan, all pre-eminent in their field at the time but soon to have competition from the court-sponsored ateliers in Florence.[6] Cosimo, in his two-prong search for such precious objects, established a tradition that would be followed by virtually all the major courts north of the Alps.

Cosimo I collected on a grand scale, as demon-strated during a visit to Rome in 1560-1561, when he made so many acquisitions – mainly antiquities – that it took four ships to transport the lot from Ostia to Pisa. The *guardaroba*'s scrupulously maintained inventories also abound in entries for large quanti-ties of Venetian majolica, antique vases unearthed in Tuscany, Chinese porcelains, Islamic works of art, gold coins and medals, bronzes of various sorts, arti-cles in semiprecious stone, antique colored marble, Oriental crystal, and Venetian glass, almost all of it lost or dispersed about Europe and the world. Still, the inventories give plentiful evidence of a luxurious mode of living, a world sparkling with jewels, articles fashioned of gold and semiprecious stones, and sil-verware virtually by the ton. Niccolò Santini made a

"bowl for washing the feet of His Excellency... with arms on the bottom and two bells," as well as "two bedwarmers with covers worked with foliage and the arms of His Excellency."[7]

Cosimo possessed numerous necklaces and chains holding the "Golden Fleece," the coveted emblem of the elite noble order established in 1429 by Philip the Good of Burgundy. The Duchess owned many rock-crystal objects, including a cup of "Oriental crystal, on a golden base and having two gold bells in the form of snakes, with Neptune engraved in the bot-tom, with two small rubies on the upper border and handles."[8] She also had a taste for coral, and, to the disgust of both the Duke and Cellini, a love of "imperfect" – eccentrically shaped – pearls, suggest-ing that she was in the vanguard of the oncoming Baroque. As drawings for caskets and vases executed by such Florentine painters as Francesco Salviati indicate, the court generally favored the decorative language of Mannerism, with its dense, elaborated configurations of *grotteschi*, elegantly attenuated fig-ures, often nude, and tendriled, sinuously curvilin-ear, and twining vegetation.

Also recorded in the inventories is a flood of rich gifts given and accepted, including a vase with "two lion's mouths as handles" and a dagger "bound in worked gold," both presented to Duke Albrecht V of Bavaria in 1565. When Ferdinando, Cosimo's second son, received his Cardinal's hat in Rome, the Duke sent him a silver-gilt casket "which opens out entirely with drawers that pull out on runners... containing inkpot, watch, and alarm... and above the top com-partment a Crucifix with Saint George and at the foot, around the sides, the signs of the four Evange-lists, with its body covered in purple velvet with a coat-of-arms in gold."[9] Meanwhile, Cosimo had received from Pope Pius IV a "blessed rose" evi-dently made of gold. From the next Pope, Pius V, he received the long-coveted title, Grand Duke of Tus-cany, granted in 1569.

Francesco I
(1541-1587)

By the time of his nomination as Grand Duke, Cosimo had lost the Duchess Eleonora and two of their younger sons to malaria. Not long thereafter His Serene Highness began leaving affairs of state to his elder son, Francesco, while he immersed himself in a series of amorous liaisons, one of which pro-duced an illegitimate child and the other a secret marriage. Meanwhile, Francesco had commenced a romantic and long-lasting relationship with Bianca Capello, which in no way prevented him from mak-ing a dynastic marriage with Archduchess Johanna of Austria, the youngest sister of Archduke Ferdinand II of Tyrol. Thirty years earlier, Alessandro de' Medici, the first Duke of Florence, had scarcely been considered eligible to marry a Habsburg bastard; now, with a Medici reigning as Queen Regent of France, the upstart Florentine family were ready for integration with Europe's most august royalty. From this new alliance with the Habsburgs came two daughters, one of whom, Maria, would marry Henri IV of France and thus become the ancestress of every Bourbon monarch thereafter, including the present King of Spain.

An indifferent statesman, Francesco I exceeded even Cosimo in his passion for the arts (fig. 82). According to the Venetian Ambassador, writing in 1576, the Grand Duke was so involved in the creation and collection of "painting, sculpture, miniatures, mounted cameos, medallions, and all sorts of curios" that "he spends almost all his time among these things in a place known as the 'Casino', wherein he doth enter in the morning and remains until the hour of luncheon, and after having taken his luncheon doth return there until the evening."[10] The place referred to was the Palazzo del Casino di San Marco, which Francesco had Bernardo Buontalenti build to house not only his collection of small bronzes but also workshops for the many artists and craftsmen invited to Florence from all over Europe. In their company he became a veritable prince/alchemist, dedicating himself to every kind of advanced experiment, from the purification and melting of crystal and metals to the manufacture of porcelain and the distillation of oils for the cure of diseases. Most of all, he helped perfect that most sophisticated of Florentine court art, *pietre dure* mosaics fashioned of colored hardstones, among them jasper, lapis-lazuli, heliotrope, cornelian, agate, and chalcedony. To celebrate his achievements, Francesco even joined in the invention of ever more spectacular fireworks, including "a fireball of such great artifice that when it leaves the cannon it can be made to burst where any man desires."[11]

In 1570, Francesco had Vasari build a *studiolo* next to his father's *tesoretto* in the old Signoria (fig. 83).[12] The *concetto* or iconological program of decoration, devised by Vincenzo Borghini, a man of letters and advisor to Cosimo, served as a symbolic foretaste of the delights to be enjoyed in the room, objects precious "both for value and for artistry, that is to say jewels, medallions, engraved stones, mounted crystals and vases, devices (locks and the like), and similar things not too large in size, placed each in its own cabinet according to type."[13] Here, systematically arranged in cupboards, would be stored the wonderful creations turned out by the talented workers recruited for the Casino di San Marco. With the Four Elements as the organizing principle, objects made of iron, steel, and glass, all forged or liquified by fire, were to appear under the images of Apollo and Vulcan; medals, goldsmith works, and semiprecious stones and minerals under the aegis of Pluto and Opi; precious stones and crystals, all shot through with light, under the gods of air, Juno and Zephyr; and pearls, together with other things of aquatic origin, under Galatea and Venus, goddesses of the sea. According to a contemporary observer, all these items had been assembled "in order to investigate in them their hidden reason and the wisdom of the Creator of nature." Francesco's *studiolo* therefore constituted a place in which "to discourse upon all the most noble subjects and of plants, animals, gems, stones, metals, and all minerals, poison antidotes, precious life-saving devices, statues, medals, paintings and machines of various purposes."[14]

At the Casino di San Marco, meanwhile, Francesco created a gallery in which to feature small bronzes, both antique and modern, works which, because cast from molten material, embodied the mysterious alchemical transformations so vitally important to the Grand Duke. The star of this venue was the Flemish-born sculptor Jean de Boulogne (1529-1608), known to Italians as Giovanni da

82

82. *Agnolo Bronzino. Grand Duke Francesco I of Tuscany, c. 1570. Oil on canvas. Galleria Pitti, Florence. Francesco, the second of the Medici Grand Dukes, neglected affairs of state in favor of immersing himself in art and alchemy. He established the Casino di San Marco for purposes of creation and experimentation, especially in the medium of pietre dure, and the studiolo as a private retreat within the Palazzo della Signoria where he could study and enjoy his collection. Thanks in large part to the Medici's politics of cultural prestige, Francesco would marry a Habsburg Archduchess and see his second daughter, Maria, become the Queen of France.*

83. *Giorgio Vasari. Studiolo of Francesco I, Palazzo della Signoria, Florence. 1570-1579. For this barrel-vaulted retreat, where Grand Duke Francesco could store and study his collection of precious objects, Vasari recruited a distinguished team of artists which included Agnolo Bronzino, Bartolomeo Ammanati, and Giovanni Bologna. The concetto or iconological program, devised by Vincenzo Borghini, called for paintings and sculptures with clear reference to the contents of the cupboards built into the walls.*

83

84

85

86

Bologna or Giambologna, the most gifted and sought-after sculptor of his time (fig. 89). In his production for the Medici family, he brought the Mannerist style to its culminating phase, as well as to the threshold of the Baroque, particularly in such famous works as *Flying Mercury*, *Samson Slaying a Philistine*, and *Rape of the Sabine Women*. In the spiraling three-figure composition of the *Sabine Women*, Giambologna triumphantly solved the age-old problem of how to design a freestanding sculpture so that it becomes equally interesting from every angle. Commissioned for the Loggia dei Lanzi, it remains there today alongside Cellini's *Perseus and Medusa*.

At work in the San Marco ateliers were Ambrogio and Stefano Caroni and Giorgio di Cristofano Gaffurri, all Milanese lapidary engravers, whose art required them to collaborate with such goldsmiths and jewelers as Niccolò Santini, Cencio della Nera, the Castrucci brothers, the Fleming Hans Domes, and the Dutchman Jacques Bylivelt. A particular favorite of Grand Duke Francesco, Bylivelt worked with Buontalenti to produce one of the most admired lapis-lazuli vases in the Medici collection (fig. 75). To him is attributed as well the new grand-ducal crown, completed in c. 1580 and then dismantled in 1788, well after the Medici family had finally died out. An inventory of 1621 describes it in detail, including the exact number of its precious stones, almost all rubies, diamonds, and emeralds.

In 1572 Francesco had Buontalenti initiate construction of a second floor over Vasari's Uffizi, at the center of which was to be an octagonal room, the *tribuna*. Planned as a "mystic site," the *tribuna* soon replaced the *studiolo* and became a repository not only for the most valuable productions of the court workshops but also for the rarest pieces from the family collections, whether old or recently acquired. The room took on the character of a *sanctum sanctorum*, its vault decorated in mother-of-pearl on a blue ground, its floor paved in polychrome marbles, and its walls embellished with paintings and niches filled with busts and statuettes. Again there were built-in cupboards to house and conceal the finest items owned by the endlessly acquisitive family. An inventory of 1589 gives proof of just how rapidly the collections had grown.[15] Among the plethora of holdings, it listed numerous hardstone vases, objects of turned ivory, including an ivory ball with a "portrait of Duke Wilhelm of Bavaria," and a "vase fashioned from half an ostrich egg carved with grotesque figures by Marchion of Germany, mounted in silver-gilt... with a crab beneath serving as a foot."[16] At the center of this treasure house stood a gem-studded altar bearing a small temple fashioned of ebony and clad in *pietre dure*. Whereas the dark and secret *studiolo* had been created for the exclusive use of the melan-

choly Prince, the new *tribuna* would now be accessible to an elite public, particularly ambassadors, the better to serve as propaganda glorifying the Grand Ducal House of Medici. Francesco also moved the workshops from the Casino di San Marco to the Uffizi, installing them in the ground-floor loggias.

When Francesco's daughter Maria de' Medici sailed for France, to become the bride of Henri IV, she traveled in a ship laden with her dowry, composed of jewels and objects so lavish they dazzled even the jaded French court.[17] For the ratification of her marriage in Lyons, the new French Queen wore a present from Uncle Ferdinando, Cardinal de' Medici: a brilliant said to have been valued at 150,000 lire. Meanwhile her elder sister Eleonora had married the Duke of Mantua, bringing to the union a dowry that included an ebony chest stuffed with treasures known from a surviving inventory.[18] The account begins with a series of four hardstone cups and continues with dozens of jeweled animal pins and pendants.

Ferdinando I (1549-1609)

In 1563, Cosimo I's second son received his Cardinal's hat in Rome, where he remained as Florentine Ambassador to the Vatican. By 1575 he had moved to a magnificent villa at Trinità dei Monti, overlooking historic Rome on one side and the spreading Pincio Gardens on the other. There he presided over a veritable court, populated not only by notables but also by artists, scientists, and men of letters. While filling the huge villa with the bronzes of Pietro da Barga (fig. 88) and Giambologna and the gardens with antique sculpture, he also enlarged his gem collection to include many pieces by Leonard Zaerles (Leonardo Fiammingo), a Mannerist goldsmith from Antwerp who specialized in fashioning precious stones and baroque pearls into bizarre naturalistic forms.

After Francesco I died without a male heir in 1587, Ferdinando resigned his position as Prince of the Church in order to succeed his brother and become Ferdinando I, Grand Duke of Tuscany. To assure the succession, he then married Christine de Lorraine, the granddaughter and heiress of Catherine de' Medici, many of whose dowry treasures would now be returned to Florence (fig. 84). Along with these, mostly gold-mounted hardstone and rock-crystal vases, went a number of new art works ordered by the French court from Milanese lapidaries and mounted by Parisian goldsmiths. Ferdinando had this gleaming collection installed next to the *tribuna*, in a room known as the Sala di Madama, or the

"Room of Idols," so called for the bronze statuettes intermingled with the hoard of vases, miniatures, cameos, and such curiosities as a "toothpick with falcon's claw trimmed in gold."

To make his mark on the *tribuna*, Ferdinando had Bernardo Buontalenti build a new gem-inlaid cabinet for the display of his collection, mainly cameos, unmounted precious gems, and curios of various kinds. As for the court workshops, Ferdinando ran them like a factory, under the supervision of Emilio de' Cavalieri, who had joined the Grand Duke's staff during his days as Cardinal in Rome. With this, interest appears to have shifted from carved hardstone vases to mosaics in *pietre dure*. Meanwhile, Ferdinando had the elderly Leonard Zaerles make him a most remarkable gold collar, composed of diamond-centered rosettes and pearshaped pearl pendants.

Cosimo II (1590-1621) and Ferdinando II (1610-1670)

From the early 17th century until the end of the Grand Duchy almost two hundred years later, the Florentine workshops of the Medici excelled at lapidary mosaics, works admired and imitated by courts all over Europe. This was particularly true during the brief reign of Cosimo II, Ferdinando's eldest son, who married Maria Maddalena of Austria. Young Cosimo won a place in history for his protection of Galileo, but he also found time to support the artists and artisans at work in his ateliers. Active there were the aging Odoardo Vallet, the Swede Jonas Falck, and the Florentine Cosimo Merlini, all of whom produced a substantial amount of sacred work, gratifying the mystical Christianity shared by the grandducal couple as well as by the dowager Grand Duchess, Christine de Lorraine. Yet even the pious objects were richly endowed with gold, enamel, pearls, and precious as well as semiprecious stones. To this repertoire of rich materials, the Habsburg Grand Duchess brought such northern favorites as ivory and amber (figs. 87, 92), furnishing her chapel in the Palazzo Pitti with amber candlesticks, altarpieces, caskets, and religious figurines, all of which would end up in the Uffizi galleries. Cardinal Leopoldo, Cosimo's younger son, emerged as a Prince with a discriminating eye for paintings and miniatures but also for bronzes, medals, marbles, inscriptions, and cameos.

Cosimo II died prematurely in 1621, leaving his mother and widow to govern as regents during the minority of Ferdinando II. In 1634, the new Grand Duke married Vittoria della Rovere, thereby inheriting a claim not only to the Duchy of Urbino but also some of the most celebrated paintings now in the Uffizi. Vittoria, according to the inventory of her possessions, quickly absorbed the Medici passion for antiquities and such curiosities as "two India nuts, one with a spout and one without... the handle for a seal in jasper."[19] In 1628 Ferdinando II visited Innsbruck, where Claudia de' Medici had married Archduke Leopold of Tyrol. While in Austria he received one of Philip Hainhofer's *Kunstschänke*, the socalled *stipo tedesco* ("German cabinet"), a wondrous, many-drawered piece of furniture decorated with painted semiprecious stones and equipped with such marvels as a small altar and an organ. It also boasted a chimed clock driving a silver automata with the figure of Christ smiting the Devil atop the cabinet.

To the dismay of Florentines, Ferdinando II, as hearty and liberal-minded as his Austrian brother-in-law, sired an heir, Cosimo III (1642-1723), who could scarcely have been more dour, self-centered, and bigoted. The general alarm increased as the new Grand Duke lived on and on, his reign, which began in 1670, coming to a close only after fifty-three dispiriting years. By 1674, his vivacious French wife, Marguerite-Louise d'Orléans, a granddaughter of Maria de' Medici and first cousin of Louis XIV, had abandoned the obsessively pious Grand Duke and their three children in favor of living out her life in a Montmartre convent. Not only did the Tuscan people and their economy suffer under Cosimo's corrupt rule, but so did art, with scarcely a major Florentine

87

88. *Pietro Simone da Barga. Satyr, c. 1580 (Florence). Bronze, parcel-gilt; height 12" (30.5 cm). Museo Nazionale del Bargello, Florence. During his career as Florence's Cardinal Ambassador to the Vatican, Grand Duke Ferdinando I conceived a passion for da Barga's small-scale interpretations of famous antique marbles, cast in green-patinated bronze. The work seen here derives from one of two figures then standing in the courtyard of the Palazzo della Valle in Rome.*

89. Giovanni Bologna. Hercules and the Erymanthian Boar, 1580/1600 (Florence). Bronze; height 17 1/3" (44 cm). Museo Nazionale del Bargello, Florence. From 1576 until 1581 the much-besought Giambologna was engaged in creating a series of small bronzes representing the Labors of Hercules. The fourth Labor seen here figured among the six models from which Jacques Bylivelt, the Medici court jeweler, made silver casts around 1589 for the tribuna in the Uffizi. The silver versions, all now lost, may have been prepared in wax by Antonio Susini. The earliest documented cast of Hercules and the Erymanthian Boar is the one listed in the 1607/1611 inventory made for the collection of Emperor Rudolf II (Kunsthistorisches Museum, Vienna). Other original casts exist at the Capodimonte Museum, the Wallace Collection in London, the Widener Collection in Washington, D.C., the Museo del Castello Sforzesco in Milan, and the National Gallery in Dublin. A silver Hercules attributed to Giambologna was in the collection of Louis XIV.

89

90. Two figures composed of shells, *17th century (Florence). Sea shells; height without bases 18 1/4 " (46 cm) and 15" (38 cm). Museo degli Argenti, Florence. The precedent for this pair of unpublished figures was set by the Milanese painter Giuseppe Arcimboldo (c. 1527-1593), an artist long in service to Habsburg Emperors Ferdinand I, Maximilian II, and Rudolf II. For these patrons Arcimboldo designed all manner of court festivities while also achieving fame for his bizarre portraits, such as the one reproduced in fig. 178.*

91. A Damned Soul in Hell, *17th-18th century (Florence). Polychrome encaustic and gilded bronze; 8 1/16 x 5 15/16" (20.5 x 15 cm). Museo degli Argenti, Florence. This colored-wax*

relief, *from a series of four, represents a novel art form that enjoyed great popularity in Florence during the long reign of the pious Cosimo III. In addition to the subject seen here, the series included treatments of Purgatory, Limbo. and Paradise.*

92. Amber casket, *1st half 17th century (Königsberg?). Amber; 22 1/2 x 11 3/4 x 13 3/4" (57 x 30 x 35 cm). Museo degli Argenti, Florence. Very likely made in the Baltic city of Königsberg, known for its amber production, this casket, together with a host of other amber works, appear to have been brought to Florence by Archduchess Maria Maddalena of Austria, the wife of Grand Duke Cosimo II. The casket is inscribed with the Medici coat-of-arms.*

91

92

93. *Giulio Parigi, Michele Castrucci, Cosimo Merlini, and Jonas Falck. Ex-voto of Cosimo II, c. 1620 (Florence). Semiprecious stones, diamonds, and gilded metal; 21 ½ x 25 ⅓"* *(62 x 64 ½ cm). Museo degli Argenti, Florence. Grand Duke Cosimo II commissioned this bas-relief - one of the most extravagant productions to come out of the Medici workshops - for a gold altar-front he hoped to present to the Church of San Carlo Borromeo in Milan as a materialization of his prayer for restored health. Part pietre dure and part mosaic, the plaque required the collaboration of an architect (Parigi), a hardstone carver (Michele Castrucci), and two goldsmiths (Merlini and Falck). Originally it had a gold mount, which was later melted down and replaced by the present frame of gilded metal.*

94. *Mounted nautilus shell. German, c. 1600. Nautilus shell, silver-gilt, and gilded bronze; height 13" (33 cm). Museo degli Argenti, Florence. The distinctive mounts holding this shell comprise a finial in the form of a triumphant nude figure riding a snail, seahorses perched on the lip of the shell, and an exotically turbaned caryatid accompanied by a leashed lion.*

painter, sculptor, or architect coming to the fore in the whole of the long reign. Still, Cosimo kept the workshops busy, albeit directed by sycophants, who, in deference to the Grand Duke, emphasized glyptics, goldsmithery, and the decorative arts in general. Much of this activity was dedicated to sacred work, particularly reliquaries, which His Serene Highness liked to keep about him in the Palazzo Pitti. To the Uffizi galleries, he added the family collection of antiquities, brought from the Villa Medici in Rome. Cosimo also acquired a vast number of coins and medals – almost 30,000. However, neither these nor any of the other Medici treasures could be seen with any regularity, since the Grand Duke found the burden of maintaining the treasures an unwelcome distraction from his religious devotions.

Prince Ferdinando (1663-1713), Cosimo III's elder son, was a discriminating aesthete as well as a gifted musician who patronized Alessandro Scarlatti and oversaw the birth of opera. Alas, he predeceased his father, which left the grand-ducal heritage to fall upon the aging shoulders of the younger son, Gian Gastone (1671-1737). Once a slender young man of good intellect and charming manners, Gian Gastone married unhappily, produced no heir, and gradually degenerated into grossness and compulsive debauchery. He had little interest in collecting and virtually none in the hoard of precious objects left to him.

Gian Gastone's elder sister, Anna Maria Lodovica (1667-1743), the childless widow of the Elector Palatine, had long since returned to Florence, bringing with her a jewelry collection of a thousand pieces: the "Electress's Jewels."[20] She also prepared the way for the Tuscan throne to be assumed by the House of Lorraine, Habsburg allies, who would have scattered the Medici collections utterly had the Electress not left a will specifying that "the successive Grand Dukes, of that which is for the ornamentation of the State, for the use of the public, and to attract the curiosity of foreigners – all the furniture, effects, and rarities... such as cabinets, paintings, statues, libraries, jewels, and other precious things – nothing shall be transported and removed from the Capital and the State of the Grand Duchy."[21] Be that as it may, Franz Stephan, who had been given Tuscany in exchange for the Duchy of Lorraine – the latter sacrificed in order for his wife, Maria-Theresia of Austria, to succeed as Empress, in lieu of a male heir – wasted no time acting upon his desire to clear out the *guardaroba*, the *tribuna*, the Sala di Madama, and the other Uffizi galleries. Within a few decades, almost everything not directly tied to Florence would be sold – the stupendous mass of precious objects long considered one of the wonders of Europe, collections so extensive that visitors were wont to tour them in wheelchairs! Then, in 1793 the heedless Leopold, who succeeded Franz Stephan, his father, as Grand Duke, had much of what remained, including the state jewels, shipped to the Hofburg in Vienna, where he now reigned as Emperor Leopold II.

Further losses occurred during the Napoleonic occupation of Florence. In 1814, however, Florence fell heir to one of the finest collections of Northern goldsmithery. This developed after Grand Duke Ferdinando III returned to Italy and brought with him 85 sumptuous pieces of medieval and Renaissance gold and silver formerly owned by the Prince Archbishops of Salzburg (figs. 95-97). Ferdinando, a Habsburg Archduke, had simply appropriated the collection during his brief tenure in 1803-1805 as governor of the Salzburg province, newly secularized by the Diet of the Holy Roman Empire in response to the expansionist policies of Napoleon Bonaparte.

Thanks to international settlements negotiated at the end of World War I, the Hofburg cache would be returned to Florence in 1923. Today what remains of the Medici collections in Florence is distributed among various museums, primarily the Museo degli Argenti. A mere fragment, perhaps, of the onetime glory, but even so, splendid beyond any comparable assemblage.

93

95

from a Virgin and Child by Kaspar Memberger, a painter at the Salzburg court of Prince/Bishop Wolf Dietrich von Raitenau. The smaller scenes around the border, narrating the Life of the Virgin, have their source in the engravings of Stradanus.

6. Fish-shaped ewer, c. 1590 (Salzburg). Silver-gilt; height 9 13/16" (25 cm). Museo degli Argenti, Florence. This aquamanile, formed like an Oriental fish, is accompanied by a basin decorated with figures of Neptune, tritons, and nereids. The earliest documentation is a Salzburg inventory of 1612.

7. Paul Hübner. Ewer and basin, 1585-1590 (Augsburg). Silver-gilt; height of ewer 17 3/4" (45 cm). Museo degli Argenti, Florence. Splendid enough to have been attributed to Benvenuto

Nuremberg goldsmith Cornelius Erb. Like the treasures in figs. 95 and 96, the ewer and basin seen here were once part of the treasury of the Prince/Bishops of Salzburg. Then, in 1805, when the Habsburg Grand Duke Ferdinando III of Tuscany ended his term as Prince/Elector of Salzburg, he appropriated some 85 works from the Salzburg hoard, including the three illustrated on these facing pages, for transfer to Florence and incorporation into the grand-ducal collections.

96

The Early Habsburgs

good argument could be made for the Habsburgs as the premier dynasty among the royal houses of Europe.[1] Early historians traced the family's descent through Julius Caesar and the Emperor Nero, even as far back as the Biblical Noah. For more than 800 years, certainly, beginning in the High Middle Ages, Habsburg Counts, Dukes, Archdukes, Kings, and Emperors played dominant roles on the world's political and cultural stage, a tradition that ended only in 1918, following the debacle of the Great War. At the peak of their power in the 16th century, Emperor Charles V could well say that the "sun never set on his Empire," encompassing as it did most of Europe, large chunks of North and South America, parts of the African and Indian coastline, and even the Philippines in the South Pacific. Moreover, such eminence did not just happen; rather, it sprang from the ability of the Habsburgs to produce, at regular intervals, capable monarchs with genuine claims to greatness, most particularly Charles V (r. 1519-1558) and Maria-Theresia (r. 1740-1780). As a family, the Habsburgs figured equally large within the realm of art patronage and collecting, where, unerringly, they went to the greatest talents – Dürer, Titian, Velázquez, Rubens – for their portraits as well as for pictures magnifying the salient events of their reigns. The masterworks assembled in the great museums of Madrid and Vienna, not to mention thousands of other works of art dispersed throughout the world, constitute monuments to the Habsburgs' passionate, grand-scale involvement with both the fine and the applied arts.

Myths aside, the Counts of Habsburg could easily track their origins to the post-Carolingian 10th century, when they held lands in Alsace and the northwest corner of Switzerland. The family name derives from the *Habichtsburg* or "Hawk's Castle" near Baden in what is now the Swiss Canton of Aargau, where an early medieval redoubt called Habsburg survives. One of the oldest objects identified with the

family is an *olifant* or "ivory horn," which, according to an inscription, was presented by Count Albrecht III of Habsburg to the Swiss abbey at Muri in 1199 (fig. 99). Five hundred years later, in 1702, it would be returned by the current Abbot of Muri, who offered the treasure to Emperor Leopold I. In 1273 the Habsburgs began their steep rise from provincial obscurity, led by Count Rudolf, whom the Electors of the Holy Roman Empire chose as King of the Germans, not only for his abilities but also for his relative lack of power. Even so, his election as Rudolf I (r. 1273-1291) provoked war with King Ottocar II of Bohemia, whose defeat and death at the Marchfeld (1278) made the Habsburgs hereditary Dukes of Austria, Carniola, and Styria. With this coup, Rudolf laid the foundations of his family's dynastic greatness, while gaining a personal reputation for shrewdness and frugality.

Rudolf's son Albrecht (c. 1250-1308), Duke of Austria and Styria, would also reign as King of the Germans, but only after his election in 1298, delayed for seven years because, unlike his father, he struck the Electors as entirely too ambitious. Indeed, he was not lacking in purpose, especially when it came to arranging the first and sometimes even the second marriages of his sons, four of whom wed the daughters of the Kings of France, Poland, Aragon, and Bohemia, as well as those of the Duke of Bavaria and

98. Portable Altar of King András III of Hungary, 1290-1296 (Venice). Silver-gilt, jasper, emeralds, rubies, pearls, rock crystal, and wood; 17 5/16 x 15" (44 x 38 cm). Historisches Museum, Bern. This gem-studded altar figured among the approximately 800 treasures taken by Queen Agnes of Hungary to the Abbey of Königsfelden (Switzerland), when she retired there in 1318 following the death of her husband, King András, who had been educated in Venice, the native city of his mother and the origin of the portable diptych altar.

99. Olifant, 11th century (Southern Italy). Ivory; length 20 1/4" (51.8 cm). Kunsthistorisches Museum, Vienna. In 1199, Count Albrecht III of Habsburg filled this olifant, a Saracen hunting horn, with relics and presented it to the Swiss abbey at Muri. Five hundred years later the current Abbot would return what is the earliest Habsburg memento, offering it to Emperor Leopold I in 1702.

98

100

100. Archduke Rudolf IV of Austria, 1360-1365 (Vienna). Tempera on parchment over wood; 15 3/8 x 8 5/8" (39 x 22 cm). Dom- und Diozesanmuseum, Vienna. This small panel may be Europe's oldest known individualized portrait. Rudolf, who wears the archducal hat, made the Habsburgs subject to the rule of primogeniture, an act that not only solidified the family-held lands but also guaranteed the survival of the family collections.

101. Heberstein-Pokal, 1449 (Burgundy and Nuremberg). Rock crystal, silver-gilt, and enamel; height 9 5/8" (24.5 cm). Kunsthistorisches Museum, Vienna. The decorative scheme on this Burgundian or Venetian "double cup" resembles that found on the court beaker of Duke Philip the Good of Burgundy (fig. 129). In 1449 the pokal belonged to Emperor Friedrich III, whose motto, AEIOU, appears on the base. It would subsequently pass to Emperors Maximilian I and Ferdinand I, then to the latter's son, Archduke Charles II of Inner Austria, and, in 1564, to a Baron Heberstein.

102. Joseph Grünpeck. Historia Friderici et Maximiliani, 1513-1514. Engraving; 11 5/16 x 8 5/16" (28.7 x 21.1 cm). Haus-Hof- und Staatsarchiv, Vienna. Here Friedrich III, the first Habsburg Emperor, is portrayed by an anonymous illustrator holding a set of scales during a visit to a goldsmith's workshop.

the Count of Savoy. Thus was firmly established the Habsburgs' successful policy of dynastic expansion through strategic matrimony. It also bred resentment, and in 1308 Albrecht was assassinated by a band of conspirators, one of whom was a Habsburg. His widow, Elizabeth, memorialized him by founding the beautiful Königsfelden Abbey in Aargau.[2]

In 1318 Albrecht's long-lived but prematurely widowed daughter Agnes (1281-1364) succeeded Queen Elizabeth as the Abbess of Königsfelden, to which she too had retired following the death in 1301 of her husband, András III, the last Arpad King of Hungary. With her came most of the 800 objets d'art she had inherited from King András,[3] including a magnificent gem-studded portable altar of Venetian origin and today owned by the Historisches Museum in Bern (fig. 98).[4] An inventory of 1357 lists dozens of jeweled sacred objects as well as scores of jewel-encrusted vestments, which, Queen Agnes stipulated, were "to be sold by no one, nor pawned, nor modified... [but rather] to be kept and cared for that they should in no way change."[5]

Again for dynastic reasons, Queen Agnes's eldest nephew, Duke and later Archduke Rudolf IV of Austria (r. 1358-1365), married the daughter of the art-loving Charles of Luxembourg (1316-1378), who in 1346 had succeeded as King of Bohemia[6] before winning the crown of the Holy Roman Empire in 1355. Archduke Rudolf, following the lead of his father-in-law in Prague, endowed Vienna with a university and furthered the reconstruction of Saint Stephen's Cathedral in the style of International Gothic. He too was a connoisseur of precious stones, and his involvement with the arts was sufficient that he became the subject of what today is considered Europe's oldest individualized portrait, a likeness made from life in which Rudolf wears the archducal hat (fig. 100).[7] In an age of proliferating, ever smaller fiefdoms, Rudolf went against the trend and declared the family's lands indivisible, a realm in which primogeniture must prevail. Thus, it is to Archduke Rudolf IV that the Habsburgs owed their initial political growth.

It was also during the reign of Rudolf that the family agreed, in 1364, to establish a jointly held Habsburg treasure of heirlooms: "Whatever each one of us owns as treasure, cash, or property, or acquires, or conquers – be it jewels, minted or unminted silver or gold, precious stones or pearls, in whatever form or denomination – this shall be our joint property, without consideration of origin. The eldest among us is to hold [these possessions] at all times in trust for each one of us, to keep and safeguard them."[8] Nonetheless, after Albrecht died in 1365, his two brothers, Albrecht and Leopold, would divide up both the family treasure and the crown

lands, thereby launching the so-called "Albertine" and "Leopoldine" lines, which would not be reunited until the end of the 15th century.

Duke Albrecht IV (r. 1395-1404) became the first Habsburg to display a talent for craftsmanship, producing carpentered and turned works – even musical instruments – worthy of preservation among his heirlooms. In 1393 the family gained access to immense wealth when Albrecht's first cousin, Leopold IV, married Catherine of Burgundy, the daughter of Philip the Bold. The Grand Duchy of Burgundy, thanks to the rich wool trade between its Flemish provinces and England, was by far the wealthiest nation in late-medieval Europe.

Further signs of a maturing interest in collecting came in the last testament of Duke Albrecht's youngest brother, Friedrich IV, Count of Tyrol, who died in 1439. Listed along with gold and silver plate, necklaces set with precious stones, numerous pendants, gold bracelets, and a crucifix rising from a mother-of-pearl Golgotha are an ostrich-egg cup and a *Natterzungenkredenz* or "mounted vipers' tongues." To the vividly imaginative Middle Ages, these were dragons' teeth, which more literal, scientific minds have subsequently downgraded to the humdrum status of fossilized shark's teeth. They were much prized as detectors of poison, at a time when poisoning was the most common means of dispatching an enemy. The credulous held that whenever the *Natterzungen* began to "sweat" they signaled the proximity of toxin. As a result, the "tongues" were often mounted on a pedestal (*Kredenz*) or combined with saltcellars, there serving as an antidote to any poison contained in the salt.

Friedrich III, the First Habsburg Emperor (r. 1452-1493)

The first Habsburg to wear the crown of the Holy Roman Empire was Duke Friedrich V (1415-1493), who would reign for more than fifty years as King of the Germans and for more than four decades as Emperor Friedrich III.[9] The son of Duke Ernst I and the ward of Friedrich IV, a Leopoldine Duke, young Friedrich needed genuine tenacity in order to wrest his father's treasures from the acquisitive and equally tenacious guardian. He not only succeeded, however; he also proved single-minded enough to reintegrate Austria's three duchies, even though he governed two of them merely as regent for their underage heirs. Mimicking Uncle Friedrich, the new Emperor appropriated his wards' *Clainatern* or "treasures." In 1455 one of the cousins, Duke

Vladislav, demanded the return of all the items which "were removed from the castle, including many valuable old and newer tapestries, Turkish carpets, valuable large and fine books in German and Latin, beautiful Bibles and other books of holy writ, in the magical arts, and in natural things, which once belonged to King Wenceslas of Bohemia and later came through Emperor Sigismund to our Lord King Albrecht and were in the little tower over the castle gate in Vienna."[10]

The other cousin and ward, Count Sigismund of Tyrol, had also been relieved of his treasures. But rather than contend with the Emperor, Sigismund utilized the proceeds of the Tyrolean silver mines to amass a vast collection of books, goldsmith works, jewels, textiles, arms, coins, and medals. The inventory drawn up at the time of Sigismund's abdication reveals signs of an incipient Kunstkammer, particularly in such items as mounted and unmounted corals, fossilized shark's teeth, curious rocks, a buffalo's horn, and the "quill of a guinea pig" (porcupine?) mounted in silver.[11]

Friedrich III, with his interest in alchemy and magic, his love of goldsmithery, jewels, precious stones, and cut gems, foreshadowed that great Renaissance maecenas, Emperor Rudolf II. A small

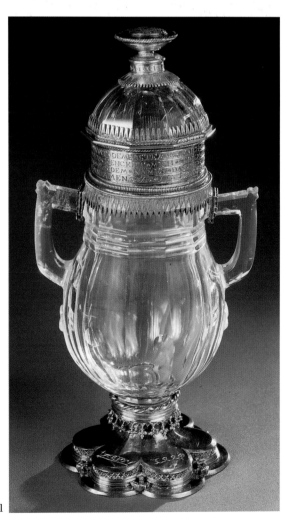

101

glimpse of Friedrich's wealth can be obtained from an inventory established between 1445 and 1453 listing 405 sapphires, 247 balas rubies (spinels), 117 emeralds, 180 pearls, 40 garnets, 82 chalcedonies, and agates, large quantities of jewelry and unminted gold, and a Burgundian saltcellar embellished with rubies and suspended pearls, gems and glass.[12] The old-fashioned Burgundian saltcellar would be refashioned into a more modern *Natterzungenkredenz*.

Friedrich employed a stone cutter and polisher, at the same time that he also became a client of Nuremberg's jewelry dealers and goldsmiths, including members of the celebrated Jamnitzer family as well as Albrecht Dürer the Elder. To such a degree did Friedrich involve himself in this aspect of art patronage and collecting that Joseph Grünpeck, in his *Historia Friderici et Maximiliani*,[13] chose to portray the Emperor during a visit to a goldsmith's workshop (fig. 102).

Friedrich inherited jewelry and other valuables from many relatives and their wives, all of which allowed him to amass a treasury of immense worth. According to hearsay, the Emperor came to possess colossal wealth, while remaining tight-fisted to the end. He was even said to own a sumptuous robe with a wide seam picked out in jewels worth 500,000 pieces of gold.

The Habsburg collections contain several objects and a number of books emblazoned with Friedrich III's device AEIOU, which may stand for the Latin phrase *Austria est imperare orbi universo*, roughly meaning: "It is Austria's destiny to rule the whole world." There is also a German reading: *Alles Erdreich ist… Österreich untertan* ("All the earth is subject to Austria"). The device can be found on two beakers and a *Natterzungenkredenz* (figs. 104, 105), pieces that would end up in Archduke Ferdinand II's huge collection at Schloss Ambras. The most remarkable of the objects so marked may be the *Heberstein-Pokal*, a magnificent rock-crystal and silver-gilt double cup bearing the date 1449 (fig. 101). Venetian or Burgundian in provenance, it passed from Emperors Maximilian I and Ferdinand I to the latter's youngest son, Charles, Count of Inner Austria.

The shrewd Friedrich had great ambitions for his only son, Maximilian – namely marriage to Mary of Burgundy, the single child of the proud Duke Charles the Bold (Charles le Téméraire) and thus the sole heiress to the largest fortune in 15th-century Europe. To advance the cause, a meeting was arranged between the would-be in-laws at Trier in 1473. The Duke of Burgundy, as usual, traveled with all the trappings of his wealth – 400 hundred carriages laden with exquisite tapestries, lavishly decorated armor, fabulous costumes, and the entire con-

102

103

103. Enameled beaker, *mid-15th century (Burgundy). Silver parcel-gilt and enamel; height 11 3/8" (29 cm). Kunsthistorisches Museum, Vienna. This silver beaker, with its enameled stars and beasts, may have been a present from Charles the Bold of Burgundy to Emperor Friedrich III in 1473 during negotiations related to the marriage of Archduke Maximilian and Mary of Burgundy, sole heiress to the greatest fortune in 15th-century Europe.*

104. Beaker, *3rd quarter 15th century (Burgundy). Silver parcel-gilt, enamel, and rock crystal; height 16 ⅞" (43 cm). Kunsthistorisches Museum, Vienna. Like the work in fig. 101, this lavish example of Burgundian craftsmanship may have been a gift from Charles the Bold to Friedrich III, whose motto AEIOU forms part of the decorative scheme, along with the arms of the Imperial provinces as well as the Imperial crown, orb, sceptre, and sword. Later Habsburgs would prize anything of Burgundian origin, especially objects related to the ancestors of Mary of Burgundy.*

105. Natterzungenkredenz, *15th century (South Germany). Silver-gilt, fossilized shark's teeth, and topaz; height 10 ⅝" (27 cm). Kunsthistorisches Museum, Vienna. The Middle Ages believed such "viper's tongues" to be dragon's teeth and prized them as detectors of poison, which, if present, was supposed to make the teeth "sweat." Once mounted on a pedestal (*Kredenz*), the Natterzungen could be ceremonially passed from guest to guest around the dinner table.*

105

106

*106. Albrecht Dürer. Emperor Maximilian I,
1519. Oil on panel; 29 1/8 x 24 1/4"
(74 x 61.5 cm). Kunsthistorisches
Museum, Vienna. Dürer based this
posthumous portrait on a chalk
drawing he had made in Augsburg in
1518. Maximilian, once an ineffectual
Archduke, matured into one of the most
powerful monarchs of his time, in part
because of his marriage to Mary of
Burgundy. As the Habsburgs' first
major arts patron, Maximilian would
be the revered ancestor and role model
for such great collectors as Archduke
Ferdinand II of Tyrol and Emperor
Rudolf II. Far from a disinterested
connoisseur, however, Maximilian
exploited the arts in order to enhance
the power and prestige of Casa Austria.*

*107. Treasure Vault of Maximilian I, 1st
edition 1517-1518. Woodcut. One of the
earliest views of a princely treasury,
this woodcut from Maximilian I's
Ehrenpforte depicts a dank vault filled
with wooden crates, their contents
separated into secular (left) and sacred
(right) objects. Like the cup in fig. 109,
some of the displayed items were
clearly inspired by designs originating
in Dürer's workshop. The theme of the
Ehrenpforte is a great triumphal arch
assembled from 192 woodcuts, most of
them the work of Albrecht Dürer.*

tents of his Kunstkammer and treasury, including
glorious works of art in silver, gold, and precious
stones. The relatively impoverished Habsburgs could
only marvel at this incomparable display of riches.
Witnesses to the occasion may be two fine Burgundian beakers made of enameled silver-gilt, now
thought perhaps to have been presents from Charles
the Bold to Friedrich III (figs. 103, 104).

Emperor Maximilian I
(r. 1493-1519)

Maximilian I (1459-1519)[14] did in fact become the
husband of the rich Burgundian heiress, as well as
the King of the Germans in 1486, Holy Roman
Emperor in 1493, and the first great Habsburg
patron of all the arts (fig. 106). A gallant Prince,
Maximilian spoke several languages and took great
interest in natural history, medicine, and astrology.
As for the much-plotted marriage to Mary of Burgundy, which took place in 1477, it brought many
complications and few advantages and ended with
the bride's premature death in 1482. Less than a
year after the wedding – staged in Brussels with such
barbaric splendor, prolonged feasting, and ribald
entertainment that it entered history as a benchmark
of vulgar excess – Charles the Bold perished in the
famous Battle of Nancy, shattering the Grand Duchy
of Burgundy. It took all of Maximilian's courage and
energy to save his wife and her Flemish provinces
from the armies of King Louis XI of France. Mary
lived long enough to bear Maximilian two children,
Philip, Duke of Burgundy, and Archduchess Margaret. They would inherit their mother's heirlooms,
most of them going to Philip.

Hardly had Mary of Burgundy died when the
Flemish provinces rose up in rebellion, while France
seized Franche-Comté and Artois, causing Maximilian to wage war on two fronts. The cost of regaining
lost ground – mainly in the Netherlands – also forced
him to send most of the Burgundian treasure to the
mint, "which hurt," as the Emperor would later
write. Moreover, the struggle over Burgundy obliged
Maximilian to betroth his infant daughter Margaret
to the Dauphin, who was to be guaranteed Franche-
Comté and Artois as part of his bride's dowry. In
1490 Maximilian made an ill-advised decision and
married by proxy Anne of Brittany after the Duchess
had sought his help against the French. The
Dauphin, now Charles VIII, thereupon broke his
engagement to Margaret of Austria and forced Anne
to marry him, by which means he assured the eventual integration of Brittany into greater France. This
double betrayal by the Valois King rankled the Habsburgs for many years to come.

To thwart French ambitions in Italy, Maximilian
married Bianca Maria Sforza in 1494, an alliance
that brought him, if not marital bliss, then a huge
dowry of 400,000 ducats and jewelry worth another
100,000 ducats. It also reinforced his Imperial claims
to power right down the boot of Italy. In a far more
effective move against France, Maximilian negotiated
a double marriage for his two children, Philip and
the rejected Margaret, to the daughter and son, Juan
and Juana, of King Ferdinand of Aragon and Queen
Isabella of Castile. Duke Philip of Burgundy, as the
husband of the mad Juana (Juana la Loca), was thus
set to become the King of Spain in 1504.

The lavish court and brilliant life-style of Burgundy left an indelible mark on the young Maximilian. Determined to endow his reign and the entire
Habsburg dynasty with glory, he produced three volumes of autobiography (*Weisskunig, Theuerdank,*
and *Freydal*), undertook major projects in the realm
of family history (*Ehrenpforte, Triumphzug,* and the
Genealogie, all three of them illustrated by Albrecht
Dürer or his circle), and planned a fantastic memorial tomb for himself at the Hofkirche in Innsbruck,
the Tyrolean city that became his political base.[15]
Even in his collecting and arts patronage, Maximilian sought to achieve princely grandeur and give pictorial form to the genealogy of the House of Habsburg. For this monarch, art offered neither recreation nor pleasure but rather a means to a political
end, the establishment of a tangible link between
past and present for the purpose of enhancing the
fame and prestige of *Casa Austria.*

At the death of his father, Emperor Friedrich III,
in 1493, Maximilian reunited Austria as it had been
before the advent of the Ernestine and Leopoldine
lines. Maximilian automatically inherited all the Habsburg treasures, those of his father as well as those
retained by his uncle, Sigismund. He kept the latter
in the castle vaults at Wiener Neustadt and Innsbruck, while storing other valuables in Vienna, Graz,
and Thaur. Since Maximilian, of necessity, led a
nomadic existence, spending much of his time in the
saddle, he never established a proper court with all
the usual trappings, or a centralized family treasury,
or even a complete inventory of his holdings in works
of art.

The Wiener Neustadt redoubt is the only one of
Maximilian's treasure troves for which there exists a
pictorial witness, a woodcut from the *Ehrenpforte*
depicting a dank vault, or storage room, filled with
crates, some sealed, others opened, their contents
clearly separated into sacred and secular artifacts
(fig. 107). Against the far wall stand religious
objects, including reliquaries and a crucifix. To the
right are church vestments and jewels, shown under
a dais, while on a ledge to the left are displayed a

which, in 1489, had been valued at 100,000 gulden for the purpose of pledging it to Tommaso Portinari, the representative of the Medici bank in Bruges. Still, when Maximilian died, his grandchildren were amazed at the riches they discovered in the Habsburg vaults.

The activity of Maximilian I as maecenas is well documented. Hans Burgkmair portrayed him in a woodcut for *Weisskunig* as a primary source of inspiration for the artist, like a priest or magus laying hands on the painter, correcting him (fig. 108). Certainly Maximilian had the power to elevate a gifted artist, such as Albrecht Dürer, from the status of craftsman to that of a master occupying a new, higher social plane. In return, Dürer, one of the very greatest of German engravers and painters, gave his Imperial patron a memorable epitaph: "He has exceeded all the Kings and Princes of his time in probity, courage, understanding, and magnanimity." The Emperor recruited for his policy not only painters, sculptors, miniaturists, woodcutters, and engravers but also printers, medalists, armorers, hardstone cutters, tapestry weavers, embroiderers, carpenters, and architects. A dozen goldsmiths and jewelers worked steadily to produce the immense quantities of plate, jewelry, and presentation pieces required by the Imperial court, wherever it might encamp (fig. 109). Maximilian appears even to have found time to practice turnery, in a workshop installed for him in the Innsbruck Hofburg. He was also humble enough to acknowledge his own mortality, as in Hans Leinberger's *Tödlein*, a *memento mori* carved from pear wood and once owned by the Emperor (fig. 110). A small masterpiece from the Late Middle Ages, the figure of Death dancing with bow and arrow would later grace one of the treasure-crammed cupboards of Maximilian's great-grandson, Archduke Ferdinand II of Tyrol, at Schloss Ambras in Innsbruck.

One of the great Burgundian relics inherited by Maximilian I was the so-called *Ainkhurn-Schwert*, a gold-mounted sword with hilt and scabbard inlaid with narwhal tusk (fig. 111). It had been the property of Duke Philip the Good and his son, Charles the Bold; even so, Maximilian found himself compelled to pawn the heirloom in 1486. Despite attempts to redeem it, the object would not return to the Habsburgs until 1630. Also very likely part of the Burgundian treasure once claimed by Maximilian I is the *Reliquary of the Holy Thorn* (fig. 7), which had belonged to the Duc de Berry and would later pass into the collection of Emperor Charles V. Another Burgundian piece, the delightful "lover's brooch" made of enameled gold (fig. 112), is also presumed to have entered Maximilian's collection through his marriage to Mary of Burgundy. It too would end up among the holdings of Charles V.

109

series of secular goldsmith works: a ewer and basin set, a marriage cup, various cups with covers, a pilgrim flask, and several dishes. Among these, some expert eyes have identified the so-called *Maximiliansbecher*, a Nuremberg lidded cup based on a design by Albrecht Dürer, its silver-gilt surface chased with pears and the arms of Austria and Burgundy. Like the so-called "Dürer Cup" in fig. 109, it would later enter the collections of Archduke Ferdinand II of Tyrol at Schloss Ambras.

More than once, however, Maximilian's costly campaigns obliged him to pawn his treasures. In 1508 the Emperor and his young grandson, Charles, had the famous Burgundian fleur-de-lis handed over to Henry VIII of England as security against a loan of 50,000 gold thalers, money needed to finance the war against Venice. Very likely this was the same lily

107

108

108. *Hans Burgkmair. Emperor Maximilian as Weisskunig in a Painter's Workshop. Woodcut; 17 1/8 x 10 15/16" (43.5 x 27.8 cm). Weisskunig, or White King, is Maximilian I's autobiography, written between 1505 and 1516. The title came from the white armor the Emperor liked to wear during tournaments. Archduke Ferdinand II of Tyrol collected the manuscripts at Schloss Ambras, but they would not be printed and published until 1775. The project included 251 woodcuts, among them works by Hans Burgkmair (118), Leonhard Beck (127), Hans Springinklee (4), and Hans Schäuffelein (2).*

109. *"Dürer Cup", c. 1500 (Nuremberg). Silver-gilt; height 18 13/16" (47.8 cm). Kunsthistorisches Museum, Vienna. This treasure, once part of the vast collections at Schloss Ambras outside Innsbruck, was probably acquired by Archduke Ferdinand II of Tyrol around 1596 from the heirs of Count Ulrich von Montfort, whose coat-of-arms it bears. The naturalistic shape and decoration may have derived from goldsmithery created within the Nuremberg orbit of Albrecht Dürer.*

110. *Hans Leinberger. Tödlein, c. 1520 (Landshut). Pearwood; height 8 ⁷/₈"(22.5 cm). Kunsthistorisches Museum, Schloss Ambras Collections, Innsbruck.* This little masterpiece of late-medieval art, with its figure of Death brandishing bow and arrows, belonged to Maximilian I, whom it served as a memento mori at a time when life was generally short. Scenes of skeletons dancing with the rich and the powerful gave the poorest members of society hope for a more equitable life in the hereafter.

111. *Ainkhürn-Schwert, 2nd half 15th century (Burgundy). Narwhal tusk, steel, gold, enamel, silver-gilt, ruby, and pearls; length 41 ³/₄" (106 cm). Kunsthistorisches Museum, Vienna.* Fashioned from a narwhal tusk, then thought to be the horn of a unicorn, this most revered Habsburg treasure once belonged to Duke Philip the Good of Burgundy and his son, Charles the Bold, father-in-law of Maximilian I. After the forever impecunious Emperor pawned it in 1486, almost 150 years would pass before the Habsburgs could reclaim the heirloom.

112. *Lover's Brooch, 1st half 15th century (Burgundy). Gold, enamel, ruby, diamond, and pearls; diameter 2" (5 cm). Kunsthistorisches Museum, Vienna.* This rare and charming Netherlandish jewel, with its pair of lovers in a garden, almost certainly entered the Habsburg collections through Mary of Burgundy. Listed in the inventory of Emperor Charles V, Mary's grandson, the precious heirloom would then belong, very likely, to Archduke Ferdinand II at Schloss Ambras.

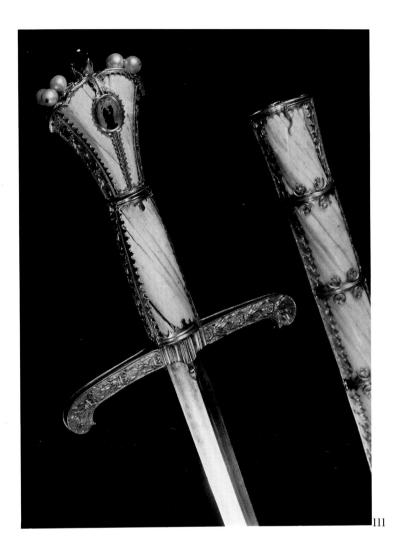

111

112

Margaret of Austria
(1480-1530)

The Spanish Habsburgs, so well known for their patronage of great painters and sculptors, remain generally unexplored as far as their holdings of objets d'art are concerned. One exception is Margaret of Austria, the daughter of Maximilian and Mary of Burgundy first encountered here as the rejected fiancée of Charles VIII of France and then as the bride of Crown Prince Juan of Aragon (fig. 113). An inventory of 1493, drawn up at Valenciennes when the Archduchess was thirteen years old, mentions all her dresses, her gold and silver plate, horses, carriages, sedan chairs, tapestries, and ecclesiastical artifacts.[16] Records also show that Margaret was exceptionally well endowed with jewelry at her wedding.[17] She had less luck when it came to husbands, for Prince Juan would die within the year following their marriage. In 1499, when she left Spain for Flanders, her jewel casket numbered 379 items, including heirlooms from her mother, as well as many presents from her onetime parents-in-law, Queen Isabella of Castille and King Ferdinand of Aragon. Level-headed, intelligent, and politically astute, Archduchess Margaret played an important role in the Netherlands, where, despite her youth, she served as Regent as well as guardian of her nephew Charles, heir to the Spanish throne and the crown of the Holy Roman Empire. To memorialize her second husband, Philibert II, the reigning Duke of Savoy, whom she married in 1501 and lost three years later, Margaret commissioned a jewel of a Late Gothic church for Brou in Bourg-en-Bresse (Burgundy). At her court in Malines she created a Humanist center, sometimes called "the capital of art and letters in the north."[18] In Margaret can be seen the transformation of Emperor Maximilian's dank treasure vault into a true art lover's collection. A worthy heiress to Burgundian opulence, the Archduchess held court in the manner of a Renaissance Princess, surrounded by a fabulous array of fine paintings, tapestries, and objets d'art. Various inventories list many remarkable works, revealing her to be a collector of genuine discernment.[19] Two brilliant prizes were signed panels by Jan van Eyck – *Giovanni Arnolfini and His Wife* (National Gallery, London) and *The Virgin at the Fountain* (Musée Royal des Beaux-Arts, Antwerp) – which evidently hung among paintings by such major masters as Hieronymus Bosch, Dirk Bouts, Jean Fouquet, Hans Memling, and Rogier van der Weyden.

Ferdinand I (1503-1564)
Founder of the
Habsburg Kunstkammer

Ferdinand I, the younger son of King Philip and Queen Juana, grew up in Spain and then went on to receive a Humanist education in the Netherlands (fig. 114). Unlike his elder brother Charles, who spent a lifetime combating heresy – the Protestant Reformation – Ferdinand, who would succeed Charles as Holy Roman Emperor, was affable, curious, and open-minded in matters of religion. After he married Anna, the daughter of King Vladislav of Bohemia and Hungary, his sister Mary became the wife of Anna's brother, King Lajos II, who in the meantime had inherited the Bohemian and Hungarian crowns. When Lajos died at the Battle of Mohács (1526), defending Hungary against the Ottoman Turks, he left his thrones without a direct heir, which provided an opportunity for Ferdinand to step in and unite his brother-in-law's lands with those of the Austrian Habsburgs. It would be another thirty years, however, before he could wear the crown of the Holy Roman Empire, once Charles V had abdicated in 1556, dividing his dynasty into the Spanish line, led by Charles V's only son, Philip II, and the Austrian line, with Ferdinand I at the helm.

Ferdinand has gone down in Habsburg lore as the founder of the family's *khunst-camer*, a "museum" first mentioned in 1550, the year in which certain valuables were transferred from the vaults in the castle at Graz to the Burg in Vienna. Among the items mentioned at this time were a glass beaker, a gaming board with stones (possibly the fine backgammon set now owned by the Kunsthistorisches Museum in Vienna [fig. 115]), a prayer book, a cased *Tafl* (very likely a Passion scene painted on panel), a *Karnierl* set with various stones, a basket holding a large ostrich egg, a serpentine spoon, and a shell.[20]

Ferdinand, a Prince for his time, clearly had an interest in clocks and other mechanical devices, as we know from orders placed with horologists in Nuremberg, Munich, and Innsbruck. It appears that Ferdinand owned and collected antiquities, at the same time that he also became an active client of the period's great armorers, commissioning many suits of armor from Landshut, Augsburg, and especially Jorg Seusenhofer in Innsbruck. Ferdinand found his court painter in Jakob Seisenegger, who produced dozens of portraits of the Habsburg family.

As a collector, Ferdinand had considerable range, extending into the realm of antique coins, where he built up a collection of 1,499 pieces, 115 of

113. Margaret of Austria (after a lost Flemish original), c. 1505. Oil on panel; 12 1/4 x 11 3/4" (31 x 30 cm). Kunsthistorisches Museum, Vienna. Archduchess Margaret, a daughter of Maximilian I and Mary of Burgundy, survived her role as a pawn in the political chess game of her time to become an astute Governor of the Netherlands, the wise guardian of Archduke Charles (the future Emperor Charles V), and the Habsburgs' first true collector.

114. Jan Vermeyen (after). Emperor Ferdinand I as Archduke, c. 1520. Oil on panel; 9 7/8 x 7 7/8" (25 x 20 cm). Kunsthistorisches Museum, Vienna. Through his marriage to Princess Anna of Bohemia and Hungary, Ferdinand extended Habsburg power far into Eastern Europe. Today he is also esteemed as the founder of the Habsburg Kunstkammer in Vienna.

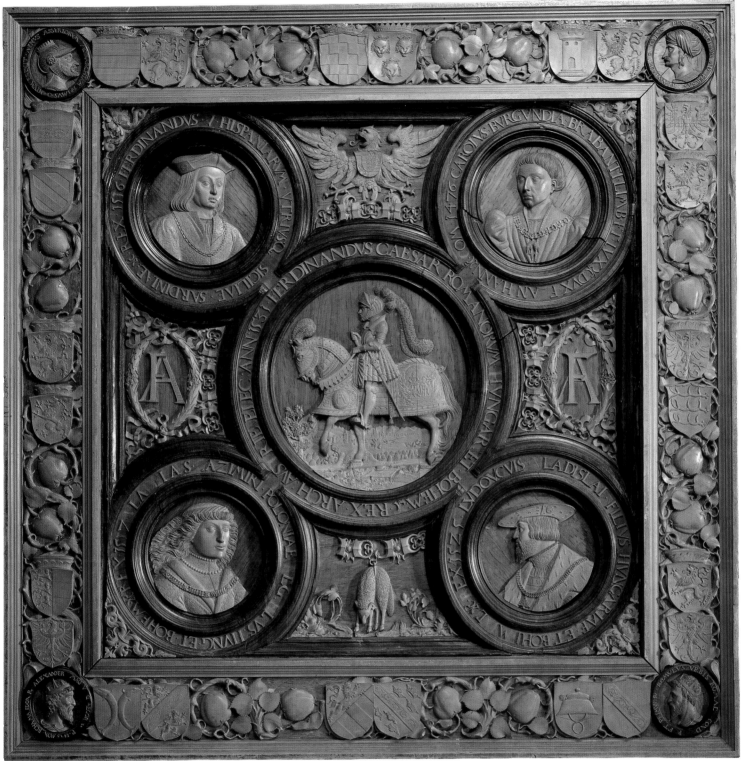

115

115. *Hans Kels the Elder.* Backgammon board, *1537 (South Germany). Oak, walnut, boxwood, ash, palissandre, mahogany, rosewood, and bronze; 22 ¹/₈" (56.1 cm) square. Kunsthistorisches Museum, Vienna. This superbly crafted board was used for playing* Langer Puff, *a form of backgammon. The applied bas-reliefs,* Düreresque in style, show a portrait of Ferdinand I on horseback surrounded by ancestors. The monogram AF signifies the ownership of Emperor Ferdinand and his wife, Anna of Bohemia and Hungary. The 30 draughtsmen are carved with mythological and biblical scenes.

116

116. *Antonio Abondio. Emperor Maximilian II, c. 1575. Wax, stone, and silver; diameter 5 ¹/₁₆" (12.8 cm). Kunsthistorisches Museum, Vienna. Abondio, a Milanese sculptor known for his medals and colored-wax portraits, worked at the Imperial court in Vienna, beginning in 1566. The art-loving Maximilian kept numerous artists in his service, among them the celebrated goldsmith Wenzel Jamnitzer, the famous clockmaker Gerhard Emmoser, and the painters Bartholomäus Spranger and Giuseppe Arcimboldo. In due course they would all be employed by his son, Emperor Rudolf II, an even greater arts patron, whose features strongly resemble those of his father.*

117. *Giovanni Bologna. Allegory of the Reign of Francesco I of Tuscany, c. 1560 (Florence). Bronze; 12 ¹/₈ x 17 ¹⁷/₁₈" (30.7 x 45.6 cm). Kunsthistorisches Museum, Vienna. According to tradition, this bas-relief is one of three bronzes by Giambologna presented to Emperor Maximilian II by Grand Duke Cosimo I of Tuscany at the time of Archduchess Johanna's marriage to Cosimo's son, Francesco. The cast seen here appears then to have entered the collection of the Dukes of Modena through another of the Habsburgs' dynastic alliances, after which Emperor Rudolf II exercised enough pressure, by way of his agent, Hans von Aachen, to acquire it from the Modena court in 1604.*

which were in gold and 754 in silver. He gathered these "heathen pennies" with painstaking care, seeking them out in Rome, Venice, Hungary, Transylvania, and Constantinople. Ferdinand particularly liked coins featuring likenesses of the Roman Emperors and tried hard to assemble a complete series of them, for, after all, Augustus and his progeny were the "ancestors" of the Habsburgs.

The pride Ferdinand I took in his coins and antiquities finds expression in his will of 1554 (made two years before he became Emperor), where he specifically mentions "… our crates with various old coins and antiquities, which we also leave to our beloved son King Maximilian with the proviso that he keep and maintain these undivided and together. Because, although such coins, according to their gold, silver, and other metal content, are only of insignificant and small value, we appreciate them for their age and for their order to be worthy to be kept as a treasure, as they would not be easy to find in this quantity and completeness in other places."[21] For the first time in Kunstkammer history, at least insofar as it concerns the Holy Roman Empire, instrinsic value was deemed less significant than quality and historical importance. While Ferdinand left his "royal crown together with the sceptre, orb, and royal mantel and clothes" to his eldest son, Maximilian, King of Hungary, he stipulated that the remainder of his "treasures, pearls, and jewels" be divided evenly between his two younger sons, Ferdinand II of Tyrol and Charles of Styria.

Within a month after Ferdinand I died in 1564, Maximilian, Ferdinand, and Charles jointly agreed to designate two particular objects from their patrimony as inalienable family heirlooms. The first chosen was the celebrated agate bowl known as the Habsburgs' *beste Hauptstück* or "best main piece," clearly thought to be the most valuable treasure owned by the family. Later it was even believed to embody the word KRISTO, naturally formed in Latin letters without the aid of human hands, which made the vessel worthy of veneration as if it were the Holy Grail. According to tradition, moreover, the *beste Hauptstück* was the largest surviving work of carved stone to have come from the booty taken during the notorious Crusader sack of Constantinople in 1204. It came to the Habsburgs as part of their Burgundian legacy. The second designated heirloom was the *Ainkhürn* or "unicorn," in reality a narwhal tusk of great length, presented in 1540 to King Ferdinand by his future son-in-law, King Sigismund of Poland. In their co-signed stipulation, Ferdinand's three sons wrote: "Both exceptional treasures will henceforth and for all time remain with our great House of Austria and are not to be sold, given away, pawned, or in any other way alienated or modified but are to

117

remain for all time with the eldest Prince of Austria in his safekeeping."[22] This unusual agreement, contrary to the more common practice of primogeniture, meant that at the death of Emperor Maximilian II in 1576 the two heirlooms would pass into the collection of Archduke Ferdinand II of Tyrol rather than into that of Emperor Rudolf II, Maximilian's eldest son.

Maximilian II (r. 1564-1576) and Archduke Charles

Maximilian II (1527-1576), who was crowned King of Bohemia in 1549, King of the Germans in 1562, King of Hungary in 1563, and Holy Roman Emperor in 1564, had a relatively short reign. One of the lesser known Habsburg monarchs, he married Maria of Austria, the strictly Catholic daughter of Charles V, which made her his aunt as well as his wife. According to a Venetian Ambassador, Maximilian II liked to "work with his hands in things of gold and silver, sometimes attending to distilling with oils, waters, and minerals, of which he knows many strange secrets." Furthermore, his greatest pleasure, "into which he puts all the time he can spare, is the making of a garden, half a league from Vienna."[23] Deeply interested in natural history, Maximilian attracted several outstanding botanists to Vienna, among them Ghislain de Busbecq, who imported lilacs and tulips from Constantinople.

Maximilian II collected antiquities with a passion, evident from considerable documentation in the Vienna archives, which are full of correspondence concerning the Emperor's acquisitions of Roman sculpture, either through purchase or through gift. The documents cite life-size figures of Venus, Hercules, and Mars, as well as a number of Roman heads, presented by the Pope or by such Princes of the Church as Cardinals Poliziano, Colonna, and Ippolito d'Este. The Imperial Ambassador to Rome, Count Prosper Arco, was charged with obtaining *statuas et simulacra*, the latter modern copies destined for Maximilian's gardens. Beginning in 1556, the well-known numismatist Jacopo Strada often appeared in Vienna, where, by 1564, he would be employed by the Emperor to serve as antiquary and thus, presumably, to advise on the collections (fig. 198).

When it came to painting, Maximilian went well beyond earlier Habsburgs, who generally concentrated on galleries of ancestral images, and seriously collected pictures as works of art. Bartholomäus Spranger, Giuseppe Arcimboldo, Giulio Licino, Lucas van Valckenborch, and Juan del Monte all worked for the Emperor. From the court medalist and wax sculptor Antonio Abondio there survives a fine profile portrait of Maximilian, an image once thought to represent the subject's son Rudolf, so closely did the two Habsburgs resemble one another (fig. 116). Furthermore, the resemblance extended even into the realm of collecting, where the influence of father on son cannot be underestimated. Indeed, most of the artists just cited would later work for Rudolf II in Prague. Maximilian, like every other prince of the day, conceived a longing for the Mannerist bronzes of Giovanni da Bologna, the great Flemish sculptor employed by the Medici in Florence. Thus, when Grand Duke Cosimo I sought the hand of Maximilian's youngest sister, Archduchess Johanna, for his son Francesco, he was advised by the Papal nuncio in Vienna to present the Emperor with works by "Giambologna." The gift almost certainly included a version of the famous *Mercury* and the *Allegory on the Reign of Francesco I of Tuscany* (fig. 117), both of which would be owned by Rudolf II.

No document from the reign of Maximilian II refers to the Kunstkammer, but some of the many art works commissioned by this Emperor may well have been intended for the museum. The collection, meanwhile, had been relocated away from the Burg to a new building, which also housed the royal stables. The Imperial archives abound in records of payments to goldsmiths, most of them having to do with presentations, which included scores of silver or silver-gilt cups and a number of gold chains. Wenzel Jamnitzer, the leading light of Nuremberg goldsmithery, crops up in relation to a part payment of 1,500 gulden for an unspecified object. Jamnitzer was also the author of a magnificent casket, described as *ein schön silbern Truhlein* ("a fine little silver chest"), presented in 1570 by the Council of the City of Nuremberg to Empress Maria,[24] who would then offer it, filled with jewels, to her daughter Anna on the occasion of her marriage to Philip II of Spain.

Archduke Charles (1540-1590), Maximilian II's younger brother, received the Duchy of Styria south of Vienna after Emperor Ferdinand I partitioned the Habsburg crown lands among his three sons. At his capital in Graz, Charles concentrated on architecture and the construction of fortifications, partly to create a fine setting for his reign and partly to defend the duchy against Turkish invasion. He housed his collection in the *Langer Saal* or "Long Hall" of his castle, where instruments, clocks, exotic objects, Chinese porcelain, and glass lay all about in no apparent order. Along with his passion for building came the need to furnish what had been erected, a need that Archduke Charles was clearly prepared to satisfy, inasmuch as he is known to have possessed 127 tapestries, of which 37 with animal subjects hung in the children's rooms.

In 1571, when Archduke Charles married Maria von Wittelsbach, the daughter of Duke Albrecht V of Bavaria, his Imperial brother staged a week-long celebration in Vienna, followed by additional festivities in Graz. These involved gigantic feasts, jousts, and hunts, simultaneously as they also provided an occasion for the duchy to garnish the couple's credenza with gold and silver plate valued at 15,000 gulden, in addition to a welcome allowance of 25,000 gulden, paid in cash. From Styria's magnificent plate survives a sumptuous gold ewer and basin made in Spain (fig. 118).

118. Ewer and basin, *1571 (Spain).*
Gold and enamel; height of ewer 13 5/8"
(34.5 cm), diameter of basin 24 1/4"
(61.5 cm). Weltliche und Geistliche
Schatzkammer, Vienna. This massive
garniture, weighing over 10 kilos, was
presented by the Duchy of Styria to
Archduke Charles, Maximilian II's
younger brother, and Princess Maria of
Bavaria on the occasion of their
wedding in Graz in 1571. It would be
inherited by their son, the future
Emperor Ferdinand II, and thereafter
serve for any number of Habsburg
baptisms.

118

Archduke Ferdinand II of Tyrol

The first Habsburg to become a legend in his own time primarily for the completeness and "universality" of his collection was Archduke Ferdinand II of Tyrol (1529-1595), the second and favorite son of the Holy Roman Emperor Ferdinand I (fig. 120).[1] In 1519, Ferdinand I had been given the Habsburgs' Austrian duchies by his brother, the long-lived Emperor Charles V, but only in 1558 did he receive the Imperial crown, after Charles retired to a monastery in western Spain. Meanwhile, Ferdinand had vastly enlarged the Habsburg domains, thanks to his marriage to Anna, the daughter of King Vladislav II of Hungary and Bohemia, lands he claimed after his brother-in-law, King Lajos II, had perished in 1526 at the Battle of Mohács, leaving most of Hungary under Turkish domination for the next century and a half. Three years later, in 1529, Suleiman the Magnificent sent a fresh army up the Danube and laid siege to Vienna, which explains in part why Archduke Ferdinand was born at Linz in Upper Austria. Vienna's vulnerability to attack also made it prudent for Ferdinand and his elder brother Maximilian, the future Emperor, to be reared at Innsbruck, the capital and cultural center of the Tyrol.

Here, in a beautiful valley protected by soaring Alpine peaks, the two Habsburg princes grew up under the tutelage of a poet, Caspar Ursinus Velius, and a mathematician, Colimitius, whose teaching set Ferdinand on the path towards intellectual pursuits that would engage him for the rest of his life. As second in line of succession to the Imperial, Hungarian, and Bohemian thrones, however, the Archduke required broader experience, and for this he was dispatched to the Netherlands, where service awaited him at the court of his uncle. He arrived at a golden moment, when, as Charles V himself liked to observe, the sun never set on the Habsburg empire, stretching as it did from the Balkans across the Americas to the Philippines. Ferdinand, already a brave knight at the age of seventeen, traveled with the Emperor to the Prussian province of Saxony

and, along with his father, took part in the historic Battle of Mühlberg (1547), at which Imperial forces prevailed over those of the Schmalkaldic League, splitting the Protestant princes and opening the way for the Counter-Reformation in Germany. The defeated Duke Johann Friedrich lost the Electorate of Saxony, which now passed to Duke Moritz, as we shall see in Chapter 10. Shortly thereafter Archduke Ferdinand found himself installed by his father as Regent of Bohemia, a post he assumed in 1547 at the age of eighteen and held until 1563. Inevitably, he would be drawn into the war with Suleiman the Magnificent, against whose formidable troops he successfully led an army in 1556 to lift the siege of Sziget in Hungary. Ten years later he was once again in the field, this time leading a squadron of cavalry in a final campaign, for the moment, against the Infidel.

Prior to his arrival in Prague, Archduke Ferdinand had lived in a relatively frugal manner. This would soon change, for it was Habsburg policy, wherever possible, to exercise power through such peaceful, and pleasurable, means as overwhelming displays of wealth. *Casa Austria* was henceforth to be seen by their Bohemian subjects as both munificent and invincible. For the next seventeen years, therefore, Ferdinand dedicated much of his annual purse – 120,000 guilders – to the acquisition of art works. It was also during this period that he began assembling, at Schloss Bürglitz, the collections of armor and *uomini famosi* – portraits of famous men – for which he would later become celebrated in his own right.

Ferdinand, moreover, would build, for, like many accomplished noblemen of the Renaissance, he loved architecture and loved to practice as a dilettante architect. Eventually he would succeed well enough to win the respect of none other than the great French essayist Michel de Montaigne, who called the Archduke *un grand bâtisseur et diviseur de telles commoditées*. This praise came, however, only after Ferdinand had returned to Innsbruck and totally reconstructed the ancient Schloss Ambras, his real home. Meanwhile, he made his architectural

120

119. Abraham I. Pfleger. Ewer and basin, 1585-1590 (Augsburg). Triton shell, four tridacna shells, two scallop shells, and silver-gilt; height of ewer 12 7/8" (32.6 cm), diameter of basin 15 11/16" (39.9 cm). Kunsthistorisches Museum, Vienna. This ewer/basin set embodies the Kunstkammer spirit to perfection. However impractical his concept, the artist transformed the enthralling products of nature - naturalia - into works of art - artificialia.

120. Jakob Seisenegger. Archduke Ferdinand II of Tyrol, 1548. Oil on canvas, 78 1/2 x 35" (184.5 x 89 cm). Kunsthistorisches Museum, Vienna. Here Archduke Ferdinand is portrayed as a handsome, strapping young man prepared for his early duties in the Netherlands.

121

122

121. *Francesco Segala. Archduke Ferdinand II of Tyrol, c. 1569 (Padua). Encaustic relief; 8 3/4 x 7 3/4" (22.3 x 19.9 cm). Kunsthistorisches Museum, Vienna. In this portrait a Paduan specialist in colored-wax reliefs represented Archduke Ferdinand at about forty, clad in a gilded cuirass and the Order of the Golden Fleece.*

122. *Philippine Welser(?), mid-16th century (Germany). Oil on canvas; 33 1/2 x 23 3/4" (85 x 60 cm). Kunsthistorisches Museum, Vienna. In 1556 Archduke Ferdinand violated Habsburg tradition and married for love rather than for dynastic politics, taking Philippine Welser, the wise and charming daughter of an Augsburg trader, as his morganatic wife, the first of many in the Habsburg family. The offspring of Ferdinand and Philippine were known as the Margraves of Burgau, a line that fell extinct after one generation, in 1618.*

debut in 1555 on the western outskirts of Prague, where, in a game preserve south of the White Mountain, he had Italian architects erect a hunting lodge or summer palace known as the *Letohrádek Hvezda* or "Star Castle." The structure, along with some of its Italian stuccoes, survives today at the center of a lush park with avenues of trees radiating from the six points of the star-shaped building.

Ferdinand, a handsome, affable, and sporting man (fig. 121), was meant from birth to make a dynastic marriage, and for this purpose eligible princesses from almost every royal house in Europe came up for consideration, only to be rejected. For no other reason than love, it would seem, this favorite and otherwise dutiful son defied his father and in 1557 married Philippine Welser, the lovely and clever daughter of an Augsburg patrician (fig. 122). Once informed, the senior Ferdinand, who would become Emperor a year later, merely insisted that the marriage remain secret until it had been recognized by the Pope and formally ratified by himself, but merely as a morganatic union, the first of many in the Habsburg family. This meant that none of the children born to the couple could be included in the line of succession or ever inherit any of the Habsburg domains. Unfazed, Archduke Ferdinand and Philippine appear to have led singularly happy, productive, and sociable lives.

In 1563 Emperor Ferdinand divided his lands among his sons, whereupon the Tyrol went to Archduke Ferdinand, who would thus be known as Ferdinand II of Tyrol. The new regency took him back to Innsbruck, where he had no desire to occupy the gloomy official residence – the Hofburg – described in 1628 by the well-known traveler Philipp Hainhofer as "vast and melancholic." The ever-fond Emperor obliged his son by spending 15,300 guilders to acquire Schloss Ambras, a dilapidated medieval castle with foundations dating back to the 11th century. It loomed southeast of Innsbruck some two miles away in the wooded foothills of the Tyrolean Alps. Almost immediately, Ferdinand deeded the property to his wife and set about drawing up plans to rebuild the castle as a private residence or

123

Lustschloss ("pleasure palace"). By 1567, when the couple made their festive entry into Innsbruck, Schloss Ambras was ready to receive them, although expansion and improvements would continue for many years. It remains one of the most impressive castles in Austria, a white-stuccoed multilevel mass with an onion-domed tower rising picturesquely against a panoramic backdrop of snowcapped mountains. Already, however, the Archduke's collections, including armor weighing 347,000 pounds, had grown so voluminous that, for the moment, they had to be housed in the Hofburg rather than at Ambras.

One of the best-preserved castles in Austria, Schloss Ambras has scarcely been altered since Matthias Merian published his famous bird's-eye view in 1648 (fig. 123). The engraving, even better than a modern aerial photograph, reveals the clear division between a lower castle (*Unterschloss*) and an upper one (*Hochschloss*), the latter a huge irregular quadrangle containing the châtelains' living quarters. The steep, many-windowed structure rises about an interior courtyard lavishly decorated in grisaille fresco with trompe-l'oeil figures in niches between windows and bands of pictorial narrative running between floors. Not only was this Renaissance pile the most modern as well as the most Italianate castle in German-speaking Europe; it was also the most comfortable, as demonstrated by Philippine's large bathroom, which survives complete with its 900-litre, copper-lined tub.

At the center of the lower castle lies another courtyard, this one spacious enough for the great bouts of jousting and other festivities in which the fun-loving Ferdinand and Philippine took such delight. The embracing structures include the entrance lodge and service buildings, of course, but also a ballroom and galleries for the collections. Lying halfway between the Upper and Lower Castles is the Spanish Hall (*Spanischer Saal*), the earliest monumental, freestanding Renaissance hall erected on German soil (fig. 124). The architects in charge were Giovanni Lucchese and his son Alberto, both from Lucca in Tuscany as their name implies. For the massive coffered ceiling and the beautifully inlaid doors, Ferdinand and his architects turned to a local talent, the Innsbruck woodworker Konrad Gottlieb. Even more spectacular are the wall frescoes, consisting mainly of portraits of Tyrolean princes and tendriled grotesques, these painted by Dionys van Halaert. Also contributing to the rich Mannerist décor are the stucco reliefs executed by Anthonis Brackh.

Spread out to the right of the Lower Castle was a formal garden, a *broderie* patterned after those of Renaissance Italy. As Merian's engraving shows, the garden boasted waterworks, in addition to an open-

124

123. Matthias Merian. Schloss Ambras, from Welttopographie. 1648. Engraving. This is the first known view of Schloss Ambras, where Ferdinand and Philippine made their home in the foothills of the Tyrolean Alps above Innsbruck. The Kunstkammer lay in the lower castle on the left side of the courtyard where the Archduke loved to stage jousting tournaments.

124. Giovanni and Alberto Lucchese. Spanish Hall, Schloss Ambras, c. 1570-1571. Commissioned by Archduke Ferdinand II, the Spanischer Saal at Schloss Ambras would be the earliest monumental, freestanding Renaissance hall built in German-speaking Europe. A local talent, Konrad Gottlieb, took charge of the coffered ceiling and the inlaid floor, while Dionys van Halaert executed the wall frescoes and Anthonis Brackh the stuccoes. The great hall would be hung with portraits of Habsburgs and stag's antlers.

125. Ambras guest book, 1570s. Paper with leather binding; 12 1/4 x 8 1/4" (31 x 21 cm). Kunsthistorisches Museum, Schloss Ambras Collections, Innsbruck. Guests who survived the Bacchic initiation rites at Schloss Ambras signed the hosts' guest book. It is divided into a section for gentlemen, headed by Archduke Ferdinand, and another for ladies, headed by Philippine Welser.

air dining pavilion, which was famous for its revolving table. Driven by hydraulic power, this remarkable piece of furniture and its surrounding seats could turn at a dizzying speed. Philippine cultivated not only a kitchen garden but also a garden planted with medicinal herbs and embellished with four hundred statues. Clearly an excellent housewife, Philippine was well known for her kindness and common sense, despite the scandal associated with a morganatic marriage. Still preserved at Ambras are her medicinal book and her cookbook, both bound in leather.[2]

No Renaissance garden would have been complete without its grotto, which at Ambras became the scene of Bacchic rites, joyously engaged in by Ferdinand, Philippine, and their guests, as we know from several books with signatures of the participants, the earliest dating from 1567 (fig. 125).[3] The ceremony involved a mechanical armchair made of iron strong enough to imprison a person until he or she had consumed a given amount of wine in a single draught (fig. 126). Ladies had to empty a glass in the form of a ship, whereas gentlemen were required to prove their manhood by downing the contents of a glass cask with a daunting three-quart capacity! Along with the signatures, the first of which are those of Ferdinand and Philippine, appear a number of amusing verses, some of them written in an obviously inebriated state.

The style of life at Schloss Ambras was opulent, as it had to be for a Renaissance prince of the blood. Virtually every day of the week the castle's many rooms were filled with visitors who, as one observer wrote, "have no business with His Royal Highness… but are all fed." The regimen consisted of processions, games, and competitions with guns or crossbows. Ferdinand, a man well known for his physical strength, took great pleasure in jousting on horseback, a noisy, rousing sport practiced on the great expanse of the lower courtyard. For more refined moments, the Archduke also kept an orchestra,

125

126

126. *Mechanical armchair, 2nd half 16th century (Germany). Iron; height 45" (114 cm). Kunsthistorisches Museum, Schloss Ambras Collections, Innsbruck. The fun-loving Ferdinand and Philippine delighted in leading their guests into the Grotto of Bacchus, where a mechanical armchair seized the initiates one at a time and released them only after each had drunk truly challenging quantities of wine.*

127. *Glass beaker, late 16th century. Glass, gold, pearls, rubies, and diamonds; height 8" (20.2 cm). Kunsthistorisches Museum, Vienna. According to tradition, the glass beaker seen here was blown by Archduke Ferdinand at the workshop he had established near Innsbruck, staffed with craftsmen imported from Murano. The attribution is supported not only by the form of the cover - an archducal hat - but also by the lopsidedness of the vessel.*

which played in the dining room as well as in the chapel on Sunday. Much of the 200,000 guilders disbursed to the Regent every year by the Tyrolean state was used to defray the cost of maintaining such an impressive household and program of entertainment. When it came to collecting, however, Ferdinand paid out of his own pocket.

A rational collector as well as one very much of his time – the age of Late-Renaissance Humanism and its Neoplatonic ideology – Archduke Ferdinand sought to form an encyclopedic collection, a *theatrum mundi* based on the principles of Pliny's *Historia Naturalis*.[4] By reflecting the whole of the known world, such an all-embracing assemblage might provide insight into the higher, divine order whence it came. Believed to be especially appropriate for this purpose were not only art works but also "curiosities," the strange, even weird, exotic, or anomalous things of nature, rare oddities in which nature was thought to be revealed in its essence. To find them, Ferdinand had his agents search throughout the Habsburg empire, at the same time that he corresponded personally with other collectors and their heirs, offering terms certain to relieve them of coveted items. One prime opportunity presented itself when Count Ulrich von Montfort died, whereupon Ferdinand persuaded his widow to part with the deceased's silver collection. To assist him in such activity, the Archduke employed a secretary, Jakob Schrenck von Notzing, who supervised the correspondence and oversaw the collections, except for the Kunstkammer, the library, and the coins, all of which fell under the purview of Gerard van Loo, a bassoonist in the castle's orchestra and later an historian.

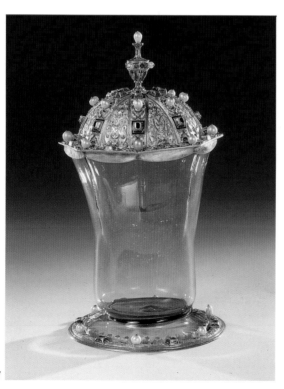

127

Ferdinand II of Tyrol went beyond collecting and vigorously patronized art, taking important steps to attract artists and craftsmen to his court, where a sort of "art collective" developed, with the Archduke himself involved in the creative process. Such commitment was in keeping with a policy designed to stimulate the local economy and encourage Tyrolean industries, among them glassblowing, introduced by craftsmen brought from Murano and set up in the nearby town of Hall. Glasses made there often had amusing shapes, such as beakers in the form of legs or hats, examples of which are preserved at Ambras. Ferdinand so taxed his lungs at glassblowing that the court feared for his life. One piece attributed to him is a lopsided beaker crowned by an archducal hat set with jewels and mounted in gold (fig. 127).

In Innsbruck, the Archduke founded a pottery where Christoph Gandtner made for his royal patron a well-known series of whimsical, picturesque figures (fig. 128). At the castle itself, Ferdinand set up a foundry as well as a carpentry workshop, the latter equipped with a lathe for his own personal use, "in part to cultivate the mind, in part to exercise the body." Two Venetian ambassadors who visited Ambras in 1577 reported that His Royal Highness "has a room furnished with arms as well as with every kind of instrument for use in the manual or mechanical arts, such as every tool required in *marangone, di favro*, turning, goldsmithery, and other such pursuits, all made with consummate – indeed singular – diligence and delicacy."[5]

At Ambras, Ferdinand employed a throng of painters – "half a hundred" by his own account – although few of them survive in history as anything more than names, unattached to works of major artistic significance. Among the better-known painters may be counted Pietro Rosa, a pupil of Titian who executed portraits for the Spanish Hall, the brothers Giovanni and Giulio Fontana, who decorated the dining room, and, most of all, Francesco Terzio, the author of many paintings for the Archduke's portrait gallery. Anecdotal evidence regarding the Flemish master Roman Fleschauer provides some insight into life at Schloss Ambras as well as into the character of the royal châtelain. When Fleschauer fell ill and remained indisposed for a long period, Ferdinand not only maintained him in every way, but he even sent the unfortunate man to a spa and had him treated by his own physicians.

Also active at Ambras were several goldsmiths, including Anton Ort, a proper court artist, and Elias Stark, their presence confirmed by the castle's archives. Ferdinand also commissioned works from craftsmen at that pre-eminent center of goldsmithery, Augsburg, doing so through an agent named August Schanternel, who, according to a 1584 account, pro-

128

vided the archducal court with twenty small silver beakers, ten larger ones, a necklace with pendant, and a silver-mounted writing table. Wenzel Jamnitzer, a Nuremberger and the greatest of the German Mannerists specializing in precious metals, also sent works to Ambras, one of which is still there. As *Kaiserlicher Hofgoldschmied*, Jamnitzer served four Habsburg Emperors, including Ferdinand's father and elder brother, who delighted in his virtuoso command of such techniques as modeling, embossing, engraving, enameling, and casting from insects, reptiles, and grasses. As we shall see, however, the Archduke was less interested in contemporary work than in historic pieces dating from earlier times.

The domestic bliss at Ambras suffered a terrible blow in 1580 when Philippine Welser died at the age of fifty-three. The big-hearted Ferdinand remained a widower for two years, but then re-wed, this time within his own class, the bride being Anna Catarina Gonzaga, the daughter of his sister, Eleonora, Duchess of Mantua. Death and remarriage brought an end to the revels at Schloss Ambras, which the Archduke and his new wife abandoned for the more formal, urban environment of the Innsbruck Hofburg. Gradually thereafter the castle became a showcase – actually the first public museum in Europe – for the vast, carefully assembled collections in which Ferdinand took such pride.

The Ambras collections could be divided into various groups, all connected, however, by a common philosophical theme centered upon man. This

was clearly reflected in the huge portrait gallery devoted to the likenesses of famous persons, for which as many as a thousand images were executed. Limitations of space finally dictated that the paintings be done in a miniature format measuring just over 6 by 4 inches. When the Archduke sent requests for portraits to agents and Habsburg relatives, he also forwarded samples of paper cut to the desired size. Given that he was less interested in artistic quality than in the personalities behind the faces, many of the pictures he received were merely copies of earlier works. Still, the gallery could boast several fine portraits by such acknowledged masters as Lucas Cranach the Younger and Agnolo Bronzino.

In the large armory, man was present mainly as an absence, given that the suits of armor were empty, a fact the Archduke may have taken into account when he jokingly dubbed the collection the "valiant assembly" (*ehrliche Gesellschaft*).[6] Filling four halls, the *Heldenrüstkammer* ("Heroes' Armory") was the most complete thing of its kind in the 16th century. Here again the emphasis fell upon personalities and the valorous deeds for which they were famous. Ferdinand meant the holdings to be a tribute to feats of bravery; thus, it was generally considered a great honor to have a suit of armor displayed at Ambras. Thanks to his prestige, the Archduke could successfully prevail upon family members and other nobility to give him armor worn by many a commander or hero noted for fearless participation in some historic battle. Ferdinand planned a book in Latin on the collection – the *Armamentarium Heroicum* – only for it to appear in 1601, some six years after his death, by which time the long-expected, pioneering work was greeted with great acclaim.[7]

Today, it is almost impossible to reconstruct the mass of coins and medals collected by Ferdinand II of Tyrol, or reassemble the almost two thousand cameos and intaglios he owned. All have become inextricably bound up with the Imperial collections in Vienna. The library at Ambras, which originally held 3,430 volumes, has also lost its most important works to Vienna, including Maximilian I's personally annotated copies of his autobiographical *Theuerdank* and *Weisskunig*.

The *Kunst- und Wunderkammer* was housed in a large, plain rectangular hall illuminated by tall windows on either side. A multitude of paintings hung from the walls and stuffed animals as well as the bones of "giants" (probably dinosaurs) from the high ceiling. Miniature portraits were stored in chests. Down the center of the hall, eighteen floor-to-ceiling cabinets stood back to back in parallel rows, which terminated at either end in two additional cabinets aligned perpendicular to the double row. Linen curtains protected the contents from dust and the dele-

130

129. Beaker of Duke Philip the Good, 1453-
1467 (Burgundy). Rock crystal, gold,
diamonds, rubies, and pearls; height
18 1/8" (46 cm). Kunsthistorisches
Museum, Vienna. This jeweled and
gilded vessel, one of the finest works of
art surviving from the opulent
Burgundian court, formed part of the
French royal treasury until 1570, when
Charles IX presented it to Archduke
Ferdinand. The repeated and
confronted E linked by cords and the
flintstones of the Order of the Golden
Fleece identify its onetime owner as
Duke Philip the Good of Burgundy.

130. Saracchi workshop. Two Herons, late
16th century (Milan). Rock crystal, gold,
enamel, cameos, pearls, precious and
semiprecious stones; height 16" (40.9 cm)
and 12 1/8" (31.8 cm). Kunsthistorisches
Museum, Vienna. Throughout the 16th
and 17th centuries objects carved from
rock crystal were deemed essential to
any Kunstkammer worthy of the name.
The prolific Saracchi of Milan, who
remained active from around 1560 until
well into the 17th century, produced
some of the most impressive lapidary
works of the Renaisssance, Mannerist,
and Baroque periods.

131

131. *Clement Kicklinger. Ostrich-egg cup and cover, 1570-1575 (Augsburg). Ostrich egg, silver-gilt, enamel, and coral; height 22 ³/₈" (56.8 cm). Kunsthistorisches Museum, Vienna. In this witty piece, a silver-gilt ostrich bears its own egg upon its back. The work also exemplifies Kunstkammer taste at its most extravagant, combining naturalia - coral as well as the egg - with the artificialia of virtuoso craftsmanship. Coral was thought, as it is today in certain parts of Southern Italy, to ward off the Evil Eye. A portent of good luck is the horseshoe the ostrich holds in its mouth.*

132. *Cornelius Gross. Dragon Horn, c. 1560-1570 (Augsburg). Tortoiseshell and silver, parcel-gilt; height 11 ⁵/₈" (29.5 cm), length 13 ³/₄" (35 cm). Kunsthistorisches Museum, Vienna. Although shaped like a buffalo's horn, this objet d'art is actually crafted from tortoiseshell, an extremely rare substance in 16th-century Europe. The presence of both tortoise and triton figures suggests an awareness of the maritime origins of the shell material. Originally, the mouth contained a Natterzunge - a so-called "dragon's tooth" - then thought to be a sure defense against poison.*

terious effects of light. In one notable innovation, Ferdinand had the cabinets' interiors color-coded – that is, painted in hues chosen to complement and identify the contents, all organized according to medium. Tables placed in front of the cabinets allowed visitors to examine art works or curiosities in a leisurely, studious fashion with the least risk to the objects.

In the first cabinet could be found the best of the goldsmith work, set forth against a blue ground. Among the pieces were four gifts from Charles IX of France, presented in 1570 when Ferdinand served as proxy for the King at the Austrian wedding ceremony that bound His Majesty to Archduchess Elizabeth, the daughter of Emperor Maximilian II, Ferdinand's elder brother. The most celebrated of these rare works is the *Saliera* or *Saltcellar* (figs. 27-29) created by Benvenuto Cellini for Charles IX's grandfather, François I. Arguably the most admired piece of goldsmithery to survive from the Renaissance – and surely a paradigm of Mannerist art – the *Saltcellar* prompted the following commentary by the great art historian H.W. Janson:

> *To hold condiments is obviously the lesser function of this lavish conversation piece. Because salt comes from the sea and pepper from the land, Cellini placed the boat-shaped salt container under the guardianship of Neptune, while the pepper, in a tiny triumphal arch, is watched over by a personification of Earth. On the base are figures representing the four seasons and the four parts of the day. The entire object thus reflects the cosmic significance of the Medici Tombs [a monumental work of architecture and sculpture by Michelangelo], but on this miniature scale Cellini's program turns into playful fancy; he wants to impress us with his ingenuity and skill, and to charm us with the grace of his figures. The allegorical significance of the design is simply a pretext for his display of virtuosity.[8]*

François I, of course, had been the nemesis of Emperor Charles V, Ferdinand's uncle; all the more reason, therefore, that the Archduke would find a prime place in his Kunstkammer for the armor once worn for the famously tall and elegant French monarch. And there it remained until 1805, when Napoleon seized the metal suit as a national treasure and returned it to France.

Among the gold and silver-gilt tributes from Charles IX was a jeweled rock-crystal beaker mounted in gold (fig. 129) and emblazoned with the device of Philip the Good (1396-1467), Duke of Burgundy, whose granddaughter, Mary of Burgundy, had become the wife of Emperor Maximilian I, Ferdinand's great-grandfather, thereby giving the Habsburgs their claim to the Netherlands.[9] Also part of the Valois package were two further works of virtuoso goldsmithery: a Flemish gem-studded cup with a lid surmounted by an image of Saint Michael and dated around 1530-1540 (fig. 17),[10] and a French

ewer fashioned of enameled onyx (fig. 24).[11] In the same cabinet there were, in addition, numerous rock-crystal vessels made primarily by the Saracchi workshops in Milan (fig. 130), as well as an amusing bear disguised as a hunter (133), the latter comparable to a piece in the Munich Schatzkammer (fig. 215).

Against the green ground of the second cabinet appeared a wide array of silver objects, among them a group of items with significant historical value. A rare Burgundian beaker embellished with enamel had once belonged to Emperor Friedrich III (r. 1452-1493), Ferdinand's great-great grandfather and the first Habsburg to wear the Imperial crown (fig. 104). It bears his enigmatic device AEIOU, an anagram traditionally thought to signify in Latin *Austria est imperare orbi universo* ("It is Austria's destiny to rule the whole world") or in German *Alles Erdreich ist... Österreich untertan* ("All the earth is subject to Austria"). Scarcely less meaningful for Ferdinand would have been a silver-gilt cup and lid bearing the arms of the revered Maximilian and Mary of Burgundy. Another rare bit of memorabilia from the Grand Duchy was a charming gold and enamel brooch decorated with a pair of lovers which had once belonged to Charles V (fig. 112).

In the same cabinet were contemporary collectibles, all of them important, including *naturalia* – specimens of botany, zoology, or paleontology – transformed into *artificialia* – works of art – through some variety of human craftsmanship. One virtuoso piece or set had come from the Augsburg atelier of the goldsmith Abraham Pfleger; it consists of a triton-shell ewer and a basin ingeniously contrived from tridacna shells (fig. 119). Also from Augsburg were Cornelius Gross's dragon formed of a tortoiseshell horn (fig. 132), a brilliant Mannerist ensemble created by Clement Kicklinger using an ostrich egg and coral branches molded together (fig. 131), and a pair of painted, silver-gilt drinking cups conceived as pilgrim figures, both of them embodying the genius of Leonhard Umbach (fig. 135). Wenzel Jamnitzer, the famous Nuremberg goldsmith mentioned earlier, was represented here by a silver writing set, including sand box and inkwell, decorated with shells, insects, and reptiles cast from nature (fig. 134). The Renaissance had dawned in northern Italy once artists, writers, and intellectuals began to study not only Classical antiquity but also nature, a practice taken up in the early 16th century by Albrecht Dürer and his Nuremberg followers, as well as by the French court potter Bernard Palissy, among many other artists and craftsmen. The use of casts after nature, a technique whose chief exponent in Germany was Wenzel Jamnitzer, evolved into a style known as *stil* or *style rustique*.[12]

The third cabinet featured a group of *lapides manuales*, specimens of mineral ore, displayed

133

133. *Gregor Baier. Bear as Hunter, c. 1580-1590 (Augsburg). Silver, ambris or musk, gold, enamel, precious stones, and pearls; height 8 ⁷/₁₆" (21.3 cm). Kunsthistorisches Museum, Vienna. This scent dispenser - an anthropomorphic bear taking aim - signifies the natural order turned upside down. When moved forward, the bear releases a miniature gaming board at his feet. Another mechanism delivers a gold monkey with a book. The figure was probably a present from Duke Wilhelm V of Bavaria, Archduke Ferdinand's nephew-in-law, whose Munich collection owns a similarly whimsical bear (fig. 215)*

134

134. *Wenzel Jamnitzer. Writing set, c. 1570 (Nuremberg). Silver; base 8 15/16 x 4 1/16" (22.7 x 10.2 cm). Kunsthistorisches Museum, Vienna. The leading Nuremberg goldsmith of his time, Jamnitzer achieved particular fame as an innovator of the stil or style rustique (fig. 22), seen here in all its freshness and novelty, complete with frogs, crabs, and insects, herbs and grasses, all cast from natural specimens.*

135. *Leonhard Umbach. Pilgrim Cups, c. 1590-1595 (Augsburg). Silver parcel-gilt and cold enamel; height: 8 1/16" (20.5 cm). Kunsthistorisches Museum, Vienna. Here an entire family - husband, wife, child, and dog - make their elegant way to Santiago de Compostella. Pilgrimages constituted a popular theme in 16th-century art, inspired by, for instance, the Brotherhood of Saint James, which took part in the courtly celebrations and processions staged during the period (Dresden 1564, Stuttgart 1575, Innsbruck 1580). Similar pairs of pilgrim figures by Umbach exist in the Museum of Applied Arts, Budapest, as well as in a private collection in Germany.*

against a red ground. The collection, much of it still preserved in Vienna as well as at Ambras, remains the most important in existence. Avidly sought in Ferdinand's time, these *naturalia* offered the added value of having been incorporated into religious or historical scenes, complete with miniature landscapes, houses, and figures, the whole mounted on silver, metal, or painted wooden bases (figs. 140-142).

The fourth cabinet, this one with a white-painted ground, contained rare musical instruments, some of them from such exotic places as China and Africa. Two pieces once in the collection present the armorial bearings of Archduke Ferdinand; the first is an exquisite, mandolin-like *zister* made in 1574 by the Brescia master Girolamo da Virchi,[13] and the second a unique keyboard instrument designed to sound on glass bells. The contents of this cabinet attested to the active musical life at the Innsbruck court.

In the pink environment of the fifth cabinet visitors could see clocks, automata, and instruments. Of the two automata presented to Ferdinand by his nephew-in-law, Duke Wilhelm V of Bavaria, one may have been made by the renowned Augsburg craftsman Hans Schlottheim. The ebony base containing the music mechanism supports an ensemble of enameled, silver-gilt trumpeters (fig. 136). Although not quite so passionate about clocks as his nephew, Emperor Rudolf II, Ferdinand managed nonetheless to collect some remarkable pieces, among them a complicated bit of horology with a mechanical astrolabe dated 1572. The painted wooden case is inscribed with the Archduke's armorial bearings. A magnificent bronze clock, with a very complicated mechanism, made by Jeremias Metzker of Augsburg and dated 1564, must also have been part of the Ambras collection.[14]

The mirrored interior of the gray-painted sixth cabinet was reserved for stone – that is, for fossils, alabaster and granite vessels (fig. 137), marble obelisks, and Hans Reichel's personification of Death as a skeleton.[15] Iron was the determining medium for the seventh cabinet, which held tools, locks of the greatest intricacy, and even instruments of torture! Housed in the eighth cabinet were the rarest volumes belonging to the castle's library, as well as Ferdinand's huge collection of engravings.[16] In cabinet nine could be discovered pre-Columbian feather mosaics and other works from the New World, including a headdress, a shield, and a fan supposedly given by Montezuma to the *conquistador* Hernando Cortez.[17]

135

The tenth cabinet sheltered works in alabaster, and the eleventh cabinet glass objects displayed against a black ground. This collection comprised a series of unique pieces made in the archducal glassblowing factory (fig. 127), as well as three exceptionally rare *commedia dell'arte* figures from Murano (fig. 138).

The twelfth cabinet was given over to a highly prized collection of works carved or otherwise made of red coral branches imported, very likely, from Genoa. Some of the pieces had been fashioned locally into grotesque landscapes (figs. 140, 141). The Ambras coral collection, although comparable to a similar hoard in the Munich Kunstkammer, was the largest ever seen in Europe.

Collections in other cabinets consisted of bronzes, ceramics, arms, and such oddities as a *Schüttelkasten*, this last a box arranged as a naturalistic habitat for a bizarre race of reptiles with nodding heads made of papier-mâché (fig. 142).

With medium as the organizing principle, works of great value sometimes stood next to items of little value, as in the eighteenth cabinet, where six toothpicks shared space with a skeletal Death beautifully carved in wood by Hans Leinberger (fig. 110). This superb sculpture had once belonged to Emperor Maximilian I.

Ferdinand also collected living *mirabilia*, such as the giant Giovanni Bona, whose suit of armor survives at Ambras, worn by a wooden surrogate. But the Archduke had a taste for the "upwardly challenged" as well, populating his court with several dwarves, one of whom had his own diminutive suit of armor. This preference for the exceptional was again reflected in portraits of cripples, but most astonishingly in a gruesome likeness of a Hungarian man whose eye had been pierced by a jousting lance. Unlike King Henri II of France, who had perished of such a wound in 1559, "Uncle Gregor," as the Hun-

137

136. *Hans Schlottheim (attrib). Automaton with trumpeters, 1582 (Augsburg). Ebony, silver-gilt, and enamel; height 13 ⅛" (33.4 cm), length 14 ¼" (36.2 cm). Kunsthistorisches Museum, Vienna. This musical automaton was a present from Duke Wilhelm V of Bavaria to his uncle by marriage, Archduke Ferdinand II of Tyrol, probably on the occasion of the latter's remarriage, to Anna Catarina Gonzaga, following the death of Philippine Welser. Attributed to the most famous automaton-maker of the period, the work seen here contains a minute organ with ten pipes. The ten trumpeters, once activated, raise their instruments while the drummer beats his tabor.*

137. *Alabaster cabinet, late 16th century (Augsburg). Alabaster, marble, wood, silver, gilded bronze, and semiprecious stones; height 25 ⁹/₁₆" (65 cm). Kunsthistorisches Museum, Schloss Ambras Collections, Innsbruck. Styled as a turret flanked by spiral staircases, this cabinet provides a stage for numerous Classical figures made of alabaster and gilded bronze. The revolving interior is fitted with 168 drawers, designed to hold medals and other precious items.*

136

138

139

138. Commedia dell'arte figures,
c. 1600 (Murano). Glass; height 8 7/16"
(21.4 cm). Kunsthistorisches Museum,
Vienna. These exceedingly rare Murano
figures represent classic characters in
the popular, impromptu theater of
Renaissance Italy. Pantalone and
Colombina do not appear in the trio
seen here, but Capitano is in the
middle.

139. Petrus Gonsalvus of Tenerife (detail),
c. 1580 (Germany). Oil on canvas; 67 x
31 1/2" (190 x 90 cm). Kunsthistorisches
Museum, Schloss Ambras Collections,
Innsbruck. Originally from the Canary
Islands and famous throughout Europe
as the "hairy man" or the "smoky man
of Munich," Petrus Gonsalvus married
a European woman and sired a
number of "hairy children." Duke
Wilhelm V sent this portrait by an
anonymous master to Archduke
Ferdinand, a well-known collector of
such mirabilia.

garian knight was called, survived his accident for many years. The collection included portraits of the "hairy man" Petrus Gonsalvus of Tenerife, his wife, and their two hirsute children (fig. 139).

The life-affirming Ferdinand of Tyrol died at the age of sixty-five. His body lies in the Silver Chapel at the Innsbruck Hofkirche, close by the tomb of Philippine Welser, in a fine Renaissance monument executed by the court sculptor Alexander Colin. Like many a serious collector, the Archduke expressed the wish that his collections be maintained intact. He bequeathed them to his second son, Count Karl von Burgau, who, in 1605, sold the Ambras treasure to that most importunate of collectors, Emperor Rudolf II, for 170,000 guilders. In 1625 the Tyrol passed to Archduke Leopold, a nephew of Ferdinand, whose wife, Claudia de' Medici, daughter of Grand Duke Ferdinando I, followed the tradition of the Florentine court and surrounded herself with scholars and artists. The result was an Ambras further enriched with works of art. Both her collection and those of Archduke Ferdinand remained at Ambras in the care of the Tyrolean Habsburgs until the line died out in 1663, whereupon everything reverted to the main Imperial branch.

In the years following Ferdinand's death, Ambras remained open to distinguished visitors. In 1655, the exiled Queen Christina, whose Swedish armies had pillaged the Imperial collections in Prague, visited Innsbruck, where she made public her conversion to the Roman Catholic faith, and spent an afternoon studying the coins, medals, manuscripts, and curiosities. More than a century later the great German poet Johann Wolfgang von Goethe arrived and remarked upon the sheer novelty of the museum's organization. Finally, Ambras fell into relative oblivion, the effect of which was to preserve the collections intact until 1805, when they were transferred to Vienna and exhibited in the Belvedere. Most of the Archduke's finest treasures would then be incorporated into the Imperial collections in Vienna, which left little of quality behind. Some pieces, such as minor arms and armor, have been returned to Ambras, where they are now exhibited under the aegis of the Imperial armory in Vienna. What survives of the Kunstkammer in situ is displayed in a successful, if much reduced, reconstruction of the original museum. The portrait gallery, supplemented with many works from the Vienna museums, now includes a large number of pictures representing various monarchs as well as members of the Habsburg family.

142

140

140. *Ulrich Caspar (attrib). Handstein, 1560-1570 (St. Joachimsthal). Silver ore, silver-gilt, and enamel; height 23 ³/₄" (60.5 cm). Kunsthistorisches Museum, Vienna.* "Hand stones" or *lapides manuales* were specimens of mineral ore, mainly of Bohemian origin, which Kunstkammer craftsmen could transform into works of art. Here, in a typical Handstein piece, silver ore has become a miniature mountainscape with figures representing David and Bathsheba, all part of a table fountain. Below the fantastic castle atop the mountain, miners are busy working in the cavities, while a lion displays the arms of Austria and Burgundy.

141. *Coral Landscape, 16th century (South Germany). Coral, wood, mother-of-pearl, pearls, plaster, glass, mirror, bronze, velvet, lapis-lazuli, and gilding; 26 x 21 ³/₄" (66 x 55 cm). Kunsthistorisches Museum, Schloss Ambras Collections, Innsbruck.* The Kunstkammern at both Ambras and Munich had renowned collections of red coral. While the Munich hoard no longer exists, the corals assembled by Archduke Ferdinand remain the largest such group in existence. Using both carved and natural corals from Genoa, an anonymous but talented local craftsman in service to the Ambras court combined them with other materials to concoct this beautiful and surreal landscape.

142. *Schüttelkasten, late 16th century (Tyrol). Wood, paper, iron wire, snail shells, moss, and plaster; 9 ³/₈ x 6 ⁷/₈" (23.8 x 17.4 cm). Kunsthistorisches Museum, Schloss Ambras Collections, Innsbruck.* When shaken, the papier-mâché heads and limbs of these bizarre "creepy-crawlies" move in unison. The Schüttelkasten, an amusing though rather frightening curiosity, is a lone survivor of many such party jokes that must have delighted Archduke Ferdinand and his contemporaries.

VII

Emperor Rudolf II of Prague

In the history of collecting there may be no figure more enigmatic and fascinating than Emperor Rudolf II (1552-1612), or one more successful in his near monomaniacal pursuit of an encyclopedic hoard of rare objects (fig. 144).[1] Crowned King of Hungary in 1572, King of Bohemia in 1575, and Holy Roman Emperor in 1576, Rudolf embarked upon his long reign at a propitious moment, a brief period of relative tranquility in Central Europe, when Renaissance Humanism and its civilizing liberality of spirit still prevailed. In 1555 Emperor Charles V had signed the Peace of Augsburg, which, for purposes of the Empire, settled the conflict arising out of the Protestant Reformation, launched in 1517 when an Augustinian friar named Martin Luther nailed his ninety-five theses to the door of the castle church in Wittenberg. And the peace, although fragile, would continue until the outbreak of the Thirty Years War in 1618, a catastrophe often blamed on the temporizing policies and withdrawn, melancholic personality of Rudolf II.

The Rudolfine era, which coincided with or overlapped the reigns of Elizabeth I in England, Philip II in Spain, Henri IV in France, and both Ivan the Terrible and Boris Godunov in Russia, had begun auspiciously enough, but then slowly deteriorated until the unhappy monarch suffered the indignity of being forced by his outraged family to abdicate. The case against Rudolf was that he had long since abandoned state affairs for self-immersion in the study of art, alchemy, astrology, and other forms of arcana.

144

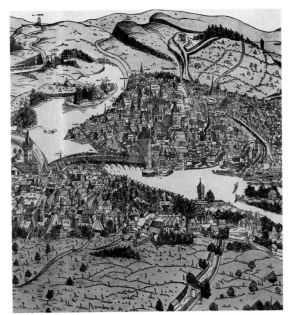

145

Worse, he had failed to produce a legitimate heir, preferring a fertile liaison with the daughter of his court antiquary, Ottavio Strada, to marriage with a crown princess. In 1609 the Emperor had even issued, under duress, a "Letter of Majesty" granting freedom of religion in Bohemia, just as the Counter-Reformation was gaining momentum in its drive to recover Protestant Europe for Roman Catholicism. Eighteen months later the deposed and aging monarch died a recluse in Prague's Hradschin (fig. 145), a towering 14th-century castle/cathedral then crammed with the Rudolfine collection, its paintings numbered in the thousands and a contemporary inventory of its other rarities – bronzes, drawings, etchings, clocks and automata, *naturalia*, *pietre dure*, books and manuscripts, minerals, coins, jewels – running to almost four hundred folios.[2]

Even the decision to rule from Prague, rather than Vienna, the Austrian capital preferred by all other Habsburg Emperors, suggested that Rudolf was a man of independent, perhaps even eccentric, mind. Yet, the choice could also be viewed as logical enough, given the divergent and polarizing pressures which then confronted the young sovereign. Prague,

143. Jan Vermeyen. Crown of Emperor Rudolf II, 1602 (Prague). Gold, enamel, diamonds, rubies, spinels, sapphire, and pearls; height 11 3/16" (28.3 cm). Weltliche und Geistliche Schatzkammer, Vienna. Inscribed: "Rudolf II, Emperor of the Romans, King of Hungary and Bohemia, ordered it to be made 1602." This glittering jewel replaced the crown of the Holy Roman Empire, which since 1424 had been in the care of the city of Nuremberg. For his crown, Rudolf had Vermeyen combine the traditional royal diadem with a bishop's mitre, the better to symbolize the sacred, priestly nature of the Habsburgs' divine-right monarchy.

144. Lucas I. van Valckenborch. Emperor Rudolf II at a Spa, 1593. Oil on panel; 9 1/2 x 15 3/4" (24.5 x 40 cm). Kunsthistorisches Museum, Vienna. It is tempting to imagine that even while taking the cure, Rudolf included in his court some of the many artists and scientists whose company he preferred to that of statesmen.

145. Imperial Prague (c. 1610), with its magnificent Hradchin crowning the heights above a city teeming with the painters, sculptors, goldsmiths, scientists, alchemists, horologists, and charlatans employed by one of the most insatiable of all royal collectors, Emperor Rudolf II.

146

146. *Benedikt Ried and Hans Spiess.*
Vladislav Hall, Hradschin Castle,
Prague. 1502. Engraving by Aegydius
Sadeler (1607). This magnificent
Gothic hall, measuring 16 by 60 meters,
rose on massive foundations laid during
the 14th-century reign of Charles IV,
the first of the two Holy Roman
Emperors to make Prague their
capital. Built by Bohemia's King
Vladislav, the hall was the largest
constructed space unsupported by
columns in contemporary Europe.
Here, below the soaring interlace of
liern vaults, unfolded all manner of life
in Prague, everything from coronations
to popular markets.

147. *Giovanni Bologna. Astronomy,*
c. 1573 (Florence). Fire-gilt bronze;
height 14 1/2" (38.8 cm).
Kunsthistorisches Museum, Vienna.
Listed in the inventory of Rudolf II as
Venus Urania, this signed masterpiece
by the Flemish sculptor at the Medici
court personifies Astronomy,
identifiable by her attributes, among
them an armillary sphere, a compass, a
prism, and a ruler. With its spiraling
pose, designed to be viewed from every
angle, the elegantly formed nude
represents the epitome of Mannerist
art. A date close to 1573 is suggested by
the proximity of style and composition
to Giambologna's mirror-image Apollo
in the studiolo of Francesco I.

after all, lay closer to the center of the Empire than did Vienna, and, by the same token, it also lay at greater remove from the Ottoman Turks, who, since Suleiman the Magnificent's victory over Lajos II at the Battle of Mohács (1526), had occupied most of Hungary, including Budapest. Not only did the Emperor, the titular King of Hungary, have to pay annual tribute to the Sultan in Istanbul; every spring the latter sent an army up the Danube, always in the hope of laying siege to Vienna itself, just as Suleiman had in 1529.

Vienna, partly because of its exposure to Turkish assault, had never been developed into a grandly monumental place, comparable to, for instance, the Escorial then under construction outside Madrid, or indeed to Prague and its Hrad or Hradschin, erected in the mid-14th century at the behest of Charles of Luxembourg, who as Charles IV had worn the Imperial crown from 1355 to 1378. Charles, the only other Emperor to reside in Prague, had also seen his Bohemian realm as a safe haven, not merely from the Black Plague ravaging the rest of Europe, but as well from the Hundred Years War in France, on whose side the French-educated Prince had fought at the Battle of Crécy, alongside his doomed father, John of Luxembourg. Hardly had the new King/Emperor appeared in Prague when he set about transforming the city into a second Paris, complete with cathedral, castle, and university, the Carolinum, the first institution of higher learning to be established in Europe east of the Rhine. His architect was none other than Peter Parler, a celebrated master who, perhaps more than any other mason in medieval Germany, grasped the French technique of using highly rationalistic designs to express the irrational. A little over a century later the sinuously interlaced liern vaults with which he crowned the cathedral nave would be recaptured when King Vladislav, from Poland's Jagiello dynasty, had the architects Benedikt Ried and Hans Spiess build the great Vladislav Hall, the largest constructed space unsupported by columns in contemporary Europe (fig. 146). It took form in the Hradschin, resting on massive foundations laid during the reign of Charles IV.

By leaving Vienna, Rudolf also escaped, to some degree, the overweening influence of Spain, whose throne had been occupied, since the abdication of Charles V in 1556, by the head of that other branch of the Habsburg line, Philip II. Rudolf knew this puritanical and uncompromising monarch's court only too well, having been sent there by his parents, Emperor Maximilian II and the Infanta Maria, Charles V's daughter and thus the sister of Philip II, to be educated in an atmosphere more rigorously pious than the one in Vienna. Yet, like all the Austrian Habsburgs, Rudolf distrusted his Uncle Philip

for having attempted to secure the whole of the Empire for himself, despite Charles V's wish that the vast, unwieldy agglomeration of kingdoms, principalities, bishoprics, and free cities, sprawling from Naples to Hamburg and from Lisbon to Budapest, be divided between the Spanish branch of the family and the Austrian branch, the latter headed by Charles's younger brother, Archduke Ferdinand I. While in Spain, moreover, Rudolf had witnessed the horrors of the Inquisition, with its auto-da-fés, expulsions, and other intolerant acts against anyone suspected of Protestant heresy, a heresy that already permeated much of the world over which Rudolf would preside as Holy Roman Emperor. To his credit, Rudolf understood that Spanish-style fanaticism would only breed revolt in the religiously diverse world of Northern and Central Europe, as Philip II himself discovered in the 1570s when he tried to impose the dread Inquisition on the Spanish Netherlands.

Among the benefits gained by the Emperor from eight years in Iberia were his high formal demeanor

147

(the Spanish code of courtly etiquette), a remarkable command of languages (German and Spanish, of course, but also Latin, French, Italian, and even a bit of Czech), a love of hunting, shooting, and riding, a passion for collecting, and, perhaps most of all, a belief in the capacity of art to endow power with splendor and majesty. How could he have doubted the latter, given the magnificence of the Spanish royal collection, with all its Titians, Correggios, Parmigianinos, Bosches, and Bruegels. Fortunately, or unfortunately as some have declared, the young Archduke arrived in Spain before the Humanism tolerated by Charles V had been anathematized by Philip II, the self-appointed champion of Counter-Reformation orthodoxy.

In 16th-century Humanism, whose roots lay in the Neoplatonic academies of 15th-century Florence, the elite of the Late Renaissance believed themselves bound up in an essentially magical world, a world wherein culture and nature were linked by correspondences, hidden sources of knowledge, the study of which, by those intelligent enough to become adept, could lead humanity from its present travails and raise it to participation in the divine order. The monarch then, especially the Christian Emperor, could be seen as a symbol of universality and equilibrium, making it morally imperative that he study not only nature and science but also art, and such occult matters as alchemy and astrology, magic, the Kabbalah, and their attendant signs and emblems. By striving to discover the key – the philosopher's stone – to the *a priori* perfection that had existed before human sin brought chaos into the world, Rudolf and his fellow sovereigns might succeed in realizing the reformation, secular as well as sacred, so longed for by Catholics and Protestants alike. In this way they might hope to salvage the mental and political unity of Christendom, preserve peace at home, and deliver Europe from the Ottoman menace. The Humanism known to Rudolf was therefore Utopian in that it believed in rehabilitation and thus a better world; yet it was also fatalistic, convinced that the better world already existed and had only to be rediscovered not so much through action as through meditation or even magic.

Beset by Calvinist inroads on his western flank, by Hussites in Bohemia, by Catholic emissaries from Rome and Madrid, and by the Turkish Infidel in the Balkans – as well as by a chronic shortage of funds owing to the elective nature of his three crowns – Rudolf could well believe that withdrawal for the sake of learning and illumination was his moral duty. Prague therefore became a magnet for important scientists, such as Tycho Brahe and Johannes Kepler, for the heretical Italian philosopher Giordano Bruno, and for magicians like the Englishmen John Dee and Edward Kelly, and for a throng of artists and craftsmen. These included the painters Giuseppe Arcimboldo (fig. 178),[3] Bartholomäus Spranger, Josef Heintz, Hans von Aachen, Roelant Savery, and Dirk van Ravenstein[4]; the miniaturist Joris Hœfnagel; the jeweler/goldsmiths Christoph Jamnitzer, Jan Vermeyen, Paulus van Vianen, and Anton Schweinberger; the engravers Hendrik Goltzius and Aegydius Sadeler; and the *pietra dura* mosaicists Giovanni and Cosimo Castrucci. Rudolf also did everything possible to recruit the great Mannerist sculptor Giovanni da Bologna (figs. 147, 148), who, held captive in Florence by his patron, the Medici Grand Duke of Tuscany, sent the Emperor a worthy substitute, the sculptor Adriaen de Vries. With him came the serpentine and elaborated Mannerist style often characterized as "Rudolfine." Many of Rudolf's artists served, along with his special agents and ambassadors, as procurers of whatever would help make the Imperial collection a burgeoning microcosm of the world the Emperor so ardently sought to understand through its linkage to higher things. Long before the end of Rudolf's reign, Prague had become the most cosmopolitan city in Europe.

One prominent member of the Rudolfine court was Karel van Mander, the Vasari of the North, who wrote in 1604: "Whoever so desires nowadays has only to go to Prague (if he can), to the greatest art patron in the world at the present time, the Roman Emperor Rudolf the Second; there he may see at the Imperial residence, and elsewhere in the collections of other great art-lovers, a remarkable number of outstanding and precious, curious, unusual, and priceless works."[5] Be that as it may, few outside the exclusive realm of art, science, and the arcane stood much chance of ever gaining access to either the Emperor or his collection. Hardly had the young Rudolf returned from Spain when the Venetian ambassador described him as a man "of few words" (*di poche parole*), and as the years went by the Emperor became ever more taciturn and saturnine, displaying symptoms that modern commentators have diagnosed as manic/depressive. Still, a later Venetian ambassador wrote that he was "of small stature, not unpleasing demeanor, and agile in his movements. His pale countenance, his noble brow, his very curly beard and hair and his large eyes, looking with a certain gentleness, cannot miss making a deep impression on all who meet him." Needless to say, the Emperor also displayed the strong, projecting chin so characteristic of the Habsburgs throughout the 16th and 17th centuries, beginning with Charles V.

After Rudolf chose to make Prague his principal residence, beginning in 1578, he moved first into the

148

148. *Giovanni Bologna. The Abduction, c. 1580 (Florence). Bronze, natural-brown patina, dark-brown lacquer; height 33 ⅝" (98.2 cm). Kunsthistorisches Museum, Vienna. First cast for Ottavio Farnese in 1579, this bronze sculpture has been interpreted as the Rape of Helen, of Proserpina, or yet of a Sabine woman. The Viennese version may reflect collaboration by Antonio Susini, who joined the Medici workshop in 1580. Another closely related version is owned by the Metropolitan Museum in New York.*

southern wing of the castle and then into the Summer House or Belvedere, finished only a few years earlier and often cited as one of the finest Italian Renaissance buildings north of the Alps (fig. 150).[6] The principal façade, with its arcaded gallery of slender Ionic columns, still faces the Royal Gardens laid out in the 1550s below the north wall of the castle complex. Gradually, however, Rudolf would have much of the medieval Hradschin remodeled and expanded into a modern Renaissance palace, with ample room for the largest and most comprehensive collection ever formed. By 1605 the bulk of the collection had been installed in the new rooms designed to receive it.[7] These consisted of two long corridors on the first and second floors above ground on either side of the so-called "Mathematical Tower." On the lower level south of the tower was the *Vordere Kunstkammer* ("Front Gallery"), which contained three vaulted chambers rising to a height of 15 feet and measuring about 16 1/2 feet wide and a total of 180 feet long. On the north side of the tower lay the big *Kunstkammer* ("Art Gallery"), a broad hall with a flat ceiling and an overall length of 99 feet. The paintings hung on the floor above in two long corridors (*vorderer* or *langer Gang*), their length the same as those of the lower corridors but their ceilings raised to a height of 15 feet, which made it possible to hang pictures in three tiered rows.

The *Vordere Kunstkammer* was furnished with seventeen cabinets and the Kunstkammer itself with twenty cabinets, the latter facing a series of windows. Larger items rested on top of the cabinets, between which hung stags' antlers, features reflecting Rudolf's passion for that most aristocratic of sports: hunting. Between and under the windows stood smaller furniture – cabinets, chests, tables – all filled with objects or serving as bases for them. On or under a long green table at the center of the room could be found rare automata, musical instruments, and precious objects.

Rudolf, as noted earlier, had sought to build an encyclopedic collection, the better to make it a mir-

ror of the real universe. As such, it served more than one purpose, not least of which was the power to impress important visitors by the magnitude, splendor, and historic significance of the holdings. To the uninitiated, therefore, the collection or collections served primarily to glorify the House of Austria and its Emperor. This was a far from irrelevant goal, given that, outside Austria itself, the Habsburgs had few dynastic claims, their three crowns being elective, and held Imperial power for some three hundred years largely by enveloping their presence in the mystique of sovereignty. As for the common ruck of humanity, access to the various galleries was all but impossible, in part because the Emperor enjoyed working at a desk placed in the midst of his favorite objects and disliked being disturbed by visitors.[8] To Rudolf and the coterie of elite who surrounded him, the collections constituted a prime source of inspiration and study; for the uninitiated, however, the concept informing the whole would have been senseless without a guide or proper explanation. Further, much of the material was stored in cases and thus not on view.

The Kunstkammer was organized into three sections, the first of which comprised *naturalia*, or specimens of zoology, botany, mineralogy, and paleontology, some of them in a natural state, others polished or otherwise refined. Here the adept could study nature and its mysteries or secrets. Rudolf, like many of his contemporaries, believed that certain minerals might have a beneficial, even magical, effect on human health, for which purpose the Emperor was known to have borrowed such items from his own collection. Hans von Khevenhüller, the Imperial Ambassador in Madrid, knew of His Majesty's interest in bezoars, ossified secretions from the stomachs of goats or camels, which were thought to constitute a panacea for melancholy, a condition from which Rudolf frequently suffered. One of the specimens the Ambassador sent from Madrid has survived, complete with its magnificent jeweled mount (fig. 149).

The second section was dedicated to *artefacta*: man-made objects. The materials could be either organic, meaning ivory, bone, horn, ostrich eggs, nuts, shells, amber, and so forth, or inorganic, a category that included armor, coins, medals, and bronzes, all made of precious or nonprecious metals. Here, for instance, were glorious vessels carved from hardstone and mounted in gold or silver, the collection one of the largest of its kind to have survived. Also classified and housed with the inorganic *artefacta* was a superb library of illustrated books.

The third section contained Rudolf's beloved *scientifica*: the automata, clocks, astronomical instruments, and celestial as well as terrestrial globes.

149. *Bezoar, 3rd quarter 16th century (Spain). Gold, emeralds, rubies, and bezoar; height 8 1/16" (20.5 cm). Kunsthistorisches Museum, Vienna. Bezoars (from the Persian Bad-sahr, meaning "poison antidote") are ossified secretions from the stomachs of goats or camels, which many in the 16th century believed to be panaceas for numerous ills. Rudolf borrowed bezoars from his Kunstkammer and wore them in the hope of curing his chronic melancholy. The South American example seen here, mounted in gold and emeralds from the New World, may have been sent to the Emperor from Spain by his mother, the Dowager Empress Maria.*

150. *Paolo della Stella. Belvedere, Hradschin Castle, Prague, c. 1538. Built by Ferdinand I as a Lustschloss or "pleasure palace" for Empress Anna, this Summer House, with its arcaded veranda and beautiful formal garden under the far wall of the Hradschin, was one of the finest Italian Renaissance buildings north of the Alps. Rudolf II made it his residence until he could have much of the old castle reconstructed for his purposes.*

150

151

*151. Venus of Cardinal Granvelle, c. 1500
(Northern Italy). Bronze and silver;
height 7 1/4" (18.5 cm).
Kunsthistorisches Museum, Vienna.
This Renaissance statuette was once
thought to be antique, which made it all
the more irresistible to Rudolf II, who
vigorously negotiated with the estate of
Cardinal Granvelle, longtime Secretary
of State to Emperor Charles V.*

*152. Pieter Bruegel the Elder. Hunters in
the Snow, 1565. Oil on panel; 46 x 64"
(117 x 162 cm). Kunsthistorisches
Museum, Vienna. The last in a series
of four Seasons by the great Flemish
master, Winter was very likely a gift to
Archduke Ernst from the city of
Antwerp.*

*153. Pieter Bruegel the Elder. Peasant
Dance, 1568-1569. Oil on panel;
45 x 64 1/2" (114 x 164 cm).
Kunsthistorisches Museum, Vienna.
Like Winter, this painting, a
characteristic Bruegel representation of
a Flemish kernesse ("fair"), belonged
to Archduke Ernst, whose rich
collection Rudolf II inherited.*

Here again was a library, this one covering all the categories just cited, but also religion and philosophy. The *Vordere Kunstkammer* boasted further collections of a similar nature, in addition to such Roman antiquities as statues, bronzes, portrait busts, and cameos, together with yet another library, this one devoted to Classical and similarly specialized literature.

Rudolf functioned as both a collector and a patron of the arts. In the first of these roles he evinced a particular interest in works associated with the Austrian Habsburgs and the history of their noble house, or in anything he deemed essential to his overall vision. For the most part, the Emperor made his acquisitions through a network of Imperial agents, by means of whom he tracked down desirable works, kept informed about potential competitors, and seized on whatever opportunity might arise from the death of a well-known collector. One such occasion presented itself at the death of Cardinal Granvelle, a leading statesman under both Charles V and Philip II who had amassed a formidable collection of art works long coveted by Rudolf, among them a celebrated bronze statuette of Venus, thought to be antique (fig. 151). Pulling rank as the premier sovereign of Europe, Rudolf sent an emissary to the Cardinal's heir, the Comte de Chantecroy, and insisted that he release certain pieces to him, all cited in a list of "curiosities which His Majesty wishes to obtain" along with the bargain prices the court was prepared to pay. Of the eleven paintings listed, one was by Raphael, four by Dürer, and two by Titian, both of them Venuses. Needless to say, Rudolf prevailed, despite the better offers received by the deeply chagrined heir.[9]

Following the death of his uncle, Archduke Ferdinand of Tyrol, in 1595, Rudolf moved heaven and earth to acquire the famous Kunstkammer at Schloss Ambras outside Innsbruck, declaring himself the rightful guardian of the family assets. In a letter to the captain of the castle, he voiced his concern for the safety of the collection, having heard false rumors about the possibility of unwanted attention drawn to the huge store of treasure. "Because you know what sorts of things are at Ambras, you are secretly to provide a guard."[10] In 1605 the Emperor ordered the Governor of the Tyrol, his brother Archduke Maximilian III, to undertake negotiations with Ferdinand's son and heir, Count Karl von Burgau, a process that lasted until 1613, by which time time Rudolf himself was dead. Still, a price for Ambras had been set, at 170,000 guilders, 100,000 of which was for the Kunstkammer. The aging and disillusioned Rudolf had even considered retiring to Innsbruck and melding the two collections, the result of which would have been a colossal family Kunstkammer.

Also in 1595, Archduke Ernst, Rudolf's favorite brother, died while serving as Regent of the Spanish Netherlands, leaving the Emperor a rich but much less complicated patrimony. It included several masterpieces by Pieter Bruegel the Elder, which today are the pride of the Kunsthistorisches Museum in Vienna (figs. 152, 153).

Eager to transform Prague into a cultural capital, the Emperor personally invited selected artists to settle in the city, where he supported them with annual stipends, in exchange for which he acquired their works. Occasionally he even bestowed titles of nobility. Those who gathered at the Rudolfine court included painters and sculptors, scientists and naturalists, goldsmiths, jewelers, and hardstone carvers. The religious tolerance shown there also proved a lure, drawing more than one Protestant artist into the Imperial service. All such factors favored the establishment of what today is known as the "Prague School," which carried the Mannerist phase of Renaissance art to its climactic moment around the turn of the 17th century, just as its antithesis, the Baroque, was getting under way in Rome.

It could be said that Rudolf's love of the arts was a legacy from his father, Emperor Maximilian II, an avid collector of antiquities, coins and medals, clocks and automata. Maximilian had decreed that his *Varnus*, or family treasure, be divided evenly by lot among his five sons. As for the *Clainater* (crown jewels), the *Achatschale*, a Roman agate, the *Ainkhürn*,

152

153

the "magic" horn of the mythical unicorn, and the collection of coins and medals, they were to be held in trust by the eldest member of the Austrian Habsburg family. This was a role which Rudolf, already a passionate collector in his own right, assumed with a vengeance, and he immediately set about trying to wrest from his brothers a number of capital items left to them by terms of Maximilian's will, especially the contents of the silver vault. More than any other particular pieces, however, he craved the agate bowl and the narwhal tusk ("unicorn's horn") earmarked for Archduke Ferdinand II of Tyrol, but they would not be his, despite numerous promises and false hopes, until after the death of Ferdinand in 1595.

Maximilian II had also employed artists at his court in Vienna, several of whom Rudolf would later co-opt for his own court in Prague. Chief among these were the painters Giuseppe Arcimboldo and Bartholomäus Spranger, the medal-maker Antonio Abondio, the clockmakers Gerhard Emmoser and Jost Bürgi, and the goldsmith Wenzel Jamnitzer. Maximilian and Rudolf both pulled every string to coax Giovanni da Bologna from Florence, but, in the end, each had to content himself with patronizing the great Mannerist sculptor from afar.

As a patron of the arts Rudolf would outdistance even his father by a very long measure. Indeed, he broke new ground by involving himself directly in the creative activities of the artists in his service, especially Spranger[11] and such fellow painters as Hans von Aachen[12] and Joseph Heintz.[13] Thus, it was the Emperor and his personal taste that set the tone for the Rudolfine style, with its erotically charged mythological or allegorical themes[14] and its strange combination of the artificial and the natural. The style is perhaps seen at its most dramatic in Spranger's paintings of voluptuous nude women elegantly or even theatrically coiled about lascivious older men in elaborate, densely packed compositions, all rendered in the most minute, searching detail.[15] Hans von Aachen was one of the artists whom the Emperor valued to the point of ennobling him. Married to the daughter of the celebrated Bavarian composer Orlando di Lasso, von Aachen was clearly more than a court painter, becoming one of Rudolf's closest companions and even serving abroad as a diplomat and art dealer.

Outside the court, Rudolf gradually found less and less comfort. His policies of religious appeasement found little favor among other members of the Habsburg family, or even in Prague itself, where his unpopularity grew apace after 1600. In response, Rudolf disappeared into the Hradschin, remaining unseen in public until, for a two-year period, he was actually thought to be dead. Far from dead, he was simply more alive to himself while working at his

154

beloved collection in the company of artists, astrologers, and astronomers, chemists, alchemists, scientists, and more than a few charlatans. Moreover, Rudolf could always muster unfailing reserves of energy and single-minded concentration when it came to the chase and acquisition of art works or any other item he deemed worthy of interest.

For Rudolf, a proud defender of the Habsburg dynasty, the memory of his great-great-grandfather, the Emperor Maxmilian I (r. 1493-1519), hovered in an almost mystical aura, some of which he saw enveloping the artist Maximilian had most patronized: Albrecht Dürer of Nuremberg. As a result, the works of this revered master stood high on Rudolf's list of *desiderata*, and they would be systematically pursued by the Emperor and his agents until the Hradschin could boast the largest collection of Dürers ever assembled. Many of them can be seen today at the Kunsthistorisches Museum in Vienna. One of the great legends deriving from the Rudolfine era relates how the Emperor obtained the large Dürer altarpiece known as the *Rosenkranzfest* or *Feast of the Rose Garlands* (fig. 154), a work commissioned by the Fondaco dei Tedeschi in Venice for the Church of San Bartolommeo and ripe with Habsburg iconography. It includes not only a self-portrait but also a profile portrait of Maximilian I kneeling to receive the Virgin's blessing. By Imperial demand, the work was packed in cotton wool, carpets, and waxed linen cloth and then hung from a bar to be transported upright across the Alps by relays of strong men.

The Hradschin collection of Dürer's landscape watercolors and animal drawings provided direct inspiration for such Prague School artists as Hans Hoffmann, Georg Bocskay, and Joris and Jakob

154. *Albrecht Dürer. Rosenkranzfest (Feast of the Rose Garlands), 1506. Oil on panel, 64 x 68 ¾" (162 x 194.5 cm). Národní Museum, Prague. Commissioned by the Fondaco dei Tedeschi in Venice for the Church of San Bartolomeo, then frequented by the German colony, this radiant altarpiece is today regarded as Dürer's first fully mature work, clearly executed under the influence of Venetian art. Rudolf II had his secretary acquire the masterpiece for 920 ducats and then ordered that it be carefully packed and hand-carried upright "by strong men, hung from poles, all the way to the Imperial residence in Prague." The Emperor venerated the painting not only because it was by Dürer but also because of its association with his ancestor, Maximilian I, who is portrayed in profile kneeling at the side of the Madonna. Severely damaged by careless handling during the Thirty Years War, the picture was left behind by the Swedish army, which plundered the Hradchin in 1648; it thus remains one of the few Rudolfine works of art still in Prague.*

155. *Nikolaus Pfaff. Dragon's Horn Cup and Cover, 1611 (Prague). Rhinoceros horn, African warthog tusks, and silver-gilt; height 19 9/16" (49.7 cm). Kunsthistorisches Museum, Vienna. Exploiting what were believed to be the horns of a dragon, a brilliant but anonymous goldsmith combined a rhinoceros horn, intricately carved by Nikolaus Pfaff, a pair of African warthog tusks, and a fossilized shark's tooth (Natterzunge) to create this terrifying vessel obviously meant to frighten and thus to ward off evil. Both the cup and its mounts crawl with snakes, lizards, spiders, crayfish, and beetles, cast from dead specimens, cold-enameled, and fully suggestive of the netherworld, not to mention the stil rustique of Wenzel Jamnitzer.*

156. *Jan Vermeyen. Bezoar cup and cover, c. 1600 (Prague). Bezoar, enamel, and gold; height 5 3/4" (14.5 cm). Kunsthistorisches Museum, Vienna. In 16th-century Europe, Oriental bezoars fetched up to ten times their weight in gold, for whoever drank from one could be certain that any poison in the draft would have been rendered harmless. To make a cup, the bezoar seen here had to be hollowed out, after which the court jeweler to Rudolf II mounted it in gold and enamel. Vermeyen is best known as the creator of the Emperor's magnificent crown, seen in fig. 143.*

157. *Anton Schweinberger. Seychelle-nut ewer, 1587-1603 (Prague). Seychelle nut and silver parcel-gilt; height 14 15/16" (37.8 cm). Kunsthistorisches Museum, Vienna. Because Seychelle nuts were considered "fruits of the sea," Schweinberger set this specimen in a highly imaginative mount which includes a triumphant Neptune riding high on a hippocamp while tritons serve as caryatids pushing up from below. Nikolaus Pfaff, Rudolf II's Hofbeinstecher ("court bone-carver"), elaborated the nut in low relief.*

156

157

Hœfnagel. In their works, art and science came together in the kind of spiritually interactive correspondence so prized by the Humanists of the Rudolfine court. The painstaking studies that Hoffmann and the Hœfnagels made of insects, mammals, reptiles, and flowers would lead directly into the art of still-life painting. While in Rudolf's service, Pieter Stevens, Roelant Savery, and Paulus van Vianen addressed nature and portrayed its many forms. At the Emperor's behest, Savery "voyaged" throughout the High Alps, drawing and painting after nature, well before this treacherous terrain was rediscovered and labeled "sublime" by the Romantics of the late 18th century.

Giovanni Bologna, or Giovanni da Bologna (1524-1608), born Jean de Boulogne in Douai, France, won fame in Italy as the leading exponent of the Mannerist style initiated by Michelangelo in the second and third decades of the 16th century. Sculptures such as the *Flying Mercury* and the *Rape of the Sabine Women*, both in Florence, made him the most besought sculptor of his time. However, even the determined Rudolf could not dislodge him from the clutches of Grand Duke Ferdinando I of Tuscany, a tight-fisted prince who not only refused to let his favorite artist go but even paid him less than the master's own pupils earned by working at other courts. Still, Rudolf managed to acquire several works, perhaps as placating gifts sent by the sculptor or his nervous Florentine patron. Rudolf registered his esteem by awarding Giambologna a title of nobility. Among the finest of the Bolognas to survive from the Emperor's collection are a *Venus Urania*[16] and a version of the celebrated *Mercury*[17]. In 1604, Cesare d'Este, the Duke of Modena, sent Rudolf a bronze relief entitled *Allegory on the Reign of Francesco I of Tuscany* (fig. 117), which, according to another legend, so thrilled the recipient that he exclaimed "Mine at last!" before carrying it personally into his Kunstkammer. Art historians have also speculated that the relief may have been one of three bronzes presented to Maximilian II by Cosimo I at the time (1565) he requested the hand of the Emperor's sister Johanna, or Joanna, for his son, Grand Duke Francesco I.[18]

Lacking the master, Rudolf made do with his pupil, Adriaen de Vries,[19] who created for him a number of superb mythological groups, animal bronzes, and portraits. Among the last is a bust of the Emperor clad in armor (fig. 158), conceived as a pendant to Leone Leoni's bust of Charles V (fig. 159). Another beautiful bronze executed for the Imperial collection is a Psyche borne by a trio of *amorini*; an early work, it is now in Stockholm's National Museum,[20] thanks to the sack of Prague carried out by the Swedish army in 1648.

Under Rudolf, the Hradschin became a veritable

158

Under Rudolf, the Hradschin became a veritable "art factory," its workshops turning out exquisite works of goldsmithery, gem-encrusted objects, carved stones, automata, and clocks. Some of them are masterpieces of the applied arts equal in quality to the masterpieces produced by the court painters and sculptors. While the Emperor retained many for his own collection and private delectation, he sent others as part of the 100,000-guilder annual tribute required to keep the Sultan's Infidel armies at bay. They also provided sumptuous gifts offered to important visitors for the sake of enhancing the Emperor's standing in the eyes of other heads of state. When, for instance, a grandiose Russian embassy arrived in 1594 bearing rich gifts – fifty wagon loads of rare furs estimated to have been worth 100,000 ducats – Rudolf responded with a present composed mainly of rare mechanized clocks.

Of all the court silversmiths and jewelers listed in Rudolf's inventories, the names Anton Schweinberger, Jan Vermeyen, and Paulus van Vianen come

most notably to the fore. Schweinberger, a native of Augsburg, was employed at the Hradschin from 1587 until his death in 1603. Nine works are attributed to him in the inventories, one of which – a ewer fashioned of a Seychelle nut and decorated with plants and mythical as well as real creatures – is often counted among the masterpieces of the Prague School (fig. 157). Other jeweled and mounted nuts are known, such as those in the Dresden Green Vaults[21] and on the Uppsala *Kunstschrank* (figs. 276, 277), but none offers so perfect a combination of rare nature and man-made setting. The Seychelle nut was believed to be a fruit of the sea, which accounts for the aquatic iconography devised by Schweinberger or his patron. The example seen here may have been the very one for which Rudolf is known to have paid 4,000 florins.

Arguably the most curious, as well as perhaps the most characteristic, work of Rudolfine art is a monstrous cup made of an artfully carved rhinoceros horn (cited in the inventory as *asino indico*) and crowned with a lid in the form of a mask sprouting tusks extracted from an African warthog, believed by contemporaries to be the horns of a dragon (fig. 155). The carving can be attributed to Nikolaus Pfaff and safely dated 1611. The anonymous goldsmith cleverly invested the object with devilish menace, emanating not only from the horned and snarling mask but also from its tongue of fossilized shark's tooth, this too thought to have come from a dragon, if not from a viper. The marriage of horns and tusks was supposed to immunize anyone who drank from the cup against poison, magic spells, or the evil eye. With its lavish decorative program featuring insects and reptiles, cast from nature, Rudolf's horned cup bears a close thematic and stylistic relationship to works in the Nuremberg tradition inspired by the great Wenzel Jamnitzer.

The Emperor's favorite jeweler/goldsmith was Jan Vermeyen of Brussels, who worked in Prague from 1597 until his death in 1606. It was undoubtedly Vermeyen from whom Rudolf commissioned the celebrated crown of 1602, a glittering diadem which Emperor Franz I would subsequently make the official Imperial crown (figs. 143, 160). The mitre shape, the iconography, and the profusion of jeweled decoration all combine to proclaim divine-right majesty. The style of the crown and its characteristic white-enameled mounts have allowed art historians to group about it a number of similarly styled vessels and cameos. These include a bezoar cup (fig. 156), a narwhal cup with snake handles (fig. 161), and a variety of beautifully mounted cameos (fig. 162). A more recent attribution to Vermeyen is an important Rudolfine hardstone vessel made, cup and lid alike, of jeweled green jasper (prasem) (fig. 164).

160

158. *Adriaen de Vries. Emperor Rudolf II, 1603 (Prague). Bronze; height 44" (112 cm). Kunsthistorisches Museum, Vienna. Rudolf II, who never went into battle, had his favorite court sculptor portray him as the heroic conqueror, after the manner of Leone Leoni's famous bronze bust of Charles V, Rudolf's venerated and truly battle-hardened grandfather (fig. 159). When Giovanni da Bologna could not gain leave of the Medici in order to serve Rudolf, he sent Adriaen de Vries, who would have a long and fruitful career in Prague.*

159. *Leone Leoni. Emperor Charles V, 1555 (Milan). Bronze; height 45 1/2" (113 cm). Kunsthistorisches Museum, Vienna. Charles V, clad in the armor he wore at the Battle of Mühlberg, is portrayed in the guise of a victorious Roman Emperor. This bust, one of two, was cast for Cardinal Granvelle, the Emperor's Secretary of State, from whose estate Rudolf II extorted it in 1600.*

160. *Jan Vermeyen. Crown of Emperor Rudolf II (detail), 1602. See fig. 143.*

159

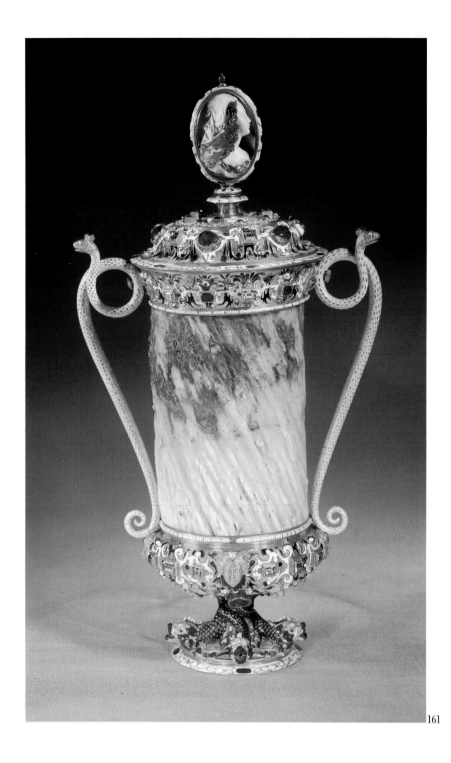

161

Museum, Vienna. Miseroni, the famous Milanese lapidary, entered the service of Rudolf II in 1588. After he crafted this stunning jug from a block of honey-colored jasper, the great Dutch goldsmith, Paulus van Vianen, another member of Rudolf's court workshop, mounted the vessel in gold, adding his signature to both base and cover. The setting includes a nereid or water nymph on the spout with a chained dragon in tow, personifications of the Four Elements on the foot interlinked with horned rams' heads.

164. *Ottavio Miseroni and Jan Vermeyen. Prasem cup and cover, 1600-1605 (Prague). Green jasper (prasem), gold, enamel, garnets, and topaz; height 9 1/4" (23.5 cm), diameter 6 15/16" (17.6 cm). Kunsthistorisches Museum, Vienna.* After Miseroni carved the rich, emerald-green hardstone, a form of jasper, to breathtaking thinness, Vermeyen mounted the vessel in gold, enamel, and gems to create one of the most lavish and harmonious works of art in the Prague Kunstkammer.

161. *Jan Vermeyen. "Unicorn" cup and cover, c. 1600-1605 (Prague). Narwhal tusk, gold, enamel, diamonds, rubies, and agate cameo; height 8 3/4" (22.2 cm). Kunsthistorisches Museum, Vienna.* In his later years, Rudolf II was increasingly isolated and thus all the more wary of poisoners. The Late Middle Ages valued unicorn horns higher than gold, believing them capable of detoxifying their contents. In same spirit, the credulous Emperor had his favorite court jeweler mount the narwhal tusk as a rare treasure.

162. *Ottavio Miseroni. Cameo Portrait of Rudolf II, c. 1590 (Prague). Chalcedony, gold, and enamel; 1 5/8 x 1 1/8" (4.1 x 2.7 cm). Kunsthistorisches Museum, Vienna.* This cameo is the first documented work by Miseroni in Prague, where it was mounted by the court workshop. A contemporary described the portrait as "so life-like that all who saw it admired it."

163. *Ottavio Miseroni and Paulus van Vianen. Jasper jug and cover, c. 1570 and 1608 (Prague). Jasper and gold; height 14" (35.5 cm). Kunsthistorisches*

163

162

164

165. *Nikolaus Schmidt. Ewer, late 16th century (Nuremberg). Silver-gilt, mother-of-pearl, and pearls; height 21 1/4" (54 cm). Kunsthistorisches Museum, Vienna. The author of this elaborately Mannerist ewer, which has lost its basin, specialized in mother-of-pearl inlays. Schmidt is also known for several silver-gilt and shell garnitures.*

166. *Christoph Lencker. Basin, late 16th century (Augsburg). Silver-gilt and enamel; 23 x 27 1/8" (58.5 x 69 cm). Kunsthistorisches Museum, Vienna. This basin, modeled in relief and designed to complement a ewer, now lost, features an ornate treatment of the Europa myth. The Mannerist figures, with their small heads and elegantly attenuated bodies, recall the paintings of Hans von Aachen and Bartholomäus Spranger, both favorites at the Prague court of Rudolf II.*

167. *Christoph Jamnitzer. Ornamental basin, c. 1605 (Nuremberg). Silver-gilt and enamel; 25 1/2 x 20 7/8" (64.7 x 53 cm). Kunsthistorisches Museum, Vienna. Here the subject is the Triumph of Love, personified by Cupid in a horse-drawn chariot leading a distinguished gang of "prisoners" - Jupiter, Caesar, the Nine Heroes, and Hercules. Jamnitzer, a nephew of the great Wenzel and a stylistic disciple of such Italian artists as Mantegna, borrowed his theme as well from an Italian source: Petrarch's Trionfi, translated by Daniel Federmann and published in 1578. Thanks to his gifts for modeling in all degrees of relief, Jamnitzer succeeded in endowing the scene with a palpable sense of atmosphere and depth.*

166

167

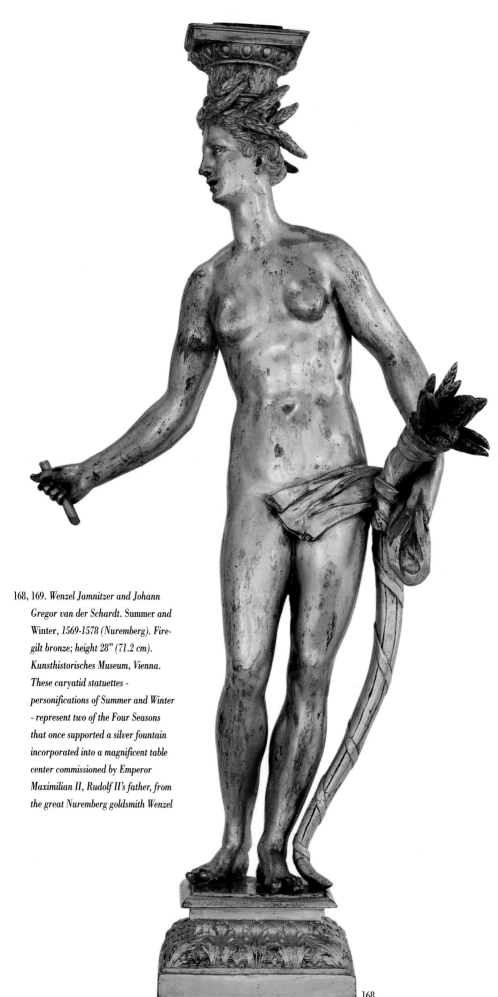

168, 169. *Wenzel Jamnitzer and Johann
Gregor van der Schardt. Summer and
Winter, 1569-1578 (Nuremberg). Fire-
gilt bronze; height 28" (71.2 cm).
Kunsthistorisches Museum, Vienna.
These caryatid statuettes -
personifications of Summer and Winter
- represent two of the Four Seasons
that once supported a silver fountain
incorporated into a magnificent table
center commissioned by Emperor
Maximilian II, Rudolf II's father, from
the great Nuremberg goldsmith Wenzel*

168

The world-renowned goldsmith Paulus van Vianen remained in the Emperor's service from 1603
until 1613. Born in Utrecht, van Vianen had worked
in both Munich and Salzburg before arriving in
Prague, well versed in his family's "auricular" style.
This was a style marked by fantastic forms so softly
modeled as to seem molten or "slithery," like the
interior of a mollusc shell. Often the van Vianens'
flowing masses resolve into such creatures as dolphins whose tails then evolve into rippling water,
which in turn develops into further bizarre imagery.
Paulus crafted several silver reliefs in a painterly
manner typical of the Prague School.[22] Through the
inventory, however, only one piece can be traced to
Rudolf's Kunstkammer, a ravishing, honey-colored
Milanese jug with a mount engraved with the artist's
initials and the date 1608 (fig. 163). Rarely has a
goldsmith's mount been so perfectly at one with the
hardstone carving.

The Emperor, with an appetite for art works
beyond the capacity of his craftsmen to produce
them, regularly commissioned pieces from artists
active elsewhere, foremost among them the famous
silversmith Wenzel Jamnitzer, his nephew Christoph
Jamnitzer, and Nikolaus Schmidt, all of Nuremberg.
Also sought out was Christoph Lencker from a family
of distinguished goldsmiths in Augsburg. For Rudolf
the elder Jamnitzer completed a magnificent table
fountain originally undertaken for Maximilian II.
Unfortunately, it disappeared into the crucible in
1747, all but four elegantly fashioned gilt-bronze
"Seasons," caryatids now in Vienna's Kunsthistorisches Museum (figs. 168, 169). Christoph Jamnitzer's ceremonial basin must figure among the odd-
est creations realized in the Mannerist style (fig. 167).
A fantastical and totally nonfunctional work, it is
elaborately chased with scenes from Petrarch and
crowned with a Venus-bearing swan. Nikolaus
Schmidt proved himself a master of Mannerist invention in a silver-gilt ewer decorated with mother-of-
pearl inlays (fig. 165). Today Christoph Lencker is
best known for a silver-gilt basin lavishly embossed
and chased with scenes representing the story of
Europa (fig. 166), erotically charged motifs derived
from Rudolfine paintings.

Well known for his interest in the sciences,
Rudolf II assembled a Kunstkammer chiming with
some 60 clocks and automata in addition to 120 geo-
metrical and astronomical instruments. As devices
for measuring time and space, they played important
roles in the period's quest for a deeper comprehen-
sion of nature and the world. By the same token, or,
rather, by the Humanist theory of correspondences,
they also provided insight into the divine order
underlying the measurable universe. The celebrated
Danish astronomer Tycho Brahe remained a year at

Rudolf's court, earning a salary of 2,000 guilders, a huge sum for the period. Brahe and his pupil Johannes Kepler, who tarried in Prague for more than a decade (c. 1601-1612), spent their time there studying the movements of the planets and the stars. The results were translated into even more elaborate instruments and clocks, produced by such skilled craftsmen as Erasmus Habermel and the Swiss Jost Bürgi, both of them regularly employed at the Hradschin. A prime example of Habermel's exquisitely precise and beautifully fashioned pieces is the ring-shaped equatorial sundial still in Prague.[24] Bürgi was regarded by contemporaries as the premier maker of timepieces, with many an invention to his credit. His mechanism for depicting a planetarium according to Copernican theory is exact to the minute, a remarkable achievement for the period.[25]

Rudolf also looked far and wide for instruments and automata, acquiring or commissioning them from specialists in Augsburg. Here he found Gerhard Emmoser, the author of a silver-gilt celestial globe clock borne on the back of Pegasus, one of the few Rudolfine objects that ever migrated to the New World.[26] Georg Roll's mechanized celestial globe, painted with 49 constellations, is the finest thing of its kind still in existence (fig. 170).[27] An enameled clock of great complication made by David Altenstetter so captivated Rudolf that he kept it for his own personal use. Hans Schlottheim's automated galleon made of painted silver-gilt once moved on wheels and could play three tunes on organs and drums and even fire a cannon (fig. 171). The work of Melchior Maier is well represented by a clockwork drinking vessel in the form of a jeweled and parcel-gilt centaur with the goddess Diana on his back (fig. 172). The mechanism comprises a clock, a musical automaton with eyes and heads that originally moved, and forward traction. When the centaur stopped it shot an arrow at the "victim," the viewer, who was then obliged to drink up the vessel's alcoholic contents. Another witty conversation piece, possibly the work of Sylvester II Eberlin and Hans Schlottheim, is a wagon on four wheels surmounted by a Bacchic group (fig. 173). Its automata include an organ with six pipes, forward traction, and figures that raise their arms or play bagpipes and a parrot capable of flapping its wings.

Among all his enthusiasms, Rudolf, like the Medici and other Princes of the period, found the greatest satisfaction in those precious and semi-precious stones known as *naturalia*. For the royal and aristocratic Humanists, such phenomena represented the natural world in its irreducible essence, which placed them at the pinnacle of the hierarchy within the divine scheme, just below the Creator himself. They were believed to embody magical prop-

Jamnitzer. The monumental composition, with its numerous allegorical figures, mechanized scenes, and water-driven music, stood 3 meters high and took eleven years to complete, after which it formed part of Rudolf's Kunstkammer in Prague. In 1747, alas, the great table center would be melted down in Vienna. The Seasons were probably modeled by Jamnitzer and then executed by van der Schardt, who had worked in Italy before establishing himself in Nuremberg in 1570.

169

170

170. *Georg Roll and Johann Reinhold.*
Celestial Globe, c. 1584 (Prague).
Bronze, brass, silver, gilt, enamel, cold
enamel, and wood; height 21 ¹/₄"
(54 cm). Kunsthistorisches Museum,
Vienna. Signed and dated by Roll, who
acted as the retailer, this superbly
designed and crafted work of art was
actually made by Johann Reinhold.
The large celestial globe, engraved with
zodiacal signs and set above a
terrestrial globe, could revolve on its
axle, completing the circuit every
24 hours. The many complications of
the automaton included a sun and
moon moving on two arcs around the
globe, a calendar, and several sundials.
Six similar globes by Roll and Reinhold
also survive. The present example,
which cost 1,500 thalers, was
apparently made for Archduke Ernst,
whose valuable estate Rudolf II
inherited.

171. *Hans Schlottheim. Clockwork Galleon,*
1585 (Augsburg). Silver-gilt, cold
enamel, and iron; height 26 ³/₈"
(67 cm), length 26" (66 cm).
Kunsthistorisches Museum, Vienna. As
this entertaining musical automaton
sails forward, driven by wheels, its
clock strikes the hours, while the
musicians on deck play their
instruments in harmony with a firing
cannon and three tunes piped by a
miniature organ. Both the automaton
seen here and a related vessel now in
the British Museum belonged to Rudolf
II. The banners on the Vienna piece are
painted with the Imperial two-headed
eagle. Schlottheim is known to have
worked in Prague in 1587.

173

172. *Melchior Maier. Diana and Centaur*
Automaton, c. 1605 (Augsburg). Silver
parcel-gilt, enamel, precious stones,
and wood; height 15 9/16" (39.5 cm).
Kunsthistorisches Museum, Vienna.
Thanks to Maier's clever mechanics,
the centaur rolls his eyes and fires off
an arrow, while Diana riding on his
back and one of the hounds turn their
heads. Another hound opens its muzzle
as if to bark. The clock strikes the
hour, and the whole group slowly
moves forward. The automaton typifies
a kind of drinking game popular at the
courts of Mannerist Europe, and
similar examples exist in Munich and
Dresden. Anyone the arrow struck or
pointed towards was obliged to drink a
cup of wine.

173. *Sylvester II Eberlin and Hans*
Schlottheim. The Triumph of Bacchus,
c. 1600-1610 (Augsburg). Silver-gilt,
cold enamel, and iron; height 15 3/4"
(40 cm), length 20 1/2" (52 cm).
Kunsthistorisches Museum, Vienna. In
this musical automaton, young
Bacchus, riding a ram, and his cohort -
bagpiper, parrot, and satyrs - triumph
atop a wagon loaded with an organ.
The mechanism driving the one-tune
organ also activates the heads, arms,
or wings of the Bacchic party. A second
mechanism in the carriage impels the
whole forward while also triggering an
arm and a head of two satyrs.
Schlottheim, Augsburg's leading master
of clocks and automata, created
several mechanized table ornaments for
Rudolf II (see fig. 171).

174. Gemma Augustea, *27 BC - AD 14
(Rome), mount 17th century. Onyx,
silver, and gold; 7 ½ x 9" (19 x 23 cm).
Kunsthistorisches Museum, Vienna.
Depicted at the center of the upper tier
of the two-layered gem are the goddess
Roma and the Emperor Augustus. The
cameo, the largest of its kind surviving
from antiquity, and the most famous,
celebrates the victory of Augustus over
the Dalmatians in 9 BC. Following its
theft in France, where it belonged to
François I, Rudolf II had the treasure
tracked down in Venice and acquired
for the colossal price of 12,000 thalers.*

175. Gemma Claudia, *49 AD (Rome). Five-
layered onyx cameo; height 4 ¾"
(12 cm). Kunsthistorisches Museum,
Vienna. This virtuoso example of cameo
carving, possibly a wedding present,
portrays the Emperor Claudius and his
wife, Agrippina the Younger, on the left
facing the Emperor's parents-in-law,
Germanicus and Agrippina the Elder,
the parents as well of the infamous
Caligula.*

176. Gian Stefano Caroni and Jacques
Bylivelt. *Lapis-lazuli vase, 1575-1581
(Florence). Lapis-lazuli, gold, and
enamel; height 14 ³/₁₆" (36 cm).
Kunsthistorisches Museum, Vienna.
Grand Duke Francesco I de' Medici
had Caroni's elegant blue vase mounted
by his court jeweler, the Fleming
Bylivelt (or Byliveldt). Two generations
later, in 1628, Grand Duke Ferdinando
II presented the treasure to Emperor
Ferdinand II.*

erties, including the power to heal. In 1609, Anselm Boethius de Boodt, Rudolf's personal physician, published a treatise, dedicating it to the Emperor, in which he revealed something of the royal attitude towards minerals: "[His Majesty] is not devoted to them in order to magnify his own dignity and splendor, but to recognize in these noble stones the greatness and incredible glory of God, which unites in so tiny a particle, all the beauty of the world and which seems to enclose the energy of all other matter, in order to have continually before the eyes a certain reflection of the Divinity's presence."[28]

Rudolf and his peers valued antique cameos for their esoteric content of rare stones in combination with such equally redemptive qualities as virtuoso craftsmanship and prestigious provenance. The *Gemma Augustea* is probably the most historic work of glyptic art to survive from the Classical world (fig. 174). A large onyx cameo carved with images of the eponymous Emperor and the goddess Roma surrounded by a host of figures, the *Gemma Augustea* had formed part of the treasure at the Romanesque Church of Saint-Sernin in Toulouse from 1246 until

174

175

1533. François I then managed to spirit the jewel away for his own collection at the Château de Fontainebleau, only for it to be stolen in 1591. Rudolf had one of his agents track the cameo down in Venice and acquire it for the incredibly steep price of 12,000 ducats. By such means, and others, Rudolf endowed the Imperial collections with some of their finest cameos, including the *Gemma Claudia* (fig. 175).

Initially, Rudolf had no choice but to acquire lapidary works from two renowned production centers: Milan and Florence. Several acquisitions, including a splendid sideboard dish fashioned of jeweled lapis-lazuli, a dragon-shaped lapis-lazuli cup, and a green-jasper cup and cover, had originated in the Miseroni workshops in Milan.[29] From Florence came a lapis-lazuli vase with jeweled mount (fig. 176). The Emperor also sent precious stones to both cities, where they were made into vessels and other works of art. Finally, to satisfy his passion for *pietre dure*, Rudolf determined to found a production center in Prague, his decision encouraged by the mineralogical wealth of Bohemia. For this enterprise he succeeded in recruiting Ottavio and Giovanni Ambrogio Miseroni, both sons of Girolamo Miseroni, the senior member of the notable Milanese family and the brother of Gasparo, a celebrated stone carver in the service Cosimo I de' Medici in Florence. To support their task in Prague, Rudolf immediately ordered a nation-wide search for rare stones and banned all private prospecting.

In his early works for Rudolf, Ottavio Miseroni displayed a rigidity of form reflecting his Milanese origins. By 1597, however, with the arrival of the jeweler Jan Vermeyen, Ottavio found himself liberated into an important and fruitful collaboration, from which came some of the finest works of Rudolfine art. In a moss-agate bowl featuring a triton (fig. 179) and a bloodstone cup in the Louvre (fig. 49), Ottavio brought his craft to full maturity, the obdurate stone seeming to melt under the warm, almost auricular softness of the virtuoso carving. The Louvre cup, dated 1608, marked the twentieth anniversary of Ottavio's debut at the Prague court. A grateful Rudolf acknowledged the fidelity and accomplishments of the Miseroni brothers by granting them titles of nobility.

The hardstone works Rudolf most prized were the *commesso di pietre dure*, Florentine mosaics made from wafer-thin sections of semiprecious stones laid in a slate or marble panel or tabletop. Here too, the Emperor began his collection by importing *pietre dure* from Italy, and he could scarcely have been more pleased when Grand Duke Ferdinando I de' Medici presented him with a table from the Opificio delle Pietre Dure. Eager for more, Rudolf commissioned another table, which cost a fortune and took

177

the Florentine workshop 78 months to complete. In Prague, the court sculptor Adriaen de Vries set it upon a base of his own design, formed as Ganymede with the eagle. This work, now sadly lost, was viewed by some as the eighth wonder of the world (*opera non più stato fatta al mondo*). By the 1590s Rudolf had his own resident masters of the *pietra dura* technique, Cosimo Castrucci and his son Giovanni, hardstone cutters brought to Prague from Italy. In the best panels from their Prague period, the Castrucci mastered their recalcitrant materials until they could produce painterly and even atmospheric effects, the very kind of interactive or magical correspondence that Rudolfine Humanists found so symbolic and meaningful. Several of their views of the Hradschin have survived, albeit moved to Vienna (fig. 177). At Rudolf's death, the works in hardstone accounted for more than half the value placed on the contents of the Kunstkammer, and of that half the Florentine mosaics represented more than 80 percent.

Rudolf II so devoted himself to the arts that the full extent of his patronage and collecting all but defies belief. In addition to the stellar names cited in these pages, the Emperor employed literally dozens of other painters, sculptors, and miniaturists, metalsmiths, jewelers, and clockmakers. Also in his pay were tapestry weavers, armorers, and medalists, cartographers, architects, and designers of waterworks, writers, poets, musicians, and librarians, all of whom contributed towards making Prague a hotbed of cultural cross-fertilization. With so many artists of so many different kinds in service to the same Imperial patron, a patron with well-defined tastes, it seems inevitable that a Rudolfine style would have evolved. The cost, however, was tremendous, adding up to hundreds of thousands of guilders every year.

To those frustrated by Rudolf's personality and policies, the vast and eclectic collection seemed a jumble signifying nothing so much as the "Babylonian confusion" of the Emperor's mind. Thus, the Tuscan ambassador would write in 1609 that Rudolf "has so delighted in the investigation of natural matters and the ornaments of painting, that he has even given up the cares of empire and the business of princes for the study of these arts... For he himself tries alchemical experiments, and he himself is busily

engaged in making clocks, which is against the decorum of a prince. He has transferred his seat from the imperial throne to the workshop stool... Now his desire for paintings is so great that he not only acquires whatever is choice in the world, and scrapes together for it great sums from the empire, but is busy painting both whole and continuous days."[30] A year earlier the alarmed Habsburg family, together with the Prince Electors, had decided to depose the incapacitated Rudolf.

Since 1605, Archduke Matthias, the Emperor's younger brother and Regent of Austria, had been commander of the Imperial armies holding off the Ottoman Turks. When the latter erupted into Hungary, the ensuing conflict allowed Rudolf to portray himself as defender of the Christian West against the forces of evil. Thus, he reacted all the more negatively after Matthias, without consultation, signed the compromising Treaty of Zsitvatorok (1606), an agreement that appeared to diminish the Imperial authority. Worse was to follow, for in 1608 Matthias would be crowned King of Hungary and in 1611 King of Bohemia, events that effectively stripped the Emperor of all power. Then, in 1612, before the inevitable could happen – the loss of the Imperial crown – Rudolf mercifully died, intestate. The animosity Rudolf bore Matthias would become the subject of Franz Grillparzer's famous 19th-century play *Bruderzwist in Habsburg*.

The Prague hardstone workshops continued well after 1612, thanks to support from Rudolf's immediate successors. Over time, of course, the vases assumed a more Baroque form, while their ornamentation became more exuberant, with the mounts lavishly gilded and jeweled. One speciality of the workshops consisted of flowers carved from citrines and other semiprecious gems (fig. 185). Many of the other artists and craftsmen also found favor with both Matthias and Ferdinand II. However, once Ferdinand, an ardent defender of the Catholic cause, revoked Rudolf's "Letter of Majesty," which had granted freedom of religious practice, Prague lost much of its attraction and rapidly declined into a cultural backwater.

A tragic fate awaited the renowned Rudolfine collections. For the remnant that survives, we must thank Emperor Matthias, who combined the extant family collections with certain works from the Hradschin to create a new family *Schatzkammer* in Vienna. The Prague pieces include the jewelry, many of the paintings, some bronzes, and part of the hardstone vase collection, the last now rated the most extraordinary group of its kind in the world.

In 1617, the Bohemian crown passed to Ferdinand II, a first cousin of Rudolf and Matthias, who immediately set about imposing the Counter-Reformation on Prague. Protestant members of the Bohemian Estates reacted by "defenestrating" the Habsburgs' Catholic governors from a window in the Hradschin, an insult that ignited the Thirty Years War, one of the most devastating conflicts in the whole of European history. It ended in Prague as well, when the armies of Protestant Sweden invaded Bohemia and sacked the capital, with precise instructions from Queen Christina to seize the most coveted masterpieces in the Rudolfine collections for removal to Stockholm. Wide dispersal followed, as some works were given away and others auctioned with the estate of Christina. In 1654 the Queen, bored with government, abdicated and slipped away dressed as a man. The following year, at Innsbruck, she became

an openly confessed Catholic, before moving on to settle in Rome, where she would die in 1689. Meanwhile, her generals, Count von Königsmark and Karl Gustav Wrangel, kept many priceless things as their share of the Rudolfine booty. These included a group of paintings ("composite heads") by Arcimboldo which now survives at Skokloster, the Wrangel family seat, and elsewhere in Sweden (fig. 178).

When the Rudolfine Age perished, so too did the special cosmology of the Late Renaissance, its unities giving way to the most brutal polarization, and its esoteric, Utopian search for innate truths crushed by the 17th century's mechanistic views of science, views articulated by those gods of the Enlightenment: René Descartes, Francis Bacon, and Galileo Galilei.

178

179

VIII

Later Habsburgs

For a time, after the death of Rudolf II in 1612, the mystery surrounding the legendary Kunstkammer on the Hradschin remained inviolate. It also continued to inspire the most extraordinary speculations about the presumed immensity of the riches hoarded by the Emperor throughout the walled-up castle on the heights above Prague. Venetian Ambassador Soranzo informed the Signoria that Rudolf had distilled two million gulden into a "soul of gold"; moreover, it was generally held "that no Prince had so many jewels accumulated as the Emperor." Three thousand paintings "fill all the halls, galleries, and rooms... there are so many that instead of adorning the palace, they make it look almost like a warehouse... Every day larger quantities of precious vases and jewels are found in every nook and cranny."[1]

Fearful of theft, Emperor Matthias (r. 1612-1619), Rudolf's brother, nemesis, and successor, ordered the collections sealed off and kept under tight guard. So fantastic were expectations that, inevitably, the actual value of the cache may have proved disappointing once an inventory was taken. The court antiquary, Daniel Fröschl, even found himself accused of misappropriation, a charge he managed to overturn. Others less fortunate went to prison. Matthias and one of his younger surviving brothers, Archduke Abrecht, Governor of the Netherlands, settled Rudolf's colossal debts and divided the remaining liquid assets between them – money, bullion, and unmounted precious stones. As a result, Albrecht returned to Brussels richer by 225,000 gulden, but not before he and Matthias had quarreled over the fate of the art works. The Emperor won and thus succeeded in maintaining the unity of the Rudolfine patrimony, "that in order to increase the fame and esteem of the House of Austria, such treasures should remain inalienable at all times with the eldest for the reputation and glory of the entire house."[2]

The break up of Rudolf's court turned out to be a more complicated matter. According to Ambassador Soranzo, the Bohemian Estates believed the treasures had been acquired with their money and thus felt justified in fearing that the new Habsburg Emperor might smuggle (*trasportare sotto mano*) their rightful legacy to Vienna. Of particular concern to them was the famous Imperial crown, estimated by some to be worth 1 million gulden. The Estates even thought of seizing the contents of the Kunstkammer in order to melt down such silver items as tables, clocks, and even the great fountain created by Wenzel Jamnitzer. Strict Protestants took a dim view of the more lascivious works, such as the classical "mythologies" painted by Bartholomäus Spranger, and prepared to have them valued and then pawned. Rudolf's chamberlains helped draw up the inventory, which estimated the gold plate at 24 hundredweight and the silver plate at 60 hundredweight, not counting the silver works of art or the gems, pearls, and other precious articles. Overall, the treasure was deemed to be worth 17 million kronen.

Emperor Matthias drastically reduced the overhead cost of Rudolf's lavish court, cutting salaries and dismissing numerous parasites. Yet he also retained the services of certain important artists, including the painters Hans von Aachen and Roelant Savery, the miniaturist Jakob Hœfnagel, the clockmaker Jost Bürgi, the engraver Aegydius Sadeler, the lapidary Ottavio Miseroni, the wax modeler Alessandro Abondio, the sculptor Paul Pfaff, and the ivory turner Hans Wecker. Favored as well was the great mathematician Johannes Kepler, while the goldsmith Andreas Osenbruck received a commission for a jeweled orb and sceptre meant to complement Rudolf's Imperial crown.

Both Matthias and his successor, Ferdinand II, compromised the integrity of the Rudolfine accumulation by having part of it transferred to Vienna. Unwittingly, however, this act of betrayal would prove a salvation, after Prague became a prime battleground for the terrible Thirty Years War. In the Austrian capital the works of art were probably installed in a new Schatzkammer within the precinct of the Burg, on the first floor of a building contiguous with the Ballhaus and under the same roof. An

180. Bratina, *1637 (Moscow). Gold, enamel, pearls, rubies, sapphires, and emeralds; height 10 5/8" (27 cm). Kunsthistorisches Museum, Vienna. This brotherhood bowl (*brat *meaning "brother"), used for serving a welcome drink, was one of the gifts sent by Tsar Mikhail Feodorovich to King Vladislav IV of Poland on the occasion of his marriage to Archduchess Caecilia Renata of Austria in 1637. The finial is in the form of Poland's white eagle.*

181

account of 1637 describes "the so-called 'gallery' with various rooms which is called the Schatzkammer. Therein is kept a multitude of most valuable things of all sorts – of gold, with gems and mounts as well as works of highest craftsmanship, paintings, including examples of feats of nature and of man and very many other rarities and curiosities. Their value is of several million. Among other things, the truly sumptuous Imperial crown, sceptre, and orb of gold set with the most valuable Eastern diamonds, worth a million pieces of gold, made for Rudolf's very own person, are worthy of attention."[3] As for the agate bowl and the unicorn's horn, "the worth of the two last mentioned items is obviously incalculable, since nothing like them in shape, beauty, quality, and size can be found in all the world."

Following the death of Matthias in 1619, the inventories made of his property at the Neue Burg in Vienna reveal that many of Rudolf's works of art had indeed found their way to the new capital. Matthias's personal estate comprised 3,909 articles, mostly paintings, but it included as well the two family heirlooms (agate bowl and unicorn's horn), the Imperial crown, and a number of objets d'art, in addition to "various Turkish porcelains, *terra sigilata*, and other metal and similar things." In order to discharge a 200,000-kronen debt, Emperor Ferdinand II, the son of Archduke Charles of Styria (see Chapter 5), sought and gained permission from his Uncle Albrecht to pawn some of Matthias's treasures, among them another work from Prague, a "fine necklace, with an 'R' and five Imperial crowns" set with seven large diamonds.[4] Significantly, five additional items – rhinoceros horns and *Eselhörner* ("donkeys' horns," meaning the horns of the mythical unicorn) – were at the same time earmarked for transfer to the "treasure of the House of Austria."

Emperor Ferdinand II (r. 1619-1637), following a first short-lived marriage to the Wittelsbach Princess Maria Anna of Bavaria, took as his bride Anna Eleonora Gonzaga of Mantua, a legendary beauty whose dowry consisted of 594,533 gulden in cash and a vast amount of jewelry. By the time she died, Empress Eleonora owned 3,600 diamonds, not counting other precious stones. The jewels included a chain with 26 little horses enameled in black, each set with a diamond, and an 80,000-kronen necklace from which hung a diamond eagle and a portrait of Ferdinand.[5]

Sadly, Ferdinand II caused, if indirectly, the destruction of the most exquisite Kunstkammer collection in Italy, that of his wife's family, the Gonzaga, in Mantua. The catastrophe occurred in 1630, when Austrian troops sacked the ducal palace, which con-

182

tained the early-16th-century *studiolo* and *grotta* of Isabella d'Este, the patroness of Ariosto, Leonardo da Vinci, and Titian. In the fabled *studiolo* hung a great wealth of paintings, including works by Mantegna, Lorenzo Costa, Perugino, and Correggio. These masterworks survived, but not much of the fine collection of antiquities and objets d'art. A tantalizing inventory of 1542 discloses the extent of the loss, listing as it does "an infinite number of rare and precious objects." These include agates, jaspers, sardonyxes, and jewels, cameos and ivories, medals, crystals, and rare articles such as "unicorn horns," vases of every sort, inkwells and saltcellars, all of which, save for a handful of objects, have disappeared. In the *grotta* stood Classical statues and replicas made from the antique by Pier Jacopo Alari Buonacolsi (figs. 181, 182), as well as the renowned Roman Imperial sardonyx vase today preserved at the Herzog Anton Ulrich Museum in Braunschweig.[6] The rampaging Imperial army wantonly destroyed "the most precious works of art, in particular the ever so valuable [rock-]crystal glasses and vessels, because of the slight value of their gold or silver mounts, [which] were thrown to earth to such an extent that hardstone [fragments] lay in heaps."[7]

The war-torn reign of Ferdinand II saw a further and finally calamitous decimation of the Rudofine collections. In 1620, following the Battle of the White Mountain near Prague, Duke Maximilian I of Bavaria, a leader of the Catholic forces, was said to

have helped himself to some of the treasures in the Hradschin Kunstkammer, but surely not the rumored 6 tons or 1,500 carloads of gold. Another myth holds that in 1632 the Protestant Elector Johann Georg I of Saxony and his army seized a further 50 wagons full of art works, antiquities, and *naturalia*. Nevertheless, prized objects – mainly silver and semiprecious hardstone vessels – were withdrawn in a steady stream to satisfy the need for gifts, among them "a Turkish present," very likely for the Sultan in Istanbul. Hans König, the treasurer of the Hradschin, was asked "to hand over the large rock-crystal jug and the cups of Bohemian agate together with five or six pieces from the remaining vessels of hardstone and crystal." In 1631 König made an inventory of 300 articles sent to Vienna, among which were three valuable gem-encrusted ebony writing cabinets, one of them equipped with a musical clock.[8]

In 1621 and again in 1635 Ferdinand II proclaimed the *Majoratsstiftung*, by dint of which all the heirlooms and treasures of the House of Habsburg, both present and future, would be subject to the law of primogeniture, thus bound to the person of the firstborn and not to the land.

One of the few Rudolfine craftsmen still in service to Ferdinand II was the famous lapidary Ottavio Miseroni, who doubled as both treasurer and keeper of the Hradschin. His son Dionysio joined the Imperial service in 1623, staying on into the reign of Ferdinand III (1637-1657), which saw the last flowering of the lapidarists' art. To Dionysio fell the high-

183

184

184. *François Dieussart. Archduke Leopold Wilhelm, 1656 (Brussels). Marble; height 28 ¼" (72 cm). Kunsthistorisches Museum, Vienna. Archduke Leopold Wilhlem, the last of the great Habsburg collectors, took advantage of his tenure as Governor of the Spanish Netherlands (1646-1656) to accumulate treasures, especially major paintings from the dispersed collection of King Charles I of England.*

185. *Dionysio Miseroni and Paul Pertz. Lapidary Vase and Flowers, 1647-1648 (Prague). Citrine, agate, jasper, chalcedony, rock crystal, gold, enamel, and silver; height 10 ¼" (26 cm). Kunsthistorisches Museum, Vienna. Dionysio Miseroni, who succeeded his father as court lapidary in 1624, gave Prague its last great flowering of the stone carver's art. His most popular works were vases carved of hard- or semiprecious stones filled with long-stemmed blossoms made of similar materials, which in the present instance came from the hand of the court gem-cutter Paul Pertz.*

risk challenge of carving the famous uncut emerald from Muzo in Colombia, a stone first acknowledged in the 1619 inventory of Emperor Matthias's estate. It took Dionysio almost two years to fashion the huge mineral into a covered bottle weighing 2,680 carats, a feat viewed at the time as verging on the miraculous (fig. 183). The master was rewarded accordingly, with the princely sum of 12,000 gulden. The only work signed by Dionysio is a rock-crystal pyramid towering over 45 inches into the air, another *mirabilium*, valued at 20,00 gulden, in which all five of its stacked and nested elements are cut from a single block of hardstone.[9] The most popular of Dionysio's works were the celebrated arrangements of hardstone flowers, a magnificent example of which has tulips and anemones carved from jasper, agate, and rock crystal, set in gold, and displayed in a relief-carved citrine vase (fig. 185).

Dionysio Miseroni, as the person responsible for the Prague Kunstkammer, evacuated its contents in 1639 as a cautionary measure against a possible onslaught by Swedish military during the Thirty Years War. And he did so again in 1642, at the sound of another false alarm. Finally, in 1648 – the last climactic year of the dreadful conflict – treachery on the part of the Swedish commander, Count von Königsmark, took the vigilant Dionysio by surprise. Threatened with torture, he surrendered the keys to the Kunstkammer, which was forthwith plundered, by explicit instruction from Queen Christina, who, in faraway Stockholm, eagerly awaited the arrival of the Rudolfine booty (see also Chapter 12).

In the following generation, Archduke Leopold Wilhelm (1614-1662), the second son of Emperor Ferdinand II, gave the Habsburgs their last great accumulator of Kunstkammer objects (fig. 184).[10] By

185

186

187

186. *David Teniers the Younger. The Gallery of Archduke Leopold Wilhelm, 1655 (Brussels). Oil on canvas; 48 1/2 x 65" (123 x 163 cm). Kunsthistorisches Museum, Vienna. One of the key artists in service to Archduke Leopold Wilhelm during his governorship of the Spanish Netherlands was the Flemish painter David Teniers, whose views of the archducal galleries provide an invaluable record of the collections and the cheek-by-jowl manner in which they were installed. Here the Archduke is shown touring the galleries attended by his retinue. Today most of the holdings can be seen in Vienna's Kunsthistorisches Museum.*

187. *Franco-Saxon School. Saint Gregory and Three Scribes, late 9th century. Ivory; 8 1/16 x 5" (20.5 x 12.5 cm). Kunsthistorisches Museum, Vienna. Archduke Leopold not only collected; he also patronized the arts, keeping 65 artists on his payroll. His collection, in addition to major paintings, boasted hundreds of marbles, bronzes, plaquettes, wood carvings, ivories, wax figures, and reliefs.*

turns Bishop of Passau, Strasbourg, Olmütz, and Breslau, while simultaneously serving as Grand Master of the Order of the Teutonic Knights, Leopold Wilhelm assembled a major collection of paintings, drawings, and sculptures, mostly, however, during his tenure in the secular role of Spanish Governor of the Netherlands, which lasted from 1646 until 1656.[11] Although his monthly salary of 30,000 kronen, promised by King Philip IV of Spain, arrived in Brussels somewhat irregularly, Archduke Leopold Wilhelm became a great maecenas, employing 65 artists and having his portrait painted 34 times. Among the better-known painters on the Governor's payroll were Peter Neefs, Jan van der Hagen, and David Teniers, an eminent figure in the history of art who produced miniature replicas of all the masterpieces owned by his patron. These included pictures by such brilliant figures as Bellini, Giorgione, Lotto, Titian, Giulio Romano, Palma Vecchio, and Veronese, many of them acquired when the Commonwealth government of England, following the regicide of 1649, sold off the fabulous collections assembled by Charles I and his ally, the Duke of Buckingham. In 1660 David Teniers published his *Theatrum Pictorium*, for which he had made 245 engravings after the Italian School paintings owned by Archduke Leopold Wilhelm. He also painted views of the archducal galleries, thereby providing an invaluable record in which most of the paintings, interspersed with sculptures, are identifi-able. As shown in fig. 186, the pictures were hung cheek by jowl, their order determined solely by decorative effect.

In 1656, Archduke Leopold Wilhelm, seriously indebted because of his ostentatious life-style and chronic lack of funds, left Brussels and returned to Vienna. There he consigned his Kunstkammer to the second floor of the Stallburg within the Hofburg complex. Crammed into long corridors, the collection would be inventoried anew. It numbered 1,397 paintings, of which some 600 have been identified, and 343 drawings. There were in addition 542 works of sculpture – marbles, bronzes, plaquettes, wood carvings, ivories, wax figures, and reliefs (fig. 187). An important artist within this part of the collection is the Mantuan sculptor cited earlier, Pier Jacopo Alari Buonacolsi, known as *L'Antico* for his partially gilt bronzes inspired by Classical prototypes. A representative, even outstanding example is the *Venus Felix*, a small-scale but beautifully modeled, chased, and patinated variation upon a marble statue unearthed in the late 15th century (fig. 181). Buonacolsi's large busts of Bacchus and Ariadne had been created for Isabella d'Este's *grotta* at the Palazzo Ducale in Mantua (fig. 182). The sculptures stood between the windows on two tiers placed 2 1/2 and 5 feet above the floor, opposite walls hung with the paintings. Even so, the immense collection spilled over into the apartments on the floor above.

188

188. *Paulus Tullner. Wenckheimscher Willkomm, c. 1570, Nuremberg. Silver-gilt; height 11 ¼" (28.5 cm). Treasury of the Order of the Teutonic Knights, Vienna. Habsburgs often served as Hochmeister of the Order of the Teutonic Knights, an office that required large cups for "welcome" libations. One such vessel is the wine ewer reproduced here, a hound with a goose in its jaws, contributed, as the title and image imply, by Grand Master Georg Hund von Wenckheim.*

189. *Leonhard Kern. Abraham and Isaac, c. 1620-1625 (Schwäbisch Hall). Ivory; height 11 ¾" (30 cm). Kunsthistorisches Museum, Vienna. When Europe's courtly taste turned from bronze to ivory, Leonhard Kern, who worked in Naples and Rome before settling in Heidelberg, Nuremberg, and Schwäbisch Hall, emerged as Germany's leading master of turned or carved ivory. His art also reflects a shift in taste, from Mannerist elegance and refinement to the more robust and naturalistic Classicism of Baroque.*

190. *Leonhard Kern. King David, c. 1620-1625. Ivory; height 10 ¾" (27.4 cm). Kunsthistorisches Museum, Vienna.*

191. *Matthias Steinl. Equestrian Portrait of Emperor Joseph I, 1693 (Vienna). Ivory; total height 27 ⅞" (70.8 cm). Kunsthistorisches Museum, Vienna. In works like this equestrian group, Baroque ivory turning attained its apogee in Europe. Here the Emperor, portrayed as a victor clad in cuirass and laurel, is shown in the aftermath of his coronation in Nuremberg in 1690.*

189

190

Archduke Leopold Wilhelm made a clear distinction between his Kunstkammer and his Schatzkammer. The latter was housed mainly in a *Schaczgewölb*, or "treasure vault," in the Neue Burg, there subdivided into eight categories: ecclesiastical treasures; objets d'art; silver; hardstone vessels; clocks and furniture; vestments from Wiener Neustadt; silver inherited from the Trautdorff estate; and church silver and plate related to the Teutonic Knights. It is interesting to note that the treasury of the Teutonic Order, today located in Vienna,[12] includes a number of typical Kunstkammer works contributed by one or another of the *Hochmeistern* ("Grand Masters"), some of them Habsburgs. One piece, a ewer made from a Seychelle nut and once owned by Rudolf II, entered the Teutonic treasury courtesy of his brother, Archduke Maximilian III of Tyrol, as did a 15th-century rock-crystal double beaker crowned with an archducal hat and possibly Burgundian in origin.[13] Highlights of the collection include two 16th-century zoomorphic cups from Nuremberg: the so-called *Wenckheimischer Willkomm* and the *Bobenhausenscher Willkomm* (fig. 188). As the names imply, both vessels are capacious cups meant for "welcome" libations, the first shaped as a hound and the second as a fox.[14] A *Natterzungenkredenz*, an example of the "dragon's teeth" seen in fig. 105, may

have been presented by Emperor Friedrich III or Emperor Maximilian I.[15] It hung from a ramified branch of coral.

At the death of Archduke Leopold Wilhelm in 1662 the Kunstkammer was inherited by Emperor Leopold I, his eldest surviving nephew. All his other worldly possessions, including the Schatzkammer, went to Archduke Karl Joseph, Emperor Leopold's younger brother, who, even though an adolescent, was Bishop of Olmütz and Grand Master of the Teutonic Order. When Karl Joseph died two years later, at the premature age of fifteen, Emperor Leopold I inherited this part of his uncle's collection as well. For the want of space, however, the whole of the estate remained provisionally wherever its various parts had been installed. In retrospect, Archduke Leopold Wilhelm's Kunstkammer, with its Italian, early Dutch, and contemporary Flemish paintings, appears to have endowed the Imperial collections with the most important array of masterpieces they ever received.

During the reign of Emperor Leopold I (1658-1705) the art of ivory turning flourished throughout Europe, its products gradually replacing bronzes in the taste of aristocratic collectors. The new Schatzkammer significantly expanded its holdings, which included two remarkable pieces by Leonhard Kern, Germany's fore-

most ivory worker: a fine Abraham and Isaac composition and a King David statuette (figs. 189, 190). Providing an impressive conclusion to this great Kunstkammer tradition were a lavishly decorated tankard – a masterpiece of virtuoso carving – by the monogrammist BC (fig. 192) and a large equestrian group with the image of Emperor Joseph I (fig. 191), both made in the 17th century.

The Habsburgs' secular and sacred Schatzkammern, as well as Leopold Wilhelm's Kunstkammer, had become relatively well known by the second half of the 17th century. Contemporary descriptions make it possible to reconstruct the installation. In a long room against a wall stood thirteen large black cupboards, each surmounted by a gilt eagle emblazoned with the monogram of Emperor Ferdinand III and protected by doors inset with valuable paintings. The contents were organized by materials, with cupboards one and two given over to ivories, three and four to clocks and automata, five and seven to silver, six to cameos, and eight to gold (fig. 193). Three succeeding cupboards contained the vast collection of hardstone vessels, after which came cupboard thirteen, crammed with the crown jewels. *Pietre dure* tables placed between the windows supported smaller cabinets with drawers full of yet more collectibles.

The last table, however, was reserved for what the Habsburgs considered their greatest treasure: the venerated agate bowl. As this overview suggests, the Imperial collections had lost the *naturalia, mirabilia,* or *exotica* so characteristic of the earlier *Kunst- und Wunderkammern*. The new Schatzkammer could therefore be said to have prefigured Augustus the Strong's Green Vaults in Dresden.

The impetus behind the *Geistliche Schatzkammer*, or purely religious treasury, can be traced to Empress Anna, the wife of Matthias. Installed next to the Schatzkammer, it contained precious vestments, relics, reliquaries, and church plate. Empress Anna also established an ecclesiastical treasury for the Capuchin Church, the Habsburgs' necropolis, where, in 1626, the collection already boasted some 400 precious objects.

Finally, there was the monumental library, combined with a huge collection of coins and medals. A splendid reflection of the Habsburgs' intellectual pursuits in the 17th century, the library struck some contemporary observers as virtually the equal of the Bibliotheca Vaticana. Together or singly, the great collections satisfied one paramount political aim: namely, the glorification, or even deification, of the Emperor and the House of Austria.

192. *BC. Ornamental tankard, late 17th century (Vienna). Ivory; height 11 3/4" (29.8 cm). Kunsthistorisches Museum, Vienna. The author of this lavish tankard is known only by his initials BG. With its lavish, virtuoso carving and its hunting/fishing scenes based on Dutch engravings, this ceremonial or parade tankard is one of the most impressive of all known works in ivory.*

193. *Jeweled ewer and basin, 14th century and 1st quarter 17th century (Antwerp). Silver-gilt, gold, enamel, rubies, diamonds, emeralds, turquoises, onyx, chalcedony, cornelian, and coral; diameter of basin 19 3/4" (50 cm), height of ewer 11 1/2" (29 cm). Kunsthistorisches Museum, Vienna. This ewer and basin set, with its multitude of cameos, must be counted among the most extravagant examples of the jeweler's or goldsmith's art to survive from the early Baroque period. The gems may have been mounted for Archduke Albrecht (1559-1621), brother of Emperor Rudolf II.*

193

The Wittelsbachs

The Wittelsbachs of Bavaria were the most durable dynasty in Europe, their reign lasting almost 700 years, from 1231 until 1918. The lands they ruled got their name from the Baiuvarii, a Germanic tribe that invaded the region in the 6th century, following the withdrawal of the Romans, and established a duchy, which then emerged as one of the five basic or "stem" duchies of medieval Germany. However, the capital, Munich, scarcely existed before 1156, when the Emperor Friedrich Barbarossa attempted to stop the brutal rivalry between the Guelph and Hohenstaufen dynasties by bestowing Bavaria upon his cousin, Duke Henry the Lion (Heinrich der Löwe), a Guelph. Two years later, Duke Henry took the radical step of destroying a toll bridge over the River Isar at Oberföring, for the express purpose of replacing it with a new span built a few miles upstream near a tiny monastic settlement known as Ze den Mönichen. In this way he gained control over the salt route across South Germany, diverted its lucrative revenues from the Bishop of Freising into his own coffers, and reinforced his authority with the power of wealth. Meanwhile, Henry, founder of such Hanseatic cities as Lübeck, Rostock, and Schwerin, understood very well how prosperous towns could contribute to the development of a province. For this purpose, he fortified Mönichen ("Little Monks") with a circle of walls and granted it the right to hold markets and mint coins, including the famous Pfennig or "penny." In 1180, however, Duke Henry lost the duchy, after he refused to support Friedrich Barbarossa in his campaign against the polities of northern Italy. Now the fiefdom, minus the Tyrol, fell to the Wittelsbachs, who thus entered upon their long reign as the resented yet fondly remembered "benevolent despots" of Bavaria.

The first Wittelsbach Duke of Bavaria was Otto I, whose grandson, in 1214, married the daughter of the Count Palatine, thereupon launching the Palatine branch of Wittelsbachs, the ultimate heirs, 500 years later, to the Bavarian crown. Not until 1240, however, did a Wittelsbach take up residence in Munich, and this after the duchy had been divided between the two sons of Duke Otto II. While Duke Heinrich remained at Trausnitz Castle in Landshut, the capital of Lower Bavaria, Duke Ludwig II the Strong moved to Mönichen and made it his capital. The arrangement became not only the cause of much bickering among the various Wittelsbachs but also an impediment to economic growth within the region. Nonetheless, it did not prevent Ludwig IV (1294-1347) from becoming Emperor in 1328 or from seizing Brandenburg, the Tyrol, and the Netherlands for his family, possessions they would not long hold. Ludwig may have won the Imperial crown, but he did so without the support of the Pope, who had favored

195

194. *Wenzel Jamnitzer. Trochus- or turbo-shell ewer, c. 1570 (Nuremberg). Trochus shell (Turbo olearius), silver-gilt, and enamel; height 12 13/16" (32.5 cm). Schatzkammer, Munich. In this exuberant work - Baroque before the fact - the great Nuremberg goldsmith Wenzel Jamnitzer married two turbo shells with a fanciful mount composed of an eagle attacking a snail, the latter cast from nature. From the very start of his career Jamnitzer revealed a gift for what would be known as stil or style rustique, based on casts made from nature.*

195. *Hans Reimer (attrib). Cup and cover, 1562 (Munich). Gold and enamel; height 10 5/8" (27 cm). Schatzkammer, Munich. Reimer (c. 1555-1604) is known through two signed works, one of which is the Saphirpokal in fig. 201. Generally he used gold and a decorative scheme of white-enamel arabesques. The vessel seen here, with its Bavarian colors (white and blue) and the arms of Bavaria and Austria, bears the initials A.H.I.B., signifying Albrecht Herzog in Bayern, and the date 1562. In 1546 Duke Albrecht had married Archduchess Anna, the daughter of Emperor Maximilian II. The cup first appears in the 1617 inventory of Duke Maximilian I.*

196. *Hans Mielich. Duke Albrecht V of Bavaria, 1556. Oil on canvas; 82 ¼ x 43 ¾" (209 x 111 cm). Kunsthistorisches Museum, Vienna. This painting was one of the many portraits of notable grandees collected at Schloss Ambras by Duke Albrecht's brother-in-law, Archduke Ferdinand II of Tyrol. And like Archduke Ferdinand, Albrecht was a merry soul actively involved in the arts, especially music; moreover, he too loved to build, beginning with the Neue Veste, the ducal residence in Munich, which he remodeled to include both a Kunstkammer and the Saint George's Hall with its glorious Renaissance interior. The Kunstkammer would house some 6,000 carefully sorted objects.*

the election of the Habsburg candidate. Indeed, John XXII excommunicated the Wittelsbach Emperor, which served to transform Munich into a center of antipapal dissent, a place, though staunchly Catholic, where even the interdicted philosopher/theologian William of Occam could find refuge.

Bavaria, in the meantime, suffered the evils of division until 1505, when Albrecht IV the Wise (1467-1508) reunited the duchy following his marriage to Achduchess Kunigunde, a sister of Emperor Maximilian I. Albrecht also made certain that his province would remain integral, by the simple act of declaring it a *primogeniture* or nondivisible heirloom. During the reign of Albrecht's son, Wilhelm IV (r. 1508-1550), the Reformation arrived, only for the Duke to side with Emperor Charles V and the Catholic cause, which prevailed against the Schmalkaldic League of Protestant Princes at the Battle of Mühlberg in 1547. To retain the interest and loyalty of their subjects, the Wittelsbachs not only encouraged religious festivals and other forms of public merriment; they also staged opulent dynastic celebrations, such as the days-long feast held during the first visit of Charles V in 1530. Thus did Munich win its reputation for *Gemütlichkeit*, that quality of easy, amiable charm, which today makes the city the one in which most Germans would prefer to live.

Wilhlem IV ushered in the Renaissance, especially at the Neue Veste, an early-15th-century fortress built outside the old city walls on a site now occupied by the Residenz at the center of Munich. Here he made a number of impressive additions, including the Rundstubenbau, a fine circular building styled in the Renaissance manner and invested with the ducal apartments. Just outside the new city walls, at the northwest corner of which the Neue Veste stood, Wilhelm had a summer house erected and a court garden laid out, these too a reflection of the growing taste for things Italian. In another sign of the times, the Duke became the first Wittelsbach known to have collected; moreover, he recruited for the court the most advanced and gifted artists, among them Hans Burgkmair and Albrecht Altdorfer, the latter famous for his visionary *Battle of Alexander* (1529), today a proud asset of Munich's Alte Pinakothek. The painting belonged to a series of fifteen pictures devoted to scenes from the lives of Classical heroes and the Old Testament, all commissioned perhaps as decoration for a small circular building located in the Neue Veste rose garden.

To house such treasures, Albrecht V (r. 1550-1579; fig. 196), Wilhelm IV's son, had the Neue Veste remodeled to include both the Ballsaal and the Sankt Georgssaal, the latter sometimes called the finest secular interior of the German Renaissance. With this campaign, he laid the foundation for what would evolve into one of the great royal palaces in Europe, today a vast complex of courtyards, state rooms, and chambers in almost every style known to the history

197

of architecture. Albrecht loved music and appointed as his court musician the celebrated composer Orlando di Lasso, paying him enough to annoy some of the more snobbish courtiers. Like Archduke Ferdinand of Tyrol, the good-nature, fun-loving Albrecht attracted parasites as well as poets into his circle, a symptom, it would appear, of a growing addiction to strong drink and gambling. Coincidentally, Albrecht was married to Archduchess Anna of Austria, a sister of both Archduke Ferdinand and the future Emperor Maximilian II.[1] Duchess Anna, much like her sister-in-law at Innsbruck, was known for her knowledge of herb lore and medicine. Albrecht, through the marriages of his own sisters, was also allied to both the Gonzaga in Mantua and the Medici in Florence. Moreover, he shared their collecting interests, but the most fascinating parallels are between the Kunstkammer in Munich and its counterpart at Ambras.

Yet for all his charm and intellect, thirty-year-old Albrecht V had not escaped criticism, as indicated by this statement of 1557: "Whatever he sees as valuable, exotic and strange [objects], he must possess! Two or three goldsmiths work for the prince constantly; what they accomplish in a year is broken up or pawned. Painters and portraitists are employed the whole year round at the Neue Veste. Added to those are sculptors, turners, stonemasons, the extraordinary expenses for clothing, tapestries, travesties, the frightful excesses in eating, drinking and banqueting..."[2] The accruing debt alarmed the Duke's advisors, given that it came to 812,000 gulden, while the income available for paying it remained at 112,000 gulden. Finally, Albrecht agreed to a serious reduction of expenditure. In 1572, however, he was again faulted, this time for being "phlegmatic," for "loving his peace and comfort above all, reveling in the enjoyment of his music and his collections, indulging in hunting and in outings around the Wurmsee, but leaving the affairs of State... as far as possible to his council."[3]

Be that as it may, Duke Albrecht found both the energy and the means to modify the Neue Veste, adding the Sankt Georgssaal, a grand, lavishly decorated banqueting hall dedicated to Saint George, and the Ballhaus, an indoor tennis court. For the arts, moreover, he developed a systematic and strategic program,[4] so that within a decade after 1563 he had founded a Schatzkammer[5] and built the Kunstkammer[6] as well as the Antiquarium.[7] Along with the Antiquarium came the Hofbibliothek, or library,[8] located in the same building.

The Silberkammer,[9] in the Silver Tower at the Neue Veste, housed the family heirlooms. And it was packed, for the amount of plate required at court was immense, as the 16th-century archives of the ducal family attest. During the reign of Albrecht V,

some 80 Wittelsbachs and guests regularly ate "from silver" at the Neue Veste and more than 400 others at the Alte Veste. For the 1568 wedding of Albrecht's son, Prince Wilhelm, to Renata von Lothringen (Lorraine), the court laid out, according to one account, "twenty silver-gilt saltcellars shaped as ships, shells and other wonderful vessels... every two steps there were four large silver chandeliers with burning candles."[10] For the entertainment of guests, Ferdinand II of Tyrol had his court dwarf pop out of a huge pie, an antic confirming the presence of the Archduke at this family event. An inventory of silver-gilt articles, prepared in 1585, lists 100 bowls, 9 ewers, 4 basins, 88 plates, 3 bottles, 63 saltcellars, 95 spoons, 22 candlesticks, 47 forks, 2 salt spoons, and 6 beakers. Apparently nothing of this collection survives, thanks to the tendency of the Wittelsbachs to melt down silver for purposes of war or changing taste.

Albrecht V enjoyed the sound artistic advice of Hans Jakob Fugger, an erudite Humanist from the family of powerful Augsburg bankers. Having failed at banking, Fugger moved to Munich, where in 1559 he married one of Duchess Anna's ladies-in-waiting and became a favorite courtier, holding such honorary titles as Director of Music and President of the Court Chamber, with a salary of 1,000 gulden. In gratitude, Fugger bequeathed his famous library to the bibliophile Duke Albrecht, after which the collection became the core of the Bayerische Staatsbibliothek. At the Wittelsbach court, Fugger was joined by Samuel Quiccheberg, administrator of the Fugger collections and author of *Inscriptiones vel tituli*, the first treatise on museology. These two scholars, together with the antiquarian and art agent Jacopo Strada,[11] played a leading role in the formation of the Munich Kunstkammer and Antiquarium (fig. 198).

Too fat to travel abroad, Albrecht V employed agents to help him remain in touch with art-producing centers throughout Europe – with the rock-crystal carvers of Milan, the purveyors of corals in Genoa, the majolica potters in Faenza, the tapestry weavers of Brussels, the goldsmiths and cabinetmakers of Augsburg. The Duke actively sought out works of art, even to the point of soliciting contributions from other rulers. One of those he approached was Elisabeth de Valois, the Queen of Spain as well as the daughter of Henri II of France and Catherine de' Medici, beseeching her to send him *selzame und hir Landes ferne Sachen* ("unusual things, unknown in this land"). The network of Fugger banks abroad also pitched in, allowing Albrecht to acquire antiquities and copies after the antique in Venice and Rome. However, the large consignments shipped by local agents, who often cheated the Duke, produced

198

197. *Hans and Elias Lencker. Writing cabinet, c. 1580 (Nuremberg). Silver parcel-gilt and enamel; 11 13/17 x 15 3/8 x 11 5/8" (30 x 39 x 28.6 cm). Schatzkammer, Munich. The work seen here is probably the finest example of translucent champlevé enamel done by the Lencker brothers, who specialized in the medium. Every serious Kunstkammer had its writing casket, with many concealed drawers containing such essential articles as inkwell, sander, ruler, scissors, small knives, or even a fan. The Munich casket, first mentioned in the 1598 inventory, culminates in a small personification of Rhetoric teaching the alphabet to a boy. The putti at the four corners symbolize Grammar, Mathematics, Astronomy, and Music.*

198. *Titian. Jacopo Strada, 1567-1579 (Venice). Oil on canvas; 49 1/4 x 37 1/2" (125 x 95 cm). Kunsthistorisches Museum, Vienna. Jacopo Strada (1515-1588) - a true Renaissance man who functioned as painter, architect, goldsmith, numismatist, art collector/dealer, and Kunstkammer advisor - could boast Wittelsbachs and Habsburgs among his royal clients. He inspired Titian to paint a singularly great portrait, showing the subject with one of his prize possessions in hand.*

199. *Valerio Belli (attrib). Charger, c. 1520 (Venice or Padua). Silver-gilt, enamel, rock crystal, rubies, and sapphires; diameter 11 13/16" (30 cm). Schatzkammer, Munich. Although first mentioned only in 1635, in an inventory of Duke Maximilian I's Kammergalerie, this sumptuous work by a leading Milanese lapidarist bears the arms of Pope Leo X, who reigned from 1512 until 1521. It may very well have been a gift from the Pontiff to Duke Albrecht's father, Wilhelm IV of Bavaria.*

200. *Annibale Fontana. Rock-crystal Shrine of Duke Albrecht V, c. 1570 (Milan and Augsburg). Rock crystal, ebony, gold, enamel, lapis-lazuli, onyx, rubies, sapphires, and pearls; 24 3/8 x 32 3/8 x 22 2/8" (62 x 82 x 50.5 cm). Schatzkammer, Munich. Duke Albrecht paid 6,000 scudi for Fontana's rock-crystal panels, engraved with Old Testament scenes, and then sent them to Augsburg for mounting in an ebony casket encrusted with 77 onyx cameos. The treasure would be declared one of the Wittelsbachs' inalienable family heirlooms.*

201. *Hans Reimer. Saphirpokal, 1563 (Munich). Gold, enamel, and sapphires; height 19 1/8" (48.6 cm). Schatzkammer, Munich. This spectacular jeweled cup was one of 19 precious works of art listed by Duke Albrecht V in 1565 as part of the Wittelsbach family treasure.*

199

uneven results. Many sculptures arrived broken, or sawn into several pieces for easier transport, much to the wrath and grief of a frustrated Albrecht.

Surviving correspondence provides an insight into the process whereby Duke Albrecht purchased entire collections of art. In one case the negotiation concerned the antiquities of the Fugger family, which, for a price of 6,000 gulden, were conveyed to the Wittelsbachs in 1566. These treasures would then be joined by the Fuggers' collection of armor. Nor did Albrecht shy away from competing with his brother-in-law, Archduke Ferdinand, for the collections of Count Ulrich von Montfort and Count Wilhelm von Zimborn, although to no avail in both instances.

The farsighted Albrecht even concerned himself with the fate of his carefully assembled collections, having grasped the contribution they could make to the fame and prestige of the House of Wittelsbach. In 1565, no doubt moved by the action of his Habsburg brothers-in-law the preceding year, the Duke and his wife stipulated in a *disposition* that nineteen precious items, all of recent manufacture, be labeled *Hausschatz* – that is, family heirlooms which "are to remain after our death in perpetuity the property of our princely house [at] the Neue Veste, and are to belong to our heirs and their heirs in descending male line of the ruling princes of Upper Bavaria . . . whether he be the firstborn, the middle or the younger [son]."[12] The Wittelsbachs were not "to sell [them], or without constraint and necessity to pawn or give [them] as security, nor to modify their aspect, nor to remove them from the princely house at the Neue Veste." In addition to various pieces of jewelry, the list of designated heirlooms describes a gold ewer enameled in blue and white (the armorial colors of Bavaria), a gold saltcellar, and a gold-framed mirror, none of which has survived, as well as four works that still exist: an elephant pendant,[13] a diamond pendant,[14] an Italian jeweled and silver-gilt casket,[15] and the *Saphirpokal* (fig. 201). The last, made by the Munich silversmith Hans Reimer and dated 1563, is a gardlanded gold cup and cover enameled with white arabesques and set with 36 sapphires.

Before 1579, Duke Albrecht expanded the heirloom collection by contributing ten further works of art. In addition to items of personal adornment, these

200

203

202. *Hans Mielich (attrib).* Regalia necklace
of Duke Albrecht V, *c. 1565 (Munich).
Gold, enamel, emeralds (replaced),
spinels, diamonds, and pearls; length
43 ³/4" (111 cm). Schatzkammer,
Munich. In their role as Grand
Masters, the Kings of Bavaria wore this
necklace at the feasts of the Bavarian
Order of Saint George. Today the
treasure lacks three pendant pearls,
and five large emeralds are later
replacements. It too was declared an
inalienable family heirloom.*

203. *Abraham Lotter the Elder and Ulrich
Eberl (attrib).* House altar of Duke
Albrecht V, *1573-1574 (Augsburg).
Ebony, gold, and enamel; 24 ³/4 x 17 ⁷/8"
(63 x 45.5 cm). Schatzkammer,
Munich. The altar displays the
armorial bearings of Duke Albrecht V
and his wife, Archduchess Anna of
Austria. The exquisite enamel and gold
figures combine with the ebony ground
to make the altar a genuine
masterpiece of Mannerist goldsmithery
as practiced in Munich.*

204

comprised two jeweled gold cups, a gold casket, an elaborately decorated gold mirror, a richly jeweled gold treasure casket, a small casket decorated with an image of Saint George (which has not survived), a large ebony casket set with engraved rock-crystal panels (fig. 200), and the Duke's regalia necklace (fig. 202). The sumptuous necklace, identified as "Spanish work," is a chain once set with large emeralds – all now replaced – and spinels alternating with pearls. The casket, also "in the Spanish manner," has an ebony framework and rock-crystal panels exquisitely engraved with Old Testament scenes by Annibale Fontana. These cost Duke Albrecht 6,000 scudi. The jewels and art works selected for the *Erb- und Hausclainoder* ("hereditary family treasure") were not only objects of great value but also virtuoso pieces of artistic worth. The treasures, never part of the Kunstkammer, were stored in the massive Silver Tower at the Neue Veste until its destruction in the early 17th century. A magnificent piece that remained apart, later incorporated into the Kammerkapelle (private chapel), is a miniature altar of jeweled ebony dated 1573-1574 and attributed to Abraham Lotter the Elder (fig. 203). It is emblazoned with the names of Albrecht V and Duchess Anna. The polychrome enamels and exuberant decoration make the piece a characteristic work of Bavarian Mannerist goldsmithery.

Under Albrecht's son, Wilhelm V the Pious (r. 1579-1597), work began in 1583 on the Michaelskirche in Munich, the largest Renaissance church north of the Alps, sometimes called the "German

Saint Peter's," just as Munich is often labeled the "German Rome" for its steadfast, if independent, Catholicism. To pay for this fourteen-year project, Duke Wilhelm opened the Royal Brewery, Munich's renowned Hofbräuhaus. During this reign, no inventories were kept of the Wittelsbach treasures. It is known, however, that three important works entered the Hausschatz: the prayer book of Charles the Bald,[16] a silver-gilt jewel case made by Wenzel Jamnitzer and set with openwork panels chased with the Labors of Hercules on a bloodstone ground (fig. 206); and a splendid equestrian figure of Saint George, patron of the Wittelsbach family (fig. 204). This reliquary, created in Munich between 1586 and 1597, is the most glorious jeweled object of its kind. The horse, partially carved from agate, sports a white-enamel saddlecloth set with rubies and diamonds. It rests upon a silver-gilt base, modified after 1623 to include the arms of Duke Maximilian surmounted by a hat identifying him as Elector.

Duke Wilhelm also founded the Reliquary Treasure, which became the Kammerkapelle or, later, Reiche Kapelle, where all the Wittelsbachs' precious relics and religious valuables could be secured.[17] Dedicated in 1607, the chapel, as its name implies, was richly decorated with semiprecious stones, scagliola, and gilded stucco; it even boasted an ebony altar and organ, both mounted in silver. Most of the reliquaries – some sixty of them, dating from between 1590 and 1640 – were placed in the chapel by Wilhelm or his son, Maximilian, and they remain there to this day.

205

204. *Friedrich Sustris and Hans Scheich (attrib). Saint George and the Dragon, 1586-1597 (Munich). Gold, enamel, silver-gilt, diamonds, rubies, emeralds, opals, agates, chalcedony, rock crystal, precious stones, and pearls; height 19 11/16" (50 cm). Schatzkammer, Munich. After Duke Wilhelm received from his brother Ernst, Archbishop of Cologne, a relic of Saint George, patron of the Wittelsbach family, he commissioned this reliquary, the most glorious piece of goldsmith work achieved during the late 16th century. First mentioned in 1617, the treasure was modified after 1623 to include on the base the Electoral arms recently bestowed upon Duke Maximilian.*

205. *Annibale Fontana. Amphora ("Jason Vase"), 1570-1575 (Milan). Rock crystal, enamel, and rubies; height 16 5/16" (41.5 cm). Schatzkammer, Munich. Ordered by Albrecht V, this vase, together with a group of 33 rock crystals, arrived in Munich in 1570, the year the Duke died.*

206. *Wenzel Jamnitzer. Jewel casket, c. 1560 (Nuremberg). Silver-gilt, diamonds, rubies, emeralds, and heliotrope (bloodstone); 9 1/2 x 14 3/8 x 8 1/4" (24.5 x 36.5 x 21 cm). Schatzkammer, Munich. One of Jamnitzer's numerous caskets (see also fig. 232), this example, which contains two drawers and an upper compartment, is decorated with the Labors of Hercules, rendered as openwork silver-gilt reliefs set against bloodstone panels.*

206

207. *Saracchi workshop. Bacchus Amphora, c. 1579 (Milan). Rock crystal, gold, enamel, rubies, and emeralds; height 20 ¹/₄" (51.5 cm). Schatzkammer, Munich. Commissioned by Duke Albrecht, this rock-crystal vase was one of the most ambitious and costly things of its kind. The decorative program consists of Bacchus in Triumph, attended by his usual retinue - satyrs, maenads, and putti - the whole based upon an engraving by Étienne Delaune.*

208. *Jakob Sandtner. Model of the city of Munich (detail), 1570 (Munich). Lindenwood. Bayerisches Nationalmuseum, Munich. This particular detail, from one of the four city models made for Duke Albrecht V, provides an overview of the quadrangular Munich Kunstkammer built by Wilhelm Egkl between 1563 and 1568. A covered corridor linked the Kunstkammer to the Neue Veste, the ducal residence (upper right).*

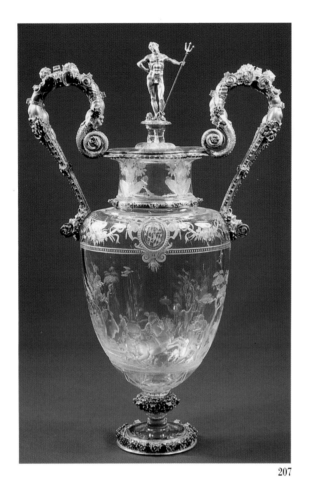

207

Duke Wilhelm moved closer to his collection after having the upper floor of the Antiquarium transformed into private apartments. Meanwhile, he also commissioned the architect Friedrich Sustris to design and build the Grottenhof, a summer residence. The eponymous grotto survives, complete with its life-size bronze figure of Mercury by Adriaen de Vries.[18] As his court sculptor, Wilhelm engaged Hubert Gerhard, whose monumental bronzes decorate the façade of the Michaelskirche. Gerhard created as well the *Perseusbrunnen*, or *Perseus Fountain*,[19] based on the Cellini figure in Florence (fig. 80), and the Wittelsbach Fountain with its multitude of figures.

Following his accession in 1597, Maximilian I, who reigned as Duke of Bavaria until 1623 and then as Elector from 1623 to 1651, added another 48 items to the official family treasure, all listed in a new *disposition*. Among them were 33 magnificent rock-crystal vessels ordered from Milan by Albrecht V, possibly for the Kunstkammer, but delivered only in 1579, following the Duke's death. The most important of these pieces are the "Jason Vase" (fig. 205), mounted in gold and superbly engraved by Annibale Fontana with scenes from the legend of the Golden Fleece, and a vase decorated with the Triumph of Bacchus by the Saracchi workshop (fig. 207). A contemporary, writing in 1579, describes the latter as "a very large vase, larger than all that have been made

of [rock] crystal, and it was of egg shape with a handle, and is all cut with figures."[20] The most celebrated of the Milanese vessels was a boat-shaped cup, unfortunately robbed in 1779 of its original mounts, which included a lavish garniture of cannon, soldiers, and sailors.[21] This cup and the Bacchus vases together cost 6,000 gold scudi, plus a special honorarium of 2,000 *lire imperiali*. The Wittelsbach family, with their pronounced interest in rock-crystal wares, counted among the most important clients of Milan's lapidary workshops.

As for the Wittelsbach Kunstkammer, it had been built by Wilhelm Egkl for Duke Albrecht V between 1563 and 1568, but then completed only in 1578 (fig. 208).[22] An oblong Renaissance or Mannerist structure with three arcaded stories facing an interior courtyard, the Kunstkammer remains in place just south of the present Residenz. Originally, the ground floor was occupied by the *Marstall* ("stables"), with the upper stories reserved for the Kunstkammer collections. The whole of the building would be taken over by the Mint in 1807. In 1611 Philipp Hainhofer, the Augsburg patrician, traveler, and art dealer, described the site: "Near the library stand the stables in a separate rectangular building... [these are] quite dark and those at Stuttgart and Heidelberg are much more to my liking. Above the stables is the *kunstCammer* [sic], into which one enters through a double door and through a small room."[23]

It is no mere coincidence that Samuel Quiccheberg published his *Inscriptiones vel Tituli* (1565), a *musée imaginaire* or practical handbook on how to structure a Kunstkammer, while employed by Duke Albrecht at the Neue Veste in Munich. The full subtitle reads: "Notes or directives for a magnificent theater, which comprises all elementary matter and exceptional images from the whole world, so that it might be said: a collection of artful and miraculous things of exquisite preciousness, testimonies of craftsmanship and of painting, a collection, the acquisition of which is counseled as a stage, where unique knowledge and admirable information can be rapidly, easily and surely obtained."[24] Drawing on

208

his personal knowledge of numerous *Kunst- und Wunderkammern* and their founders, Quiccheberg wrote his *Inscriptiones* with the clear purpose of inspiring his Wittelsbach patron and providing ideal guidelines for the formation of his museum. Such a museum, according to Quiccheberg, would serve as a *theatrum mundi*, or "world theatre," reflecting every aspect of the complex universe.

Quiccheberg's *Theatrum*, believed to be the first museological treatise ever published, visualized a museum in five sections, each of them divided into ten or eleven subsections:

• Decorative paintings of all kinds (including portraits of the founder, his family, his domains, portraits of notorious personalities, freaks, etc.), city models, and models of machinery.

• Works made of such materials as stone, metal, wood, or ivory (including sculpture, artifacts, goldsmithery, instruments, arms, wrought-iron pieces, coins, etc.).

• A cabinet of natural history involving organic matter (stuffed animals, casts after nature, skeletons, seeds, pressed flowers) or inorganic matter (corals, shells, and hardstones such as rock crystal, lapis-lazuli, chalcedony, etc.), whether natural or modified by human hands.

• Musical, medical, and mathematical instruments, toys and exotic objects.

• An art collection composed of fine paintings, drawings and prints, portraits of *uomini famosi*, coats-of-arms, carpets, and fitted cases for the art works.

The museum, furthermore, was to be complemented by a scholarly library, covering all fields of modern knowledge, as well as by workshops and classrooms for practical studies.

Still, neither the original layout of the Kunstkammer in the time of Albrecht nor its relationship to the Quiccheberg treatise is known. In 1578, however, Prospero Visconti, one of the Duke's Italian agents, described the contents in Latin as *museum non solum rarum, sed unicum in tota Europa* ("a museum not only rare but unique in all of Europe"). Twenty years later Maximilian I received an inventory drawn up by Baptist Fickler, a lawyer who had very likely compiled the list for Wilhelm V.[25] Philipp Hainhofer visited the museum twice, in 1603 and again in 1611, and set down his personal impressions, which serve well to complement Fickler's inventory.[26] Together these documents allow us to reconstruct, with relative accuracy, the layout of the building and even that of the collection, at least as they were constituted under Wilhelm V if not under Albrecht V. Quiccheberg had died in 1567, some ten years before the completion of the Munich Kunstkammer. Thirty years later, however, his elaborate system of classification could still be detected in Fickler's inventory,

209

which confirms that the Wittelsbach Dukes had indeed followed the guidelines established in the *Inscriptiones*, even if loosely.

It appears that the upper floor of the Munich Kunstkammer was rectangular in shape and divided into two corridor-like rooms, each measuring approximately 180 by 20 feet, and two shorter rooms, these measuring 120 by 20 feet. All together, the rooms, which opened on to the interior courtyard, provided over 12,000 square feet of exhibition space, making this Kunstkammer the largest thing of its kind. Fickler's inventory lists around 6,000 items dispersed in 3,407 locations and disposed upon some 60 tables. Smaller tables reserved for more precious objects stood against the walls between windows. Larger tables or cabinets were aligned in rows throughout the four wings of the quadrangular building, with objects placed both on and underneath the tables as well as in their drawers. Paintings, reliefs, and plaster casts of Roman Emperors hung on the walls, whose running cornices provided shelf space for hunting trophies, statuettes, receptacles, and modern as well as antique busts. Stuffed animals dangled from the ceiling. Visitors must have found the collection and its installation not only innovative but also quite overwhelming.

The formal entrance to the Kunstkammer lay in the northwest corner through a corridor connecting it to the Neue Veste. The north wing, dedicated to objects of better quality, was illuminated by large windows. Here the collection consisted of 45 coral "mountains" similar to those at Ambras (fig. 141), all displayed upon 12 small square tables painted gray. On or under twelve larger gray-painted tables, or in their drawers, were exhibited thousands of articles, all generally grouped according to material. They included a mass of *lapides manuales* – mineral ore

209. Mounted prayer bead, *c. 1500 (bead, Flanders), c. 1600 (mount, Munich). Boxwood, gold, and enamel; diameter 2 ½" (5.7 cm). Schatzkammer, Munich. A typical* Kunststück, *or outstanding feat of craftsmanship, the boxwood bead has been minutely carved with a host of figures, ornaments, and inscriptions accounting for all the joyful mysteries or meditations of the first rosary decade: Annunciation, Visitation, Nativity, and Presentation in the Temple. The bead appears in the first Kunstkammer inventory of 1598.*

210

210. Plaquette with fishing scene, *late 16th century (Nuremberg). Lead; diameter 6 ¹/₁₆" (15.3 cm). Bayerisches Nationalmuseum, Munich.*

211. Portrait medallion, *c. 1440 (Burgundy). Gold, enamel, and chalcedony; diameter 3 ⁹/₁₆" (9 cm). Schatzkammer, Munich. The Kunstkammer inventory of 1598 identifies the subject as Emperor Maximilian I, which neither date nor style allows. A more likely candidate would be Duke Philip the Good of Burgundy, who visited Munich in 1454. Whoever it may be is shown wearing the Order of the Golden Fleece.*

212. Terrestrial and celestial globes, *c. 1570- 1580 (Nuremberg). Ivory, gold, enamel, and pearls; height 2 ³/₄" (7 cm). Schatzkammer, Munich. These jeweled miniatures are first cited in the Kunstkammer inventory of 1598.*

specimens comparable to the *naturalia* so prized by Archduke Ferdinand at Ambras – many of them mounted, embellished with figurative additions, and presented under glass. One of the room's outstanding pieces was a nef-shaped, striated bowl of brown agate, which contemporaries mistook for petrified wood. The treasure, with its exquisite silver-gilt mount, fashioned between 1611 and 1614 by the Augsburg goldsmith Johannes I. Lencker, was fitted into a specially made leather case. Elector Maximilian I later transferred the piece to his Kammergalerie. Another virtuoso showpiece was a turbo shell whose mount, by the distinguished Nuremberg goldsmith Wenzel Jamnitzer, included a foot in the form of a snail, six coiling snakes, and a predatory eagle (fig. 194). On a table among objects of little intrinsic value, such as an intricately carved rosary bead (fig. 209) and a pair of miniature globes (fig. 212), lay a 15th-century gold Burgundian medallion of great refinement, its profile image thought at the time to portray Emperor Maximilian I (fig. 211). Other extant items are a lead plaquette chased with a fishing scene and a relief carved from Solnhofen stone depicting the Judgment of Paris (figs. 210, 213).

The Kunstkammer's most valuable works of art, assembled in a room located at the northeast corner

211

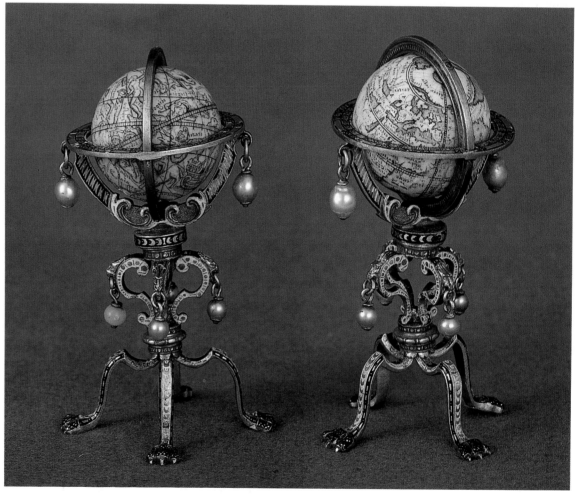

212

of the building, were objects of both exceptional workmanship and "antiquarian" interest, meaning older rather than "modern" pieces eligible for inclusion in the Treasury. The collection included a characteristic group of 16th-century gold and silver-gilt flasks, beakers, chargers, and tazzas exhibited on a four-tier buffet. Among the few surviving items are a ravishingly illuminated prayer book, with its fine, silver-gilt Florentine binding, commissioned by Lorenzo de' Medici around 1485,[27] and a silver-gilt and enamel bookbinding made by Hans Lencker of Nuremberg in 1574. Inside is a prayer book thought to have been presented to Elector Maximilian I by Emperor Ferdinand II on the occasion of his visit to Munich in 1619.[28] On a second buffet rested "white" or ungilded silver, a collection made up of ewers, sweetmeat dishes, saltcellars, and reliefs, all of which disappeared into the crucible over the course of centuries, for the usual reasons: war or the desire for new, more "modern" works. The silver pieces in today's Schatzkammer date chiefly from the 18th and 19th centuries. Placed in splendid isolation on separate small tables were two mid-16th-century ivory caskets, delivered in 1577 from Ceylon by way of Lisbon and Antwerp (fig. 214), and the celebrated *Goldene Tafel*, a 12th-century gold Byzantine plaque with an enameled Crucifixion scene.[29] A large rectangular table in the corner held a number of hardstone vessels, together with a bear-shaped cup fashioned of ambergris, silver-gilt, and jewels by Hans II Ment (fig. 215), and an amusing automaton conceived as a mountain (fig. 216).[30]

The Wittelsbachs' Renaissance collection abounded in rare and exotic objects from every corner of the earth, some of them labeled "Egyptian," "Mauritanian," or "Muscovite," others "Indian," "Persian," "Turkish," "Moorish," or simply "Barbaric." Included as well were articles sent by Grand Duke Cosimo I from a shipload of ethnographic material that had arrived at Livorno in 1572. The range of holdings embraced Latin American artifacts, Chinese porcelains, Mexican feather headdresses, Japanese lacquer boxes, and a pair of fur shoes from Lapland. A Greenland kayak, presented to Duke Wilhelm V sometime after 1577, can be seen today at Munich's Ethnographic Museum.[31] Until the outbreak of World War II, the Bayerisches Nationalmuseum exhibited a stuffed elephant from the Kunstkammer; it had been given to Duke Albrecht V in 1572 by Emperor Maximilian II.[32]

Among the interesting items listed by Fickler is a group of ivories turned and presented by such passionate collectors as Emperor Maximilian II, Archduke Ferdinand II, and Elector Augustus of Saxony. The 15 majolica pieces cited in Fickler's inventory may belong to a unique and extant 82-piece Faenza service painted by Don Pico and emblazoned with the arms of Duke Albrecht.[33] Other odds and ends included costumes from a revered ancestor, Duke Wilhelm IV; the bridal shift of Empress Eleonore, wife of Emperor Friedrich III (r. 1452-1493); the tunic and sword of François I of France; the obligatory micro-carved cherry pit; and a Florentine *pietre dure* table. Something unique in the world of Renaissance Kunstkammern were architectural models repesenting Bavaria's five principal cities, works that still survive at the Bayerisches Nationalmuseum (fig. 208).

The Munich Kunstkammer had its Wunderkammer aspect as well, identified by Fickler as bezoars, deformed calves' heads and pigs' trotters, roebuck horns, the head of an aurochs (a wild ox once plentiful in German forests), the "leg of a giant," "growths" from the sea, "wood looking like bread," "four heads of sea wonders," "*miracula naturae*," "wheat that fell from heaven," and "a wooden clock made by a blind man."

After the turn of the 17th century, Duke Maximilian I curtailed visits to the Kunstkammer because of mounting thefts, which the open displays on tables all but encouraged. By 1606-1607 Maximilian had installed a Kammergalerie contiguous with his own apartments, where the most select treasures were kept in cupboards. The 1635 inventory of this collection makes the first mention of Wenzel Jamnitzer's silver bell, a prime example of the *style rustique* with its swarm of small creatures cast from nature (fig. 217). Also cited for the first

215

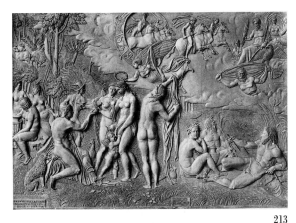
213

214

213. *Hans Ässlinger. Judgment of Paris, 1550 (Munich). Solnhof limestone; 11 7/8 x 12 5/8" (30.1 x 44.7 cm). Bayerisches Nationalmuseum, Munich. For this relief, the court sculptor to Albrecht V relied upon Marc Antonio's celebrated engraving after a drawing by Raphael. Inscribed A.H.I.B. for Albrecht Herzog in Bayern, the relief appears in the 1598 Kunstkammer inventory.*

214. *Ivory casket, c. 1555 (Ceylon). Ivory, gold, rubies, and sapphires; length 11 13/16" (30 cm). Schatzkammer, Munich. The relief-carved ivory panels narrate scenes from the life of the last Buddhist King of Ceylon. This casket and a second one in the Munich Kunstkammer are probably identical with the two jewelry-filled boxes acquired at Lisbon in 1566 by the emissaries of Marc Fugger, Duke Albrecht V's agent.*

215. *Hans II Ment. Bear, c. 1570 (Augsburg). Silver-gilt, ambergris, enamel, diamonds, rubies, and pearls; height 7 7/8" (20 cm). Schatzkammer, Munich. Closely related to the Bear as Hunter at Schloss Ambras (fig. 133), this example, also from Augsburg, has lost the "surprises" cited in an inventory of 1598: a compässl and a string of precious stones.*

216. Automaton, c. 1560-1570. Silver, gold, enamel, rubies, diamonds, emeralds, pearls, and ebony; height 5 ⅝" (14.2 cm), length 7 ¹¹/₁₆" (19.5 cm). Schatzkammer, Munich. A rare "conversation piece" of an amusing sort once typical of Kunstkammer collections, the silver and enamel mountain is flanked by trees and surmounted by a music-reading mechanical monkey with an audience composed of a stag, a hind, and a roe. The drawers in the base contain three animal "calls" or whistles.

217. Wenzel Jamnitzer. Silver bell, c. 1560-1570 (Nuremberg). Silver; height 5 ⅛" (13 cm). Schatzkammer, Munich. One of the foremost examples of Jamnitzer's stil or style rustique (see also figs. 43, 134), this little bell swarms with nature - lizards, snails, frogs, snakes, etc. - cast from dead specimens. The arms of Bavaria and Lorraine, for Duke Maximilian I and his wife Elizabeth, were added later. The bell first appears in the Munich Kammergalerie inventory of 1635.

216

time is a magnificent rock-crystal and silver-gilt charger from the hands of Valerio Belli of Vicenza (fig. 199). The presence of Pope Leo X's arms suggests that the work may have been a gift to Duke Wilhelm IV.

Remarkably enough, the original Kunstkammer in Munich was open to both scholars and distinguished visitors. By the 17th century, however, many of the finest pieces had wandered from the Kunstkammer into the Kammergalerie, the exclusive museum assembled for the sovereign's own private "recreation." The Kunstkammer, thus degraded to a secondary status, had entered upon its long decline, a process exacerbated by the Thirty Years War, which caused Munich, a Catholic stronghold, to be invaded twice by marauding Protestant armies. The turmoil cost the Kunstkammer two of its most important collections: the coral mountains and the *lapides manuales*. Fortunately, the objects in both the Kammergalerie and the Reichekapelle, as well as the Wittelsbach family treasure, had been secured far from harm's way.

In 1651 the long reign of Elector Maximilian I, a great collector of fine paintings, notably those of Dürer and Rubens, came to an end, after which the contents of the Kammergalerie were moved into the Schatzkammer. Almost a century later, Elector Karl Albrecht had the great Rococo architect François

217

Cuvilliés create a mirror-lined room in the Munich Residenz, a project very likely inspired by similar "cabinets" at Versailles. It became a venue for choice works from the Kammergalerie The Schatzkammer would receive a number of exceptional works after 1777, when the Palatine branch of the Wittelsbach family succeeded to the Bavarian throne. Elector Karl Theodor von Pfalz-Zweibrücken, the first in this line of succession, was also heir to the treasury of the Palatinate, which in part harked back to the Kunstkammer of Ottheinrich von der Pfalz at Heidelberg, a cousin of Duke Albrecht V.

The Palatine accumulation had been augmented by treasures from the Pfalz-Neuburg branch as well as from its scion, Elector Johann Wilhelm (d. 1716), husband of the childless Anna Maria Ludovica de' Medici, whose death in 1743 in Florence had brought an end to Tuscany's first grand-ducal dynasty (see Chapter 4). More than one object from the court of Johann Wilhelm and Anna Maria Ludovica at Düsseldorf would later enter the collections in Munich. The most important of these works may be the so-called "Holbein Cup," a 14th-century rock-crystal vessel with a jeweled and enameled cover based on a design by Hans Holbein the Younger.[34] This object, which once belonged to Henry VIII, had formed part of the Royal Treasury in London's Jewel Tower until 1649, the year in which the Commonwealth government, following the execution of King Charles I, began selling off the royal collections. Two other exceptional pieces can be identified in an inventory prepared for the Mannheim court in 1730: a jeweled gold cup made for Janusz Radziwill, Duke of Sluzk, possibly in Nuremberg around 1600[35]; and a silver-gilt ewer and basin studded with turquoises, the set created by an anonymous Augsburg goldsmith in the years 1570-1580.[36] In 1770, as part of the

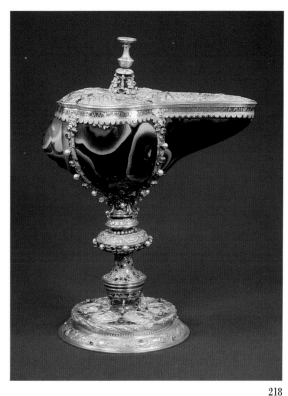

218

Pfalz-Neuburg patrimony, the Munich Schatzkammer gained a gold-mounted agate cup designed in 1536 by the Nuremberg master Melchior Baier the Elder for Margrave Georg zu Brandenburg-Kulmbach (fig. 218).

By this time the Kunstkammer had been stripped of its finest works of art and relegated to the status of a *garde-meuble*, a storage hall for furniture and textiles. To make room for the Royal Mint, which took over the building in 1807, after Napoleon made Bavaria a kingdom, the remaining parts of the collection were reassigned variously, to the Schatzkammer, the Alte Pinakothek, the Bayerisches National-museum, and other local institutions.

218. *Melchior Baier the Elder. Agate cup, 1536 (Nuremberg). Agate, gold, enamel, diamonds, rubies, and pearls; height 12" (30.5 cm). Schatzkammer, Munich. Baier was the leading Nuremberg goldsmith during the second quarter of the 16th century. His snail-shaped cup, splendidly jeweled and mounted in gold, was commissioned by Margrave Georg zu Brandenburg-Kulmbach in 1536. Listed in the 1770 inventory of Duke Clemenz von Bayern in 1770, who presumably had inherited it from his grandmother, Anna Maria, wife of Philipp Wilhelm, Count Palatine of Neuburg.*

219. *Rock-crystal basin, c. 1600 (Milan). Rock crystal, gold, enamel, silver-gilt, rubies, and diamonds; diameter 19 3/4" (50.1 cm). Schatzkammer, Munich. This basin, presumably a late product of the Milanese lapidary workshops, first appears, with its ewer, in a 1711 inventory of the Electors Palatine in Düsseldorf, after which it passed in 1782 into the Munich branch of the family. The vessel is engraved with the Polish royal arms and the initials SR for Sigismund III Rex, King of Poland from 1587 until 1632. In 1592 Sigismund Vasa married Anna, daughter of Archduke Charles of Styria and then, in 1605, her sister Constanze. The daughter of this second royal alliance married Philipp Wilhelm, Count Palatine of Neuburg.*

219

X

The Electors of Saxony

hen the smoke finally cleared in February 1945, following the firestorm set off by wave after wave of Allied bomber raids, the exquisite Baroque/Rococo city of Dresden on the River Elbe had been smashed to bits and its population, swollen with refugees from the East, reduced by some 135,000 dead. Among the few structures solid enough to survive this devastating assault were the so-called "Green Vaults," built deep inside the old Renaissance castle by the Elector Augustus of Saxony (r. 1553-1586) as a secure place in which to house his Treasury. Originally, the *Geheime Verwahrung* ("State Storage Vault"), with its green decorative details, contained state documents, unminted bullion, minted coins, jewels, and objects of value. Established in 1560, it marked the beginning of the Dresden Kunstkammer, which very quickly evolved into a kind of universal museum, with constituent collections made up not only of art works but also of objects more technical, scientific, historical, or merely decorative in nature. Thanks to the dedication of the Wettin dynasty, which ruled Saxony from the mid-14th century to the end of the German monarchies in 1918, Dresden's universal museum would continually expand until, by the mid-18th century, it had become the most comprehensive and distinguished galaxy of specialized museums in Central Europe. This steadiness of purpose, as rock-solid as the tough old storage site, saved the day even in 1945, when the collections survived, in caves and other havens beyond harm's way, even though the elegant buildings designed to shelter them succumbed to the horrors of war. The oldest and some of the most fascinating and beautiful items in the

Dresden hoard are those associated with the princely *Kunst- und Schatzkammer* – the works of goldsmiths, medalists, lapidaries, clockmakers, armorers, gunsmiths, and ceramists employed by the Saxon court. This was a court, moreover, that could supply its workshops from the rich lodes of silver, tin, copper, iron, and semiprecious stones available in the mountains of southern Saxony.

The Duchy of Saxony, one of the five basic or "stem" duchies of medieval Germany, came into being in the late 9th century. Extending from the Elbe in the east to the Rhine in the west and from Holstein in the north to Franconia and Thuringia in the south, it constituted a much larger state than the Saxony known since the Renaissance, which nonetheless encompasses the important cities of Dresden, Leipzig, Meissen, Magdeburg, and Wittenberg, all located in east-central Germany near Poland and Bohemia. Political power arrived after Duke Heinrich I (Henry the Fowler) was elected King of the Germans in 919, a rise in the world that could only increase once Heinrich's son Otto established the Holy Roman Empire. Thus began the justly celebrated Ottonian dynasty, which would retain the Imperial crown until the death of Heinrich II in 1024. A struggle between Duke Heinrich der Löwe (Henry the Lion) and Emperor Friedrich I caused the vast Saxon duchy to be broken up into numerous small fiefdoms, with the ducal title going to Bernhard von Anhalt, the founder of the Ascanian line of Saxon dukes, who received, in addition, Lauenburg and the country around Wittenberg. Come the Golden Bull of 1356, the Duke of Saxe-Wittenberg would be elevated to the permanent rank of Elector,

220. *Balthasar Permoser, Johann Melchior Dinglinger, and Martin Schnell. "Blackamoor" with Emerald Lode, c. 1724 (Dresden). Pearwood, silver-gilt, emerald lode, emeralds, rubies, sapphires, topaz, garnets, and tortoiseshell; height 25 ⅛" (63.8 cm). Grünes Gewölbe, Dresden. Arguably the most famous work in the Green Vaults, this exotic statuette was created for Augustus the Strong by two of the most gifted artists in his service: the sculptor Permoser and the jeweler/goldsmith Dinglinger. A final, gleaming touch was provided by the lacquerer Martin Schnell. In 1581 Emperor Rudolf II presented Elector Augustus, founder of the Dresden Kunstkammer, with a rare mineral specimen from Colombia comprising sixteen emerald crystals, of which only five large and five small stones survive. Early in the 18th century, Augustus the Strong had his premier artists combine the New World naturalia into a stunning Old World artefacta. The figure, despite its title, is not the conventional Rococo "blackamoor" but rather a Florida Indian, based on a contemporary print.*

221. *Olifant, 11th/12th century (Sicily). Ivory; 18 ¾" (47.5 cm). Rüstkammer, Dresden. Ivory horns found a place in numerous Kunstkammern, many of them from sources in Saracen Sicily. A similar horn, once owned by the Habsburgs, was seen earlier in fig. 99.*

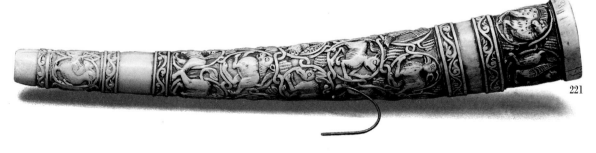

221

222

223

222. *Zacharias Wehme. Elector Augustus,
1586 (Dresden). Oil on canvas; 48 x
37" (122 x 94 cm). Rüstkammer,
Dresden. In this posthumous portrait,
the Elector, who died at the age of 60 in
1586, is presented as a sturdy man,
clad in his favorite suit of armor and
armed with his sword of office.
"Father" Augustus won the affection of
his subjects by dedicating himself less to
war than to economic development, a
fact apparent even in the way he went
about giving the Wettins their first
great collector. More than a princely
hoard, the Dresden Kunstkammer
founded by Augustus became a museum
of science and art, designed for the
improvement of his sons, his people,
and the Saxon state.*

presiding over a Saxony enlarged to include the Margraviate of Meissen, long ruled by the increasingly powerful House of Wettin. In 1425 Margrave Friedrich the Warlike emerged as Elector Friedrich I of Saxony, only for his lands to be partitioned in 1485 between the two sons of Elector Friedrich II: Ernst, founder of the Ernestine branch of Wettin, who gained electoral Saxony, with Wittenberg and most of the Thuringian lands; and Albert or Albrecht, founder of the Albertine branch, who accepted ducal rank and the Meissen territories, including Dresden and Leipzig.

When the Augustinian friar Martin Luther, a professor of theology at Wittenberg University, posted his 95 theses to the door of the chapel at Wittenberg Castle, he found a staunch if self-interested ally in Elector Friedrich III, the chief beneficiary of the Church properties whose seizure the Reformation sanctioned. The next Elector, Johann Friedrich I, even became a leader of the Schmalkaldic League, formed by Germany's Protestant princes to defend the Reformation against the campaign by Emperor Charles V to restore traditional Catholicism. At the Battle of Mühlberg (1547), however, the League suffered defeat, just as Johann Friedrich did a year later, when the victorious Emperor forced him to relinquish his electorate to Duke Moritz of Saxony, an Albertine Wettin, whose descendants would hold the electoral title until the dissolution of the Holy Roman Empire in 1808.

In the meantime, prosperous Saxony, a veritable crossroads of European history, culture, and commerce, had begun to exploit its silver mines and nurture craftsmen skilled in the techniques needed to create sacred objects endowed with a wealth of decorative detail. There survives, for example, a printed inventory of 1509 listing the 117 reliquaries housed in the chapel of Wittenberg Castle, where they had been assembled by Elector Friedrich the Wise around 1500. Published with illustrations by none other than Lucas Cranach the Elder, the inventory bears witness to a lost treasure, for the chapel door was the very one to which Luther nailed his theses in 1517. By calling for reform, Luther triggered a wave of Protestant iconoclasm, which very quickly destroyed much of Germany's rich patrimony of carved and painted altarpieces, stained-glass windows, stone-carved statuary, decorative reliefs, and all manner of holy objects made of gems and precious metals. Moreover, it halted the production of such works within those lands converted to the puritanical values of the avenging Luther. By the same token, however, Lutheranism helped advance the cause of secular art, already in the ascendancy as a consequence of the Humanistic Renaissance then being imported across the Alps from Italy.

Elector Augustus (1526-1586)

Saxony, with its natural resources and developed industries, could well afford the great quantities of plate stashed away in a *Silberkammer* ("Silver Vault") known to have existed as early as 1469 in Dresden's ducal palace. By 1530 the treasure would be estimated at a value of 128,393 *Guldengroschen*, and some of the older Kunstkammer items now on display in Dresden are believed to have survived from that hoard, despite the mischief wrought by the Reformation. Twenty years later, Duke Moritz, now Elector (r. 1547-1553), decided to mark his recent accession by transforming the castle in Dresden into an imposing Renaissance *Schloss*, a structure that remains the core of the present Residenz. It was on the ground floor of what today is the west wing of the castle that his brother and successor, Elector Augustus, had the Geheime Verwahrung installed, its four vaulted chambers protected by thick walls and by iron doors and windows reinforced with strong bars and shutters. So that one of the rooms could serve for official functions, it was lavishly furnished and decorated with stuccoes and architectural details picked out in green, the eponymous source of the term *Grünes Gewölbe* or "Green Vaults," which came into usage as early as 1572. The fire- and theft-proof cells lay directly below the Elector's own apartments, to which they were connected by a spiral staircase.

Augustus, a ruler less interested in war than in economic development, won the gratitude of his people, who affectionately dubbed him "Father Augustus" (figs. 222, 223). Zacharias Wehme portrayed him as the kindly ruler he was, an image reinforced in life by the Elector's wife, Princess Anna of Denmark, a herblorist known for her kindness towards the sick. By reason of his policy, Augustus was also the first serious collector among the Wettins, eagerly assembling his universal museum of arts and sciences as a means of educating his sons and his subjects for the economic betterment of the state. In the Germany of this period, the Kunstkammer of Elector Augustus constituted a major innovation, as well as an institution of high prestige, a fact witnessed by a guest book full of princely signatures.

The visiting dignitaries would have been especially taken with the *Rüstkammer*, or "Armory," which, despite serious losses, remains one of the leading collections in Europe. In addition to the magnificent parade, tournament, and battle armor made for the electoral family, the collection included exotic Turkish equipment as well as items presented to the Wettins by Archduke Ferdinand II of Tyrol, Duke

Albrecht V of Bavaria, and Emperors Maximilian II and Matthias. In 1560, Augustus integrated parts of the old Silver Vault and the Green Vaults to establish the Kunstkammer, housed in seven rooms in the west wing under the eaves of the castle.[1]

An inventory of 1587, drawn up following the Elector's death, contains 9,586 entries, and even these do not account for a large group of engravings bound in volumes. Inevitably, the collections reflected the personal tastes and values of the founder, who, adhering to a medieval tradition, saw no reason to separate works of art from such objects as scientific models, historical, ethnographic, and geographic materials, and a shimmering array of 442 mechanically precise clocks, spheres, astrolabes, and automata. The nucleus of the Kunstkammer, in fact, consisted of a truly impressive assemblage of 7,353 tools and implements associated with Saxon

industry – mining, geodesy, hardstone carving, cabinetry, armaments, and glassmaking. Since the collection over all was practical as well as didactic in purpose, the tools and instruments could be checked out by the craftsman in the Elector's service. Moreover, Augustus himself, as well as his sons, frequently took a place at the work benches and strove to develop his skills, especially ivory turning. Also represented in the Kunstkammer were the fields of anatomy and medicine, geometry and mathematics, writing and printing, hunting and fishing, often explained in a supplementary collection of illustrated scholarly books. Indeed, the Elector's library, with its beautiful bindings designed by the best artists available to the court, was one of the most important of the time.

The paintings and watercolors were remarkable primarily for their number, some ninety in all, most of them portraits, hunting scenes, and views of

223. *Jörg Seusenhofer.* Suit of armor made for Elector Augustus, *before 1588 (Innsbruck). Iron; weight 30.5 kg. Horse armor, c. 1515 (Italy). Iron; weight 33.6 kg. Rüstkammer, Dresden. The suit, made by one of the most celebrated armorers in 16th-century Europe, was a bespoke gift to Elector Augustus from his good friend, Archduke Ferdinand II of Tyrol, one of the period's greatest collectors. The horse armor was a wedding present to Giuliano de' Medici, Duc de Nemours, at the time of his marriage in 1515 to Philiberte de Savoie.*

224. Unicorn, *before 1587 (Augsburg). Brass (Gelbguss); height 14 ⅞" (37.8 cm). Grünes Gewölbe, Dresden. This little sculpture is listed in the first inventory of the Dresden Kunstkammer, made in 1595, as having been purchased from one Hans Reisiner of Augsburg before 1587. Also acquired at an early date were a number of bronzes by Giambologna, presented by Grand Duke Francesco I to Prince Christian I at the time of his nomination as co-regent of Saxony.*

224

225. Cup of Queen Jadwiga of Poland, *mid-14th century (France), mounts late 14th century (Krakow). Rock crystal, silver-gilt, and enamel; height 9 1/2" (24 cm). Grünes Gewölbe, Dresden. A black-enamel inscription declares his cup to have been a present from an unnamed bishop to Queen Jadwiga of Poland (r. 1382-1399). Jadwiga, the youngest daughter of King Lajos the Great of Hungary, had married Grand Duke Vladislav Jagiello of Lithuania and Poland in 1386. The cover is probably a later addition.*

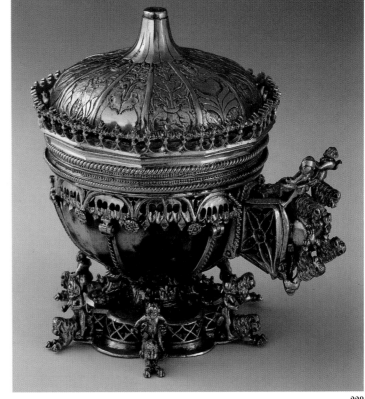

228

226. Duodecagonal cup, *mid-14th century (France). Rock crystal, silver-gilt, and enamel; height 6 11/16" (17 cm). Grünes Gewölbe, Dresden.*

227. Three buffalo-horn cups, *late 14th/early 15th century (Germany). Buffalo horn and silver-gilt; height (left to right) 13 3/8", 8 7/8", and 11 7/16" (34, 22.5, and 29 cm). Grünes Gewölbe, Dresden. These Late Gothic drinking vessels entered the Dresden Kunstkammer at a very early date. They figure among a group of eight items in the collection known as Greifenklauen ("griffin claws").*

228. Amethyst cup, *late 15th century (Burgundy). Amethyst and silver-gilt; height 5 1/2" (14 cm). Grünes Gewölbe, Dresden.*

229. Two Syrian glass beakers, *c. 1300 (Syria), mounts early 15th century (Germany). Glass, enamel, and silver-gilt; height 13 3/8" (34 cm), 10 5/8" (27 cm). Grünes Gewölbe, Dresden.*

229

230. *Andreas Riehl the Younger. Elector Christian I, c. 1590 (Dresden). Oil on canvas; 26 11/16 x 21 1/4" (67.7 x 54 cm). Historisches Museum, Dresden. Elector Christian I reigned only five years, but he left his mark, mainly through an overweening love of pomp and luxury. Characteristic were the two silver suits of armor he ordered in 1591, not to mention the twelve identical suits delivered by the leading armorer Anton Pfeffenhauser at the behest of the Electress, Sophia von Brandenburg.*

231. *Abraham Jamnitzer. Daphne, late 16th century (Nuremberg). Silver parcel-gilt and red coral; height 26 3/4" (68 cm). Grünes Gewölbe, Dresden. Abraham Jamnitzer, one of the three sons of the celebrated Wenzel, made this unusually large Daphne from a mold earlier employed by the senior Jamnitzer for an almost identical figure now in Paris. Obsessed with metamorphosis, the Mannerist period often turned to Ovid's* Metamorphoses, *as here, in the legend of the chaste nymph whose prayers for deliverance from the amorous god Apollo were answered when she turned into a laurel tree, represented by a brilliant, ramified branch of coral.*

fortresses. They did include, however, a series of small landscapes by the Dutch painter Hans Bol. Among the *naturalia*, pride of place went to the famous emerald lode from Colombia, presented to the Elector by Emperor Rudolf II in 1581 and later mounted by Dinglinger and Permoser, who transformed it into one of the most celebrated works of the Dresden Baroque (fig. 220). The collection also had its obligatory bronzes by Giovanni da Bologna, a gift from Grand Duke Francesco I de' Medici to the Elector's son, Christian, at the time of his nomination as co-regent of Saxony. Alongside these works stood an Augsburg unicorn cast in brass (fig. 224). The Dresden Kunstkammer could even accommodate a luxurious backgammon set, each of its thirty stones overlaid with a portrait bust modeled in wax.[2]

Elector Augustus and his successors collected objects in semiprecious stones mounted in silver and gold, but apparently kept them in the safety of the old Green Vaults rather than in the Kunstkammer. An inventory made in 1587 cites six cupboards filled with specimens of mineral ore, gold and silver caskets, works in amber, and sixty vessels in rock crystal. What survives from this early group of objects forms one of the core elements of the present Saxon royal collections.

231

Today the Dresden Green Vaults, albeit diminished in numbers from the zenith attained during the reign of Elector Augustus, are breathtaking for both their quality and their size, the catalogue running to more than 3,000 works of art or craft. Among the earliest pieces are a rock-crystal cup in a Gothic silver-gilt mount inscribed with the name of 14th-century Poland's Queen Jadwiga (fig. 225); a duodecagonal vessel carved from rock crystal, also dated to the 14th century and probably French in origin (fig. 226); a late-15th-century amethystine quartz cup and cover with mounts thought to be of Burgundian manufacture (fig. 228); two rare 13th-century Syrian glass beakers with bright enameling and an early-15th-century German mount (fig. 229); and a group of equally rare buffalo horns with Gothic silver-gilt mounts dating from around 1400 (fig. 227). There is no record of how these medieval objects came into the possession of the Saxon royal family, although they could have been there since at the least the time of Friedrich the Wise.

While other rulers frequently found themselves obliged to melt down or sell their treasures, the early Wettins, who enjoyed steady revenues from the mining industry, could afford to retain their cache of silver and gold. The Dresden Kunstkammer is therefore rich in silver works from Nuremberg, whose silversmiths outranked all others during the 16th century. An elegant casket for writing implements dated 1562 was made by the renowned Wenzel Jamnitzer and very likely for Elector Augustus, whom the artist knew personally. The crowning figure personifies Philosophy, seated upon a simulated rockwork base crawling with small animals cast from nature. Many of the pieces in precious metal joined the collections during the reigns of Electors Christian I (1586-1591; fig. 230) and Christian II (1591-1611). The former, Augustus's son, acquired, as a Christmas present for his wife Sofia, a large and lavish jewel casket designed by Jamnitzer and executed by Nikolaus Schmidt, who specialized in works encrusted with mother-of-pearl (fig. 232). The piece entered the Kunstkammer in 1589. It would be followed by another work from the hands of Schmidt, this time a particularly elaborate Mannerist ewer fashioned from a turbo shell matched to a basin inlaid with mother-of-pearl (fig. 235). Another instance of Nuremberg originality and brilliant craftsmanship is a silver-gilt group by Christoph Lindenberger representing the Devil clad in a barrel as he pushes a glutton in a wheelbarrow (fig. 234).

Elias Lencker, another Nuremberg master, crafted the 1577 Crucifixion or Calvary encrusted with shells, monstrous pearls, and jewels, producing a work reminiscent of objects owned by Archduke Ferdinand of Tyrol (fig. 236). Abraham Jamnitzer

232

233

232. *Wenzel Jamnitzer and Nikolaus
    Schmidt. Jewel casket, c. 1585
    (Nuremberg). Wood, silver parcel-gilt,
    mother-of-pearl, velvet, silk, glass, and
    precious stones; 19 ³/₄ x 21 ¹/₄ x 14 ³/₁₆"
    (50 x 54 x 36 cm). Grünes Gewölbe,
    Dresden. Evidently begun by Jamnitzer,
    whose presence can be felt not only in
    the creatures cast from nature but also
    in the quality of the niched figures, the
    casket may have been finished by
    Schmidt, who would have added the
    mother-off-pearl inlay. The topmost
    figure reclining in a garden of crystals
    originally pointed the staff towards a
    clock at her side. The whole radiates
    color, thanks to cold enamel used on the
    figures, set forth against a background
    of glass, velvet, or silk. The casket was
    a Christmas present from Elector
    Christian I to his wife Sophia, who in
    turn left it to the Kunstkammer.*

233. Jewel casket of Elector Christian I, *c.*
    1590 (Nuremberg?). Wood and silver
    parcel-gilt; 16 ¹/₂ x 19 ¹/₄ x 14 ¹/₈" (42 x
    49 x 36 cm). Grünes Gewölbe, Dresden.
    In an age eager to overpower by some
    means other than armed conflict,
    sovereigns such as the Electors of
    Saxony required impressive jewels, as
    well as regalia, and thus places in
    which to store their accumulations of
    cameos, necklaces, collars, diadems,
    badges, and brooches. The caskets in
    turn had to be as beautifully made as
    their contents, all which made them
    ready candidates for the Kunstkammer
    once the Elector or Electress had
    moved on to still more glittering
    containers.

234

234. *Christoph Lindenberger. Devil and
Drunkard, 2nd half 16th century
(Nuremberg). Silver-gilt; height: 7 ½"
(19 cm). Grünes Gewölbe, Dresden.
This Trinkspiel, a typical conversation
piece, pokes fun at the alcoholism and
gluttony of the period. The Devil, clad
in a barrel, masquerades as a cook,
who drives a wheelbarrow laden with
an obese drunkard, while various
inscriptions warn about the dangers of
excess.*

235. *Nikolaus Schmidt. Ewer and basin,
c. 1600 (Nuremberg). Turbo shell,
trochus shells, mother-of-pearl, and
silver-gilt; height of ewer 16 ⅛" (41 cm),
diameter of basin 22" (56 cm). Grünes
Gewölbe, Dresden. As seen in fig. 232,
Schmidt, a pupil of Wenzel Jamnitzer,
had a special gift for shells and mother-
of-pearl, as well as for casts of*

*creatures made from nature. In the
present instance the model appears to
have been the Jamnitzer masterpiece in
the Wittelsbach collection (fig. 194).*

236. *Elias Lencker. Calvary, 1577
(Nuremberg). Silver-gilt, wood, shells,
pearls, emeralds, turquoises, garnets;
height 26 ⅜" (67 cm). Grünes Gewölbe,
Dresden. As the image suggests,
Lencker may have been a Catholic in
Lutheran Nuremberg, where he excelled
at translucent champlevé enamel, a
technique acquired during several years
of service in France. The reptiles, ferns,
and flowers cast from nature may have
been inspired by Wenzel Jamnitzer.
Stylistically, this Calvary bears
comparison with a work at Schloss
Ambras (fig. 140). Lencker's best-known
creation is the writing cabinet in
Munich (fig. 197).*

235

worked from an earlier model by his father, Wenzel, to create the breathtakingly beautiful parcel-gilt figure of Daphne metamorphozing into a tree of ramified red coral (fig. 231). In the realm of fine silversmithery, Nuremberg had a would-be competitor in the prosperous Hanseatic city of Luneburg, where, in 1587, Christian II obtained from Dirich Utermarke a monumental mirror featuring a chased allegory of Good and Bad Government (fig. 237), this too a gift for Electress Sofia. With its profusion of figures and ornament, Utermarke's mirror constitutes one of the finest pieces of German Mannerist silver in existence.

Given the eclecticism of the Saxon collections, it can scarcely surprise to find in the 16th-century Green Vaults such Kunstkammer works as a cherry pit carved with countless tiny faces and mounted in 1589 (fig. 238). It belongs to a group of micro-carvings, a genre of *mirabilia* much prized at the time. An enameled-copper basin by the 16th-century Limoges master Martial Courteys or Courtois (fig. 239) was added to the collection in the 18th century by Elector Augustus the Strong. This monarch acquired as well the magnificent Muscovite kovsh made of gem-studded gold and dated 1563 (fig. 241). It came from the collection of Ivan the Terrible courtesy of Peter the Great, the father of modern Russia.

The Wettins' group of hardstone carvings ranks among the largest and the best, particularly the formidable array of 16th-century rock-crystal vases derived mainly from the Milanese workshops of the Saracchi. The models are the same as those used for comparable works found in princely collections everywhere, from Florence, Paris, and Madrid to Munich and Vienna. Among the later works, however, is an original rock-crystal jug from post-Rudolfine Prague; made by Dionysio Miseroni, it stands out by virtue of its exuberant dragon-shaped mount embellished with gems.[3]

As for the future direction of the Saxon collection, a straw in the wind appeared in 1587 when Christian I received a "memoir" from Gabriel Kaltermarckt, a widely traveled artist, suggesting that the Elector build a Kunstkammer similar to the one assembled by the Medici, who had "achieved princely, yea, almost royal status, through their patronage of the Arts." For the sake of concentrating on works of art, Kaltermarkt advised the removal of "instruments for

238

239

237. *Dirich Utermarke. Mirror, 1587-1592 (Lüneburg). Silver-gilt, wood, glass, rock crystal, and amethyst; height 45 1/4" (115 cm). Grünes Gewölbe, Dresden. Elector Christian I ordered this grandiose mirror from Luleff Meier, a retailer in the Hanseatic city of Lüneburg, who had it executed by one of the leading goldsmiths of the 16th century. The iconography about the elaborate frame, taken from the Book of Daniel, narrates the dream of King Nebuchadnezer in which the end of the four great empires - Assyria, Persia, Greece, and Rome - is announced, to make way, as told here, for the Holy Roman Empire.*

238. *Micro-carved cherry pit, before 1589 (Germany). Cherry pit, gold, enamel, and pearl; height 1 3/4" (4.5 cm). Grünes Gewölbe, Dresden. This kind of Kunststück, with its host of minuscule heads, was an essential curiosity in every major Kunstkammer.*

239. *Martial and Jean Courteys. Ewer and basin, c. 1580 (Limoges). Copper and enamel; length of basin 21 5/8", height of ewer 11" (28 cm). Grünes Gewölbe, Dresden. The Green Vaults own thirty Limoges enamels, making the collection one of the largest outside France. The scene painted on the basin involves the Whore of Babylon cited in the Apocalypse of Saint John. The ewer, meanwhile, features the Triumph of Diana.*

240

music, astronomy, geometry, and the tools for the analysis of materials, for goldsmiths, sculptors, cabinet-makers, turners, surgeons and others... because they are not works [of art], but mere instruments and tools, to produce different works."[4] Not only would the Renaissance Prince thus achieve fame; he would also establish a moral example for himself as well as a source of studies for his people, for the "art-thirsty" young.

After the turn of the 17th century, when the ateliers of Nuremberg and Luneburg failed to keep up with stylistic changes, Elector Johann Georg I (r. 1611-1656) commissioned important silver articles from Augsburg in Bavaria as well as from Dresden and Leipzig in Saxony itself. The little-known Augsburg silversmith Elias Lencker is the author of two large clockwork cups and covers shaped as Hercules and Atlas respectively holding aloft a terrestrial and a celestial globe. In 1629 the visiting Philipp Hainhofer described them as follows: "Two fine globes which are carried by Hercules and Atlas, which move forward on a table, and can be used as drinking vessels" (fig. 240).[5] In Dresden, Daniel Kellerthaler, who emerged as the leading silversmith of this production center, received the colossal sum of 2,700 guilders for a contorted Mannerist ewer and basin made of silver-gilt and dated 1629.[6]

Dresden's proximity to the North Sea helps explain the number of amber works present in the Saxon Kunstkammer. Two early 17th-century tankards with amber panels have jeweled mounts fashioned in Königsberg (fig. 243). A treatment of the Three Graces, carved in amber, bears the signature of Christoph Maucher, an artist also known for his ivory carvings (fig. 244).

Ivory, in fact, figures large in the Green Vaults, which contain over 200 works crafted from this material, making the collection the finest of its kind.[7] Ivory turning was long considered a pastime noble enough to be taken up even by princes.[8] Among the Wittelsbachs, Wilhelm IV, Albrecht V, and Wilhelm V all indulged their passion for working with ivory. Blue bloods encouraged one another in the craft through mutual lending of ivory turners and by exchanging their finished products. Georg Wecker, professional ivory carver from Munich, settled in Dresden in 1578 and taught his craft to Elector Augustus, who, according to a posthumous inventory, turned at least 165 articles, only one of which survives. In 1599 Wecker was summoned to Prague to teach his art to Emperor Rudolf, notorious for spending unconscionable hours among his throng of court artists. Such was the Emperor's appetite for works in ivory that Elector Christian II sent no less than thirteen pieces to the Hradschin, where they were received with great delight. Rudolf's inventories list five ivories by Wecker alongside others turned by Elector Augustus. Hans Wecker, Georg's son, became *Kammerdrechsler* ("court turner") to both Rudolf II and his successor, Emperor Matthias, but then returned to Dresden in 1622. Elector Christian II learned the art of ivory turning from Egidius Lobenigk, who created many of the fine ivories in the Dresden Kunstkammer. In 1610 Christian II found his court turner in the Regensburg master Jakob Zeller, who then created for Johann Georg I the extraordinary ivory frigate seen here (fig. 245). In 1619 this Elector added to the Kunstkammer a further 23 objects by Zeller, at a cost of 2,300 guilders. The sheer virtuosity of the ivory carving done for the Wettins can be seen in a quartet of works still in the Green Vaults (fig. 246).

Philipp Hainhofer, quoted earlier, left a vivid description of the Dresden Kunstkammer as it was in 1629,[9] when eclecticism reigned, without discernible order, throughout six galleries preceded by an anteroom. The first gallery contained not only *naturalia*, such as crabs, snails, *Natterzungen* (fossilized sharks' teeth), and the molar of a "big man," but also paintings, porcelains, animals carved from coral, and busts of Roman emperors and Saxon princes. In gallery or room two were to be found lapidary works, *pietre dure* tables, hardstone vessels, automata, clocks, and yet more paintings and *naturalia*. The remaining rooms all but overflowed with tools, maps, more clocks and automata, works in gold or silver, turned-ivory objects, minerals, "horns of unicorns," and paintings by Lucas Cranach.

The Kunstkammer and the Treasury or Green Vaults remained separate entities until the late 17th century. For over a century and a half, the descendants of Elector Augustus had continued adding to the Wettin collections, gradually shifting, however, from the applied arts to the "high" art of painting. This process had already begun when Christian I acquired major works by Albrecht Dürer, not only the *Seven Sorrows of the Virgin* but also a group of almost 200 drawings and prints. His successor,

241

Christian II, assembled so many hardstone vessels that he found it expedient to display them in the Belvedere recently completed on the ramparts overlooking the Elbe. Then came the outbreak of the Thirty Years War (1618-1648), when Saxony found itself once again at the crossroads of European history, repeatedly invaded and occupied by opposing Protestant and Catholic forces. Not until the end of the 17th century did the electorate recover from the devastations, or the Wettin family bring fresh energy and purpose to their collecting.

Augustus the Strong (1670-1733)

Renewal began in 1694 with the accession of Elector Friedrich Augustus I, one of the most colorful personalities ever to occupy the electoral throne (fig. 242). History knows him better as Augustus the Strong, because of his legendary strength, or perhaps prowess, given the vast number of illegitimate children attributed to him. A true Prince of the Baroque era, Augustus reveled in hunting, theatre, festivities, and fireworks. He was also endowed with boundless political aspiration, first manifested in a determined quest for the elective throne of Poland, fallen vacant in 1697 at the death of King Jan III Sobieski. Augustus won, thanks to massive bribes, a last-minute conversion to Catholicism, and a contingent of Saxon troops. He also had enjoyed the support of Russia, which proved to be a devil's bargain, inasmuch as it antagonized Sweden and thus set off the Northern War, during which the Saxon forces fared badly. Faced with a new Swedish occupation of Saxony, Augustus gave up the Polish crown in 1706, only to recover it ten years later.

From this date until his death in 1733, there was no stopping Augustus the Strong (King Augustus II of Poland), empowered as he was by the economic upsurge flowing from the combination of Saxon industrial might and Poland's agrarian economy. Dresden soon evolved from its rather old-fashioned Renaissance aspect into the royal Baroque capital immortalized in the magically precise views painted at mid-century by the Venetian master Bernardo Bellotto (fig. 249). Leipzig, with its excellent university, burgeoning middle class, and liberalized censorship, emerged as an important center of the book trade, famous even today for the Leipzig Book Fair. Music flourished as well, particularly after Johann Sebastian Bach arrived in 1723 to take up the post of music director at Leipzig's Church of Saint Thomas.

Inspired by the splendors of Versailles, Augustus the Strong wanted not only to endow Dresden with requisite pomp and splendor; he also set out to trans-

242

243. *Georg Schreiber and circle (attrib). Two amber tankards, 1st quarter 17th century (Königsberg). Amber, silver-gilt, enamel pearls, gold, enamel, and diamonds; height 5 ¼" (13.4 cm) and 8 1/16" (20.5 cm). Grünes Gewölbe, Dresden. Königsberg and the neighboring Baltic city of Danzig, in Poland, were well-known centers of amber-carving in the 17th century. The Margraves, Electors, and Kings of Prussia often chose amber vessels as prestigious gifts for such distinguished peers as the Elector/Kings of Saxony.*

244. *Christoph Maucher. Three Graces, c. 1680 (Danzig). Amber; height (without base) 7 ½" (19 cm). Grünes Gewölbe, Dresden. Unlike ivory, amber, a fossilized resign in plentiful supply along the shores of the Baltic Sea, seldom lends itself to high-quality carving. Thus, it served mainly for functional objects and small pieces of furniture, except in rare instances, such as the celebrated Amber Room in the Catherine Palace at Tsarskoie Selo, whose ultimate fate, since World War II, remains a matter of conjecture.*

243

245. *Jacob Zeller. Ivory Frigate, 1620
(Dresden). Ivory and gold; height 45 1/4"
(115 cm). Grünes Gewölbe, Dresden.
Created by an ivory turner at the
Dresden court, this stunning sculpture is
inscribed with the name of every Saxon
ruler from Widukind to Johann Georg I,
whose arms appear on the main sail
together with those of his wife,
Magdalena Sybilla von Brandenburg.*

246. *Georg Friedel, Jacob Zeller, and others.
Four ivory carvings, early 17th century
(Dresden). Ivory; height (left to right)
22 7/8", 16 1/8", 23 5/8", and 19 11/16" (58,
41, 60, and 50 cm). Grünes Gewölbe,
Dresden. Bravura carvings like these
were known as Kunststücke ("showpiece
art works"), and every major
Kunstkammer boasted a large number of
them. The Green Vaults collection alone
counts 200 works in ivory, only a few of
which remain on view. The Renaissance
regarded ivory turning as a suitable
pastime for blue bloods, who gave
themselves to it with pride and gusto,
most of all the Wittelsbachs in Munich,
the Wettins of Saxony, and, of course,
Emperor Rudolf II in Prague. Jacob
Zeller turned the cup and cover on the
far right and Georg Friedel the daringly
intricate column next to it.*

245

247. *Matthäus Daniel Pöppelmann and Balthasar Permoser. The Zwinger, Dresden, 1709-1736. In 1723, the Rococo masterpiece known as the Zwinger, for its location between Dresden's electoral palace and the city ramparts, prompted the diplomat Johann Michael von Lön to write: "It is difficult to see something more beautiful and magnificent than the new Zwinger - or palace garden. This building would be perfect if it had been completed according to the plans of the King together with the new castle, that I have seen in the admirable plans of the architect Pöppelmann." Commissioned by Augustus the Strong as an orangerie but then utilized mainly as a festival arena, the Zwinger captivates through its harmonious marriage of architecture and sculpture - especially the airy intricacy of the lavish relief decorations gracing the pavilions which punctuate the arcaded arena at its cardinal points. The restless, ambitious Augustus never authorized the start of the new castle, even though it figured large in his scheme to compete for the crown of the Holy Roman Empire, now that the male line of the Habsburgs was about to die out. Instead, he rechanneled his energies into other palaces, Pillnitz and the Japanisches Palais, both on the Elbe. In due course, the Elector/King would use the Zwinger to house the Mathemathisch-Physiklaische Salon and other collections.*

form the capital into a cultural metropolis on a par with Paris, Vienna, and London. This demanded extravagant monuments, such as a lavish new Baroque palace to replace the Renaissance castle begun by Duke Moritz and finished by Elector Augustus in the 1560s. What actually came forth was something both less and more: the Zwinger, or "Outer Courtyard," a deliciously Rococo festival arena enclosed by low arcaded buildings and a punctuating series of tall pavilions, the latter arcaded as well, but open below, glazed above, and crowned with a lacy profusion of confectionery sculpture (fig. 247). Here, the architect Matthäus Daniel Pöppelmann and the Bavarian sculptor Balthasar Permoser accepted the Vitruvian rules so dear to Renaissance and Baroque architects, but then distended and contracted, dismantled and recombined them until Roman massiveness and decorum had given way to airy richness, intricacy, and grace, more like a Rococo interior or stage set than true architecture. Originally conceived as an *orangerie*, the Zwinger came brilliantly into its own in 1719 as the backdrop for celebrations marking the marriage of the Saxon Crown Prince, Friedrich Augustus, and Maria Josepha, the eldest daughter of Emperor Joseph I.

To prepare for the wedding, Augustus started acquiring large pieces of Augsburg silver at the Leipzig Easter Fair. In Augsburg itself, he commissioned a suite of silver furniture from members of the Biller family.[10] These "modern" pieces were then combined with the "old" ones from the Kunstkammer to create a splendid *Buffet* in the Hausmannsturm, the castle's new tower. The lavish display of plate filled an entire room from floor to

ceiling, an arrangement that became permanent when it was reassembled in two rooms in the Green Vaults (fig. 248).

Lacking a cultural administrator as effective as Louis XIV's Charles Le Brun, Augustus the Strong took it upon himself to urge his court artists to scale the heights of artistry and craftsmanship. He supervised their activity, discussed their projects, and took pride in their achievements. Moreover, his vision of Dresden as a great cultural center included a complete reorganization and consolidation of the existing collections, the program consistent with Cartesian or Age of Reason principles. To the Armory, the Royal Library, and the Coin Cabinet, he planned to add a painting gallery, a museum of antiquities, a *Kupferstich Kabinett* ("Graphic Arts Cabinet"), a porcelain collection, the Salon of Mathematics and Physics, and a museum of natural history. So vast was this campaign of renewal and expansion that it could be only partially realized during the lifetime of Augustus the Strong. Meanwhile, the avid and optimistic Elector collected everything imaginable – Netherlandish, German, and Italian paintings, Roman marble statues and Egyptian antiquities, Chinese and Japanese porcelains, Limoges enamels, German 15th-century prints, drawings and etchings by Rembrandt, clocks and scientific instruments, coins and medals, arms, gemstones, and Indian miniatures.

One of the great triumphs of the reign was the Meissen porcelain manufacture, an enterprise made possible by a deposit of kaolin found around 1708 in Saxony. Previously unknown in Europe, kaolin, or white china clay, happened to be the secret ingredient of the Chinese porcelain for which European roy-

248

249

alty had developed a passion, beginning in the mid-17th century. Discovering how to make hard-paste porcelain, with its special qualities of dense, translucent whiteness and bell-like resonance, had become a goal almost as pressing as the search for the philosopher's stone. Upon hearing that an alchemist who knew how "to make gold" was now in Saxony, as a refugee fleeing the disappointed and irate King of Prussia, Augustus the Strong ordered this miracle-worker confined to Meissen's Königstein fortress until he could make good on his boast. Instead of gold, however, Johann Friedrich Böttger reinvented Chinese porcelain, a product then worth its weight in precious metal. According to legend, the breakthrough arrived after Böttger became curious about the powder he was using for his wig. Be that as it may, the onetime alchemist did not turn the trick without the help of the Saxon mathematician/physicist Ehrenfried Walter von Tschirnhausen, whose experiments in burning mirrors and optics had given rise to the lucrative glassworks of Saxony. Even more profitable would be the Meissen porcelain potteries, which, until the mid-18th century, enjoyed a monopoly on the manufacture of hard-paste porcelain in Germany.

Credit for Meissen's success was also owing to a pair of remarkable sculptors, Johann Gottlob Kirchner and Johann Joachim Kändler, whose enchanting, naturalistically modeled animals – hundreds of them – Augustus the Strong enshrined on the upper floor of the Japanese Palace in Dresden, where he would also house his vast collection of Oriental porcelain. The venue, originally known as the Holländisches Palais, had been acquired by the court in 1717 and renamed *Japanisches Palais*. In that same year Augustus traded dragoon regiments for masses of Oriental porcelain kept by Friedrich

Wilhelm I of Prussia at Schloss Oranienburg north of Berlin. The collection had been installed in a mirror-lined "cabinet" or room, which would serve as a model for Augustus's ambitious refurbishment of the Green Vaults.

In 1721 Augustus the Strong began to concentrate his efforts on the Green Vaults Treasury, which he redecorated and then enlarged in two successive stages. For this he marshaled a team composed of his best architects, sculptors, modelers, cabinetmakers, and lacquerers, who cooperated to create a *Gesamtkunstwerk*, a total, all-embracing work of art. A phenomenon without precedent or parallel, the new Green Vaults are today regarded as the perfect expression of Dresden's "Augustan" Baroque – that is, German Rococo in its early phase. With visitors specifically in mind, the great Elector/King personally conceived and had designed a suite of rooms or galleries, each with its own identity. For the same reason, he set aside works from the Kunstkammer, the Treasury, the Silver Vaults, and his own private collections and had them installed in the specially prepared spaces. In this way the monarch created a unique and innovative museum of the decorative arts, the ultimate model for similar institutions established almost 150 years later.[11]

Work got under way during the summer of 1721, with the architect Pöppelmann in charge, and it would be essentially finished a year later. The four rooms of the original Green Vaults, situated in the northwest corner of the castle, were modernized and then furnished with mirrors, consoles, and tables. They became the setting for a selection of magnificent jewelry, fine plate, and objets d'art. A 1722 inventory, running to 141 pages, itemizes the jewelry consigned by the Elector, including parures set with emeralds, sapphires, rubies, diamonds, and cor-

250. *Matthäus Daniel Pöppelmann. The Green Vaults (Bronze Room, photographed before 1913), 1723-1724. Built in 1548, deep inside Dresden's new Renaissance castle, the fire- and theft-proof Geheime Verwahrung ("State Storage Vault") became known as the Grünes Gewölbe ("Green Vaults") after the Elector Augustus had one of its four vaulted chambers lavishly installed as a reception room with stuccoed decorations and architectural details picked out in green. For the next two centuries these chambers housed the Saxon state archives, the Electors' hoard of gold and silver, and some of their most precious jewels and objets d'art. Then, beginning in 1723, Augustus the Strong had Pöppelmann transform the old Green Vaults into a series of Rococo, mirror-lined venues for the display of works from the Kunstkammer, the Treasury, the Silver Vaults, and his own private collections. After a major reorganization and expansion launched in 1727, the Green Vaults emerged as the first modern museum, open not merely to the privileged few but to anyone who could pay a 1-ducat entrance fee.*

251. *Balthasar Permoser. Hercules and Omphale, c. 1700 (Dresden). Ivory; height 10 1/4" (26 cm). Grünes Gewölbe, Dresden. The Bavarian sculptor Permoser, encountered earlier at the Zwinger (fig. 247), may be even better known for his ivory groups and his figures in lacquered wood. In their elegance and refinement, these small sculptures anticipated the products of the Meissen porcelain manufacture, which they eventually influenced.*

250

nelians. A second, 273-page inventory, dated 1723, takes account only of white and gilded silver, a collection whose gleaming beauty required the full-time attention of a butler aided by eight servants, assistants, and silver washers. Finally, a third inventory, this one 300 pages long and dated 1725, lists an exceptional range of art works, among them complete services and *Kabinettstücke* (literally "cabinet pieces," meaning virtuoso productions) made of semiprecious stones, enamel, glass, or ivory, mounted shells and corals. When completed, the first version of the Grünes Gewölbe prompted Baron von Pöllnitz to describe them in 1727 as "three vaulted rooms which contain immense riches, [where] one sees but Gold, Precious Stones, and Diamonds everywhere. It is one of the most beautiful places on earth."[12]

In that very year, however, Augustus the Strong launched into a complete reorganization of the Green Vaults Treasury, his active engagement with the process registered in the many vigorous autograph amendments he made to an existing plan.[13] With a few strokes of the pen, the Elector added four new galleries, a reception room, a vestibule, and administration facilities, along with an itinerary for the visitor. Conceptually, at least, the first modern museum had been born. The architect in charge of executing the plan was again Pöppelmann, abetted by the court sculptor Benjamin Thomae, who was responsible for decorating the interiors. These would be clad in mirrors and fitted with tiers of consoles for the display of smaller art works, with large ones placed on tables aligned next to the walls. Three years later Thomae had finished most of the sculptural embellishments, his task shared by Christian Kirchner and the young Johann Joachim Kändler of later porcelain fame. Lacquered wall panels, by Martin Schnell and Christian Reinow, and floors of polychrome marble inlaid by local craftsmen completed the sensational scheme. Yet, however rich this environment, the rooms functioned perfectly as a setting for the innumerable treasures presented within them, enhanced by the stunning, even theatrical effect of multiplying mirror reflections.

Yet more revolutionary was the decision to make the collection available to the public, who could enter through the castle's inner courtyard. As a cautionary measure, however, the Elector had the original connecting staircase to his private apartments walled up. And to keep the riffraff at bay, he required that visitors obtain permission from the *Geheime Camerirer* ("Secret Chamberlain"), who then exacted a 1-ducat entrance fee.

An inventory reveals that the new Green Vaults contained almost twice as many works as the old rooms. Entry was through the vestibule, where sword and hat had to be left behind. On the north side of the vestibule lay a small room, of approximately 480 square feet, paneled in stained oak and filled with 103 bronzes standing on tables, on a shelf above the cornice, and against mirrors. The largest piece in the Bronze Room was an equestrian figure of Augustus the Strong modeled in the workshop of François Girardon, Louis XIV's court sculptor, from whom it had been commissioned in 1715, along with a group of other contemporary works (fig. 250).

On the west side of the Bronze Room was the Ivory Room, its walls decorated with brownish-purple *faux marbre* lacquered, incised, and polished by Reinow. Here the Elector had transferred from the Kunstkammer the Wettins' huge collection of turned-ivory vessels and figures, some 300 of which have survived, mostly from the late 16th and early 17th centuries. Thanks to Balthasar Permoser, already encountered at the Zwinger, ivory carving attained new peaks of brilliance in 18th-century Dresden. The gifted and prolific Permoser, appointed court sculptor in 1690, would remain active for over forty years. His signed group representing Hercules and Omphale (fig. 251), executed around 1700, had a profound and lasting effect on Meissen porcelain figurines.

After the Bronze Room came the *Emaillezimmer* ("Enamel Room"), a 950-square-foot gallery reserved for "white" or ungilded and "modern" silver. At the center rose a structural pier, which, like the surrounding walls, was faced with mirrors framed by gilded architectural panels. One contemporary visitor noted that "works in silver, piled up in pyramid shape, standing on tables and window seats in great profusion" filled the room all way to the ceiling.[14] Much of this treasure would be melted down in 1772, following the death of Augustus III in 1763, when the Wettin dynasty lost the Polish throne to the Russian candidate, Stanislaus Poniatowski.

After the Emaillezimmer came a gallery of identical shape and dimensions, the *Silberzimmer* ("Silver Room") crammed with works made of gold and silver-gilt (fig. 253). It differed, however, in décor, which consisted of mirrors surrounded by green-lac-

Overleaf:

252. *Johann Melchior, Georg Friedrich, and Georg Christoph Dinglinger. The Court of the Grand Moghul, 1701-1708 (Dresden). Gold, silver parcel-gilt, enamel, precious stones, pearls, lacquer, and wood; length 56" (142 cm), width 45" (114 cm). In this masterpiece among Kabinettstücke, Dinglinger, together with his two brothers, used 5,600 precious stones and pearls, as well as great quantities of gold and silver, to restage in miniature a ritual weighing of Shah Auranghzeb and the presentation of gifts on his birthday. The silver base is thronged with 132 figures surrounded by 32 presents, all which took the artist and his workshop eight years to complete, on speculation and at such expense that it took Augustus the Strong five years to pay the 58,475-thaler price.*

253. *Matthäus Daniel Pöppelmann. The Green Vaults (Silver Room, photographed in 1904), 1727. The Silver Room, which came after the Ivory Room, with its 200 ivories, and the Enamel Room, housing the Wettins' "white" or ungilded silver, served for the display of gold-plated silver, modern as well as antique, in a décor dominated by green-lacquer and mirror revetments.*

254. *Matthäus Daniel Pöppelmann. The Green Vaults (Valuables Room, photographed in 1904), 1727. The largest and most impressive room in Augustus the Strong's Green Vaults was the Pretiosenzimmer, its walls also mirror-clad and further embellished with masses of gilded detail. It contained a vast collection of hardstone vessels, Limoges enamels, silver animals, Schwarzenburger's colorful mantelpiece, and Dinglinger's Court of the Grand Moghul.*

253

254

quered paneling. The walls, moreover, bristled with 300 brackets bearing a multitude of silver-gilt vessels. It was here that Augustus the Strong exhibited most of the 16th- and 17th-century display pieces from Nuremberg, Augsburg, Leipzig, and Dresden.

At the core of the new Green Vaults was the *Pretiosenzimmer* ("Valuables Room"), actually the main room of the original Geheime Verwahrung, still intact with its 16th-century stuccoed vaults sprung from a trio of piers. Now, however, the walls had been decorated with inset mirrors and a profusion of carved and gilded detail (fig. 254). Hundreds of gilded brackets held the electoral family's vast collection of hardstone vessels, carved from rock crystal, onyx, jasper, agate, chalcedony, and lapis-lazuli and mounted in jewels and precious metals. Against one wall stood all the marvelous animal figures – lions, elephants, griffins, sea monsters – fashioned of silver, ostrich eggs, and nautilus shells. On the western wall of the Pretiosenzimmer, in a place of honor between two windows, glittered Johann Bernhard Schwarzeburger's mantelpiece of composite semi-precious stones. Its original location is visible in the old pre-1914 photograph seen in fig. 254.

Among the starring attractions in the Pretiosenzimmer were pieces created by the celebrated court goldsmith Johann Melchior Dinglinger (1664-1731),[15] a Swabian who worked with great success in the Mannerist tradition of Benvenuto Cellini and

Wenzel Jamnitzer but proved more fortunate in the number of his surviving creations (fig. 255). His elaborate enameled and bejeweled ornaments, often with an exotic *chinoiserie* theme, took the Saxon court by storm. However, they should perhaps be seen as co-productions with other members of the court "factory," which included Dinglinger's brothers as well as various Dresden jewelers, sculptors, and enamelers. Even Permoser carved ivory and wooden sculptures for incorporation in some of the larger productions.

Dinglinger's masterpiece, the glorious *Court of the Grand Moghul*, stood at one end of the Pretiosenzimmer under a gilt-wood canopy (fig. 252). For this characteristically exotic scene, the artist re-imagined the weighing of Shah Auranghzeb and the presentation of gifts on his birthday, staging it on a silver base measuring 142 by 114 centimeters. Here 132 gold figurines stand surrounded by 32 presents brought by the dignitaries of the Moghul Empire. The composition, set with 4,909 diamonds, 160 rubies, 164 emeralds, 1 sapphire, and 16 pearls, took eight years to realize, with Georg Friedrich and Georg Christoph Dinglinger applying both the gems and the enamels. Even Augustus the Strong needed five years in which to pay the 58,485 thalers asked for the witty, extravagant work. In a note to the Elector, Dinglinger wrote: "... without wishing to cover myself with any premature glory, I can state that such a work has never been executed by an artist and probably never will be, as few are capable [of it] and those who are, have neither the necessary money nor the time. This is the reason why no such work will be found in any other art cabinet of a great lord."[16] Dinglinger's *Kabinettstücke*, with their fantastic, often overladen look, represent the quintessence of Augustan *joie de vivre*.

Also in the Pretiosenzimmer was the only surviving treasure documented as having been in the original Kunstkammer: the Rudolfine emerald lode artfully mounted by Dinglinger and placed in the hands of a black "Indian" carved by Permoser (fig. 220). The two artists collaborated as well on several other known blackamoors, albeit smaller, jeweled ones (fig. 263). For Dinglinger's *Bad der Diana* or *Bath of Diana*, an exquisite piece completed in 1704, Permoser carved an ivory goddess seated on the rim of a chalcedony bowl filled with water spewed by a pair of dolphins (fig. 258). The vessel is held aloft upon the curving antlers of a stag's head under siege from two hounds. Cascades of rose-cut diamonds stream from the accessories surrounding this virtuoso piece, which cost 8,000 thalers. *The Labors of Hercules*, on which Dinglinger worked for over twenty years, comprises a jasper bowl dripping with cameos as well as diamonds and surmounted by the

255

Classical hero in contest with the Nemean lion (fig. 257). It symbolizes, of course, Augustus the Strong – the "Saxon Hercules" – whose enameled portrait can be seen on the back.

In the wake of the gifted Dinglinger, a number of other craftsmen labored to assuage the insatiable appetite of their royal patron for jewels and precious objects. Among these lesser artists was Johann Heinrich Köhler, whose major known work is a jeweled table clock which serves as a base for a staging of the Legend of Saint Hubert (fig. 259).

In a small cabinet in the northwest corner of the Pretiosenzimmer, Augustus placed his much-loved collection of jeweled miniature objets d'art – droll figures of dwarves, cooks, dancers, beggars, and craftsmen, many of them fashioned of baroque pearls. From a total of about one hundred pieces, forty survive, some of them made in Dresden, others acquired from jewelers in Berlin and Frankfurt. Two of the figurines – a jolly toper and a fiddle-playing cook dancing on a grill – were bought in Frankfurt from a Frenchman named William Ferbecq (fig. 256). Groups of similar statuettes exist in Florence and St. Petersburg, but there is nothing anywhere like Dresden's host of grotesque yet graceful and precious miniatures. Produced around 1720, they anticipated the carefree Rococo world of Kändler's Meissen sculptures.

The *Wappenzimmer* ("Device Room"), a dimly lit gallery featuring nothing more than stained-oak cupboards inlaid with 44 sets of gilt-copper armorial bearings, allowed visitors some relief from the inexorable crescendo of treasure building from room to room. This restful interlude arises in part from the failure to execute the life-size wax busts of Augustus the Strong, Friedrich Augustus II, and their spouses originally planned for the venue. In their place came lesser works added in subsequent times.

The tour of the Green Vaults culminated in the eighth and final gallery, the *Juwelenzimmer* (fig. 260). In this "Jewel Cabinet" were gathered the Wettin family's extraordinary hoard of gems, parures, and jeweled insignia, considered the finest collection of its

255. *J. G. Wolfgang, after Pesne. Johann Melchior Dinglinger, 1722. Engraving. The Swabian-born Dinglinger (1664-1731), shown here proudly displaying his* Bad der Diana *(Bath of Diana), served as court jeweler to Augustus the Strong in Dresden, where he produced works of great beauty, many of which survive. A century and a half later they would have a profound influence on Peter Carl Fabergé, whose family lived in Dresden.*

256. *The Merry Vintner and The Musical Cook, c. 1725 (Frankfurt). Pearls, gold, silver-gilt, precious stones, and enamel; height (left to right) 3 ¹/₁₆" (7.9 cm) and 4 ³/₄" (12 cm). Grünes Gewölbe, Dresden. Augustus the Strong doted on his collection of tiny grotesques fashioned of Baroque pearls, those irregularly shaped gems much admired in the Late Renaissance and Baroque periods. The Elector/King so prized the whimsical miniatures - jolly beggars, harlequins, soldiers, topers, cooks - that he had them installed in a cabinet in the great Valuables Room. There can be no doubt that the collection influenced the early porcelain figurines produced by the Meissen manufacture.*

256

257. *Johann Melchior Dinglinger. The Labors of Hercules, 1708-1712 (Dresden). Jasper, gold, silver-gilt, enamel, pearls, diamonds, emeralds, rubies, and cameos; height 23 5/8" (60 cm). Grünes Gewölbe, Dresden.* One of a select group of spectacular *Kabinettstücke* by Dinglinger, this richly decorated cup glorifies Augustus the Strong as Hercules, a demigod whose twelve labors won him a place among the Olympian gods. Atop the cup the hero overcomes the Nemean lion, while cameos hung from the lip depict his other labors. Although inscribed with the date 1712, the treasure remained in production until after Dinglinger's death in 1731, when it finally entered the electoral collection.

258. *Johann Melchior Dinglinger and Balthasar Permoser. Bath of Diana (Bad der Diana), 1704 (Dresden). Chalcedony, gold, silver, steel, ivory, diamonds, pearls, and enamel; height 15" (38 cm). Grünes Gewölbe, Dresden.* This is generally deemed the finest of Dinglinger's *Kabinettstücke,* a work in which the cup becomes the pool in which the nude goddess prepares to bathe, accompanied by Cupid, while below a pair of hounds besiege the antlered head of the spying Actaeon metamorphosed by Diana into a stag. Permoser supplied the ivory figure of Diana and Georg Christoph Dinglinger the enamels. A French epigram, picked out in diamonds, runs about the base: Discretion sert, effronterie perd ("Discretion is laudable, indiscretion unwise").

257

kind in 18th-century Europe. Here again the room was revetted in mirror, the reflecting sheets set within frames made of gold as well as blue and red lacquer beneath ceilings of white lacquer. The finest pieces sparkled against black velvet stretched over slanted *présentoirs* in four recessed vitrines. For Augustus, the pride of the collection were the nine magnificent parures made of, respectively, agates, brilliants, diamonds, cornelians, rubies, sapphires, tortoiseshell, emeralds, or topazes and, for the most part, based on designs by Dinglinger. Less important jewels, including pieces from earlier Wettins, lay hidden away in the drawers below. The most famous of the Green Vault diamonds – the "Dresden Green," a 160-carat stone of greenish hue – entered the collection later, after its acquisition by Augustus III in 1742, allegedly for the sum of 400,000 thalers. Together, the Wettin crown jewels – those prerequisites of absolute monarchy – constituted a singular political statement of power, prestige, and authority.

Against the central, mirror-faced pier in the Jewel Cabinet stood the celebrated *Goldene Coffee- und Thee-Zeug*, another Dinglinger masterpiece, this one dating from 1701 (figs. 261, 262). It was the world's first large *chinoiserie* coffee and tea service, for which the Elector paid an astronomical 40,000 thalers. A veritable *surtout de table*, the complex service comprises a multitude of vessels, variously made of silver, gold, enamel, ivory, and some 3,500 diamonds. The elegance and lightness of the touch transcend the Baroque, with its ponderous monumentality, and anticipate the Rococo vivacity of the Régence period in France. From Warsaw, the forever impatient Augustus sent word to Dinglinger threatening him with "loss of favor" if he did not immediately convey the finished work across the snowbound plains and forests of mid-winter Poland.

Dinglinger also made the *Obeliscus Augustalis*, a freestanding piece placed at the center of the Jewel Cabinet (fig. 260). This paen to the fame of Augustus cost the Elector 60,000 thalers, which no doubt seemed a bargain given that the elaborately classicized obelisk served as a vehicle for the display of some 240 cameos and intaglios from the Wettin collection. Three further *Kabinettstücke* represent the Ages of Man: *The Spring of Life*, *The Highest Joys of Life*, and *The End of Life*.[17] Each centers upon a magnificent cameo carved by Christoph Hübner, for which Dinglinger and his "factory" created an elaborate jeweled mount. Offered to Augustus for 48,000 thalers, the Ages of Man trilogy would be acquired only in 1734, following the accession of Augustus III. In the extraordinary *Altar of Apis* (fig. 264), Dinglinger created what must surely be the earliest example of *égyptiennerie*, the Egyptian equivalent of *chinoiserie*. It was, however, the final work to come

260

from his inventive hands, to which had been joined those of the collaborating Johann Gottlieb Kirchner. Augustus III acquired the piece in 1738, after Dinglinger's death.

Augustus III added only a small number of works to the Green Vaults, Old Master paintings being more to his taste than *Kabinettstücke*. It was to this monarch, therefore, that we owe most of the glories of the Dresden *Gemäldegalerie* ("Paintings Gallery"). The Green Vaults, meanwhile, would both gain and lose works as the generations rolled by. In 1772, as noted, most of Augustus's "white" silver was melted down, a consequence of the economic dislocations caused not only by the loss of Poland but also by the Seven Years War (1756-1763). During this deadly conflict Friedrich II of Prussia had bombarded Dresden, destroying the Late Gothic Kreuzkirche whose great spire soars above the capital in Bellotto's panoramas. Yet, in 1832, hundreds of items would be transferred to the Green Vaults from the old Kunstkammer, with the remainder auctioned off in 1835, after Saxony had been made a kingdom in 1806. At the end of World War I, when all the German monarchies were finally abolished, a number of precious articles went in compensation to Friedrich Augustus III, the last King of Saxony.

Thanks to their massive 16th-century walls, doors, and windows, the Green Vaults and their unique decoration survived the firestorm set off by Allied aerial bombardments throughout the nights of 13 and 14 February 1945. While, all about, the beau-

261

261. *Johann Melchior Dinglinger. Goldene Kaffee- und Thee-Zeug, 1697-1701 (Dresden). Gold, silver-gilt, enamel, diamonds, peridots, pearls, ivory, lacquer, wood, glass, and iron; height 39 1/4" (96 cm), length 30" (76 cm). Grünes Gewölbe, Dresden. The guiding genius behind this "Golden Coffee and Tea Service" was Dinglinger, who however drew on the talents of his brother, Georg Friedrich, for the enamels and Paul Heermann for the ivory sculptures. Together* these artists moved Kunstkammer art beyond the grandiloquent Baroque into the wit and delicacy of the Rococo. Well before Meissen, they also created one of the first large-scale works in the chinoiserie mode, an épergne with 45 gold and glass vessels disposed over a terraced pyramid rising from a polylobate and footed base to culminate in an ornate teapot.

262. *Detail of Dinglinger's Goldene Coffee- und Thee-Zeug (fig. 261).*

263. *Johann Melchior Dinglinger and Balthasar Permoser. Pearl-bearing Blackamoors, c. 1720 (Dresden). Ebony, gold, silver-gilt, enamel, precious stones, cameos, pearls, and mother-of-pearl; height c. 8" (20 cm). Grünes Gewölbe, Dresden. In addition to the famous "Indian" bearing the Rudolfine emerald lode (fig. 220), Dinglinger and Permoser collaborated on other such sculptures, which the 18th century, with its love of the exotic, quickly saw as ready Kunstkammer fare.*

264. *Johann Melchior Dinglinger and workshop. The Altar of Apis, 1724- 1738 (Dresden). Kehlheim stone, agate, silver-gilt, enamel, precious stones, and pearls; height 78 1/4" (195 cm). Grünes Gewölbe, Dresden. The prolific and gifted Dinglinger continued to innovate even in this last work, completed after his death in 1731 by such colleagues as the lapidary Christoph Hübner and the sculptor Gottlieb Kirchner of Meissen fame. Having introduced chinoiserie and demonstrated his deft way with Classicism (Obiliscus Augustalis), the elderly master was forging ahead into égyptiennerie, inspired by Bernard de Montfaucon's L'Antiquité expliquée et representée en figure, published between 1719 and 1724. Perhaps the artist sensed his own end when he chose to depict the death and transfiguration of Osiris.*

tiful old city – "Florence on the Elbe" – lay in charred ruins, the Green Vaults lost merely three galleries: the Bronze Room, the Pretiosenzimmer, and the Wappenzimmer. The rest had been miraculously spared. The collections, removed at the onset of war to Königstein Castle, were at first "salvaged" by the occupying Russian forces but then returned to

Dresden almost intact in 1958. Approximately half the works are today on view at the Albertinum. The Residenz – the great Renaissance *Schloss* begun by Duke Moritz in the mid-16th century – has been painstakingly and wonderfully restored, but the Green Vaults must await the turn of the millennium for their reopening.

XI

Two German Kunstkammern
and the Augsburg Kunstschrank

The Brandenburg
Kunstkammer, Berlin

The princely Hohenzollern family trace their line to the 11th century and their name to a medieval castle in Swabia. The dynasty's rise to prominence, however, did not commence until 1415, when Emperor Sigismund named Friedrich VI of Hohenzollern Regent of Brandenburg and then, two years later, Elector Friedrich I. Henceforth, the onetime Mark or Margraviate of Brandenburg would be the center of Hohenzollern power, with Berlin, a tiny fortified village on the River Spree, as the political capital, after Friedrich II (r. 1440-1470) enlarged his domains to include New Mark and Lusatia. In 1525 Prussia came under the Hohenzollerns thanks to Albrecht of Brandenburg, a grandson of Elector Albrecht Achilles, who, following his election as Grand Master of the Teutonic Knights, secularized the order's lands, at the advice of Martin Luther, and declared them the Duchy of Prussia. Indeed, the electorate would emerge as a major German state largely because of the Reformation, which allowed the Hohenzollerns to expropriate a vast amount of ecclesiastical property. This included Prussia itself after Elector Johann Sigismund of Brandenburg (r. 1608-1619) inherited the duchy, at the same time that he acquired Cleves, Mark, and Ravensburg.

Territorial expansion by such means had already begun with the conversion to Lutheranism of Elector Joachim II (r. 1535-1570). A contemporary of Duke Albrecht V of Bavaria and Elector Moritz of Saxony, Joachim may also have initiated the Hohenzollerns into the aristocratic habit of collecting precious objects. He is known, at least, to have commissioned "artful things to be made abroad," and to have sent out agents "to purchase rarities and strange objects." According to Hohenzollern tradition, moreover, it was during the reign of Joachim that the family amassed their first coins and antiquities. Still, much has to be

assumed here, for the origins of the Brandenburg Kunstkammer lie shrouded in darkness.[1] Little is known about its location or locations in the 16th and 17th centuries, and most of the original inventories were lost during World War II. Only a few photographs taken in the 1930s give some idea of the interiors of the castle precinct where the Kunstkammer once stood in the 18th century (fig. 266). Virtually all the city's museums possess several works that could very well have formed part of the Hohenzollerns' first collections. Yet, an exhibition organized in Berlin in 1981 presented only 128 pieces associated with the Kunstkammer, and it included nothing in the way of *naturalia*, antiquities, coins, or medals.[2] Moreover, few of the objects on view could match the quality of the treasures owned by the Green Vaults in Dresden, the Kunsthistorisches Museum in Vienna, or the Museo degli Argenti in Florence.

Thanks to the diplomatic skills of Friedrich Wilhelm, the Great Elector (r. 1640-1688), Brandenburg/Prussia emerged from the Thirty Years War considerably enhanced in both territory and status. The electorate now embraced part of Pomerania, a number of secularized bishoprics, and even Magdeburg. For present purposes, however, Friedrich Wilhelm looms large because there is, at last, tangible evidence of his collecting, which, as it turns out, focused

266

265. *Christoph Jamnitzer. Elephant Ewer, c. 1600 (Nuremberg). Silver and gilt; height 17" (43 cm). Kunstgewerbemuseum, Berlin. After his celebrated uncle, Wenzel, the prolific Christoph Jamnitzer (1563-1618) emerged as the foremost goldsmith of his extensive family (see fig. 231). The sculptural qualities of Hannibal's battle mount and the African warriors riding it are pronounced. Elephants as pouring vessels were not uncommon in the late 16th and early 17th centuries, as witnessed by a fine example, probably by Wolf Christian Ritter, in Amsterdam's Rijksmuseum, and a drawing prepared for Frederick II of Denmark by the Hamburg goldsmith Jakob Mores, now in the Berlin Kunstbibliothek. A better known work by Christoph Jamnitzer is the magnificent ewer and basin from the collection of Rudolf II, seen in fig. 167.*

266. *Naturalienkammer, Stadtschloss, Berlin, 18th century (photographed c. 1930). It was in this room that the Electors of Brandenburg installed their collection of naturalia in the early 18th century. The architect Andreas Schlüter had prepared the space, on either side of the Rittersaal ("Knights' Hall"), as part of his plans for the new Royal Palace. The Schloss and most of the Kunstkammer inventories were destroyed during World War II, leaving only a few photographs to suggest what the interior arrangements were like.*

267. *Jonas Silber. "Weltallschale" of Emperor Rudolf II, 1589 (Nuremberg). Silver-gilt; height 13 ¹/₂" (34.3 cm). Kunstgewerbemuseum, Berlin. The iconography of the Universal Cup, fashioned by a goldsmith once apprenticed to the great Wenzel Jamnitzer, glorifies the Imperial House of Habsburg; it also reflects a deluded hope on the part of Emperor Rudolf II that he might gain the thrones of Spain, Portugal, and even France, by virtue of a marriage with the Infanta Isabella, eldest daughter of Philip II of Spain. Rudolf never made a dynastic marriage, nor did he win any additional crowns.*

268. *Wenzel Jamnitzer. Kaiserpokal of Maximilian II, 1565-1570 (Nuremberg). Silver-gilt; height 27 ¹/₈" (69 cm). Kunstgewerbemuseum, Berlin. The Imperial Cup and its iconography extol the virtues of the Habsburg Emperor Maximilian II, portrayed in full regalia atop the cover, above the figures representing Duke Albrecht V of Bavaria, the Archbishops of Salzburg, Würzburg, and Bamberg, and the arms of Nuremberg, Augsburg, Windsheim, and Weissenburg, all members of the Protestant-friendly Landsberger Bund. It was evidently Nuremberg which planned this gift to the Emperor, whose Protestant sympathies were well known.*

267

on books and Classical antiquities. An inventory dated 1649 lists 4,900 antique coins housed at a castle in Cleves on the Rhine; it also accounts for the Elector's bronzes, intaglios, and cameos, ceramics and glass, all itemized in an appendix. By 1688 the *Kunst-Kammer* boasted 320 articles, not counting books, antiquities, and coins. The collection was divided into eight categories: 1) turned objects; 2) *naturalia*; 3) sculpture; 4) objets d'art and rarities; 5) paintings and architectural plans; 6) Oriental arms; 7) minerals; and 8) mechanical models.

Friedrich Wilhelm, having introduced absolutism into Brandenburg/Prussia, paved the way for his son, Elector Friedrich III (r. 1688-1713), to have himself crowned in 1701 as King Friedrich I of Prussia. Meanwhile, he had also become the foremost collector among the Hohenzollerns, whose Kunstkammer grew until it included 600 objects by 1694 and 1,500 by the end of the reign. Among the acquisitions were the mathematical, optical, and scientific instruments assembled by Professor Johann Jacob Spener of Halle. In 1698 the Elector imported from Rome the 232 antiquities his agents had purchased from the estate of the antiquarian and seminal theorist Giovanni Pietro Bellori. Sometime before 1689 Friedrich Wilhelm also received the celebrated *Pommersche Kunstschrank* created between 1610 and 1617 by Philipp Hainhofer for Duke Philipp II of Pomerania (fig. 274). According to an inventory of 1689, the Hohenzollern collections included Mathias Walbaum's *Diana Riding a Stag*,[3] an automated group, made around 1600, presented to the Elector around 1689 by the Principality of Minden. An inventory prepared in 1694 cites Christoph Jamnitzer's *Elephant Ewer*, it too a turn-of-the-century work, this one presented to the Elector by the Duchess of Simmern in 1694 (fig. 265).

Today the most important piece of virtuoso silver associated with the Berlin Kunstkammer is the so-called *Weltallschale* of Emperor Rudolf II (fig. 267). Signed by Jonas Silber of Nuremberg and dated 1589, the "Universal Cup" is decorated with allegories glorifying the Holy Roman Emperor and his divine-right role in the world, a role inherited from the Caesars of ancient Rome. The iconography may illustrate the Habsburg Emperor's fancied claims to the thrones of France, Spain, and Portugal, which, if realized, would have given Rudolf dominion over much of the world – hence the name of the cup. Such hopes appear to have sprung from his betrothal in 1579 to Isabella, the daughter of Philip II of Spain and Elisabeth de Valois, who was herself the daughter of a King, Henri II of France. Since the inventories reveal no trace of the *Weltallschale* in Rudolf's collection, the Emperor may have disposed of it as an embarrassment after 1599. It surfaces for the first

268

269. Jeweled snuffbox, c. 1765 (Berlin).
Gold, mother-of-pearl, diamonds,
rubies, and semiprecious stones;
4 x 3 ³/₁₆ x 2 ¹/₁₆" (10 x 8.1 x 5.2 cm).
Arthur Gilbert Foundation Collection,
London. The otherwise frugal Friedrich
the Great indulged a passion for
French culture, especially the paintings
of such Rococo masters as Watteau,
Pater, and Lancret. An addicted
snuff-taker, he also amassed an
enormous collection of richly jeweled
snuffboxes, about 26 of which survive,
many of them in the private collections
of the Hohenzollern family.

270. Katzenelnbogische Willkomm, 2nd
quarter 15th century (Rhineland?).
Silver-gilt; height 16" (40.5 cm).
Landesmuseum, Kassel. This
"welcome" libation cup, designed in
imitation of a wooden jug or tankard,
displays the arms of the Counts of
Katzenelnbogen, whose silver treasures
were inherited by the Landgraves of
Hessen/Marburg and ultimately by
their Hessen/Kassel relatives.

time in 1703, when it served as a present from the Jews of Halberstadt to King Friedrich I of Prussia.

Another Habsburg gem won by the Hohenzollerns is a silver-gilt cup and cover made around 1565 by the great Wenzel Jamnitzer (fig. 268). Originally the property of Emperor Maximilian II, it became available after the Empress pawned the treasure in the wake of her husband's death in 1576.

Shortly after 1703 the Berlin Kunstkammer collections were transferred from a location near the King's private apartments on the third floor of the castle to the fourth floor, where they would be installed in a series of rooms on either side of the "Knights' Hall," recently built by Andreas Schlüter, the court architect in charge of the new Royal Palace. At Schloss Oranienburg north of Berlin, King Friedrich installed the famous mirror-lined porcelain "cabinet" or room, the contents of which his successor, Friedrich Wilhelm I, would barter in 1717 to Augustus the Strong of Saxony and Poland for dragoon regiments (see Chapter 10).

As this exchange implies, Friedrich Wilhelm I (r. 1713-1740) had little interest in art or collecting. Although the real architect of Hohenzollern greatness, owing to his administrative, fiscal, and military reforms, the *Soldatenkönig* or "Soldier King" even withdrew numerous objects from the Kunstkammer in order to have them melted down or simply to give them away. One such present was an amber cabinet, offered in 1716 to Tsar Peter the Great, who also received "on loan" a statuette of Priapus from the Bellori collection. By 1735 the Berlin Kunstkammer collections were being dismembered, the *naturalia* transferred to the Academy of Sciences and the objets d'art as well as the instruments to various royal residences.

Thanks to Friedrich Wilhelm's stern reforms, power arrived in Prussia with a vengeance once Friedrich II – the enlightened despot known as Friedrich the Great (r. 1740-1786) – used the controlled economy, obedient bureaucracy, and efficient

military bequeathed him by his father to launch a major campaign of conquest. By the end of his reign Friedrich II had seized most of Silesia, a province immediately south of Poland traditionally claimed by Austria, then ruled by the young Empress Maria-Theresia. He had also connived with Russia and Austria to partition Poland, so that "East Prussia" (the original Teutonic Duchy of Prussia taken over by Albrecht of Brandenburg) could be fully integrated with Brandenburg/Prussia. Yet for all his so-called "Prussian" qualities – especially military genius – Friedrich had a pronounced taste for French art and literature, wrote mainly in French, invited Voltaire to his court, corresponded with d'Alembert and other French *philosophes*, played and composed music for the flute, and relaxed at Potsdam in an elegant country villa called Sans Souci. Here the *roi-philosophe* hung a collection of over 80 paintings by his favorite artists, mainly French Rococo masters such as Watteau, Pater, and Lancret.[5]

Friedrich, an addicted snuff-taker, indulged an even greater weakness for extravagantly jeweled snuffboxes, gradually amassing some 300 examples, about 26 of which survive (fig. 269).[6] In 1742 the newly anointed King purchased, unseen, the collection of 300 antique sculptures owned by Cardinal Melchior de Polignac in Paris. To these holdings he then added a celebrated hoard of 3,444 intaglios and 400 pastes, acquired from Baron Philipp von Stosch in 1764. As for the old-fashioned collections assembled by his ancestors, the only items with any meaning for Friedrich the Great were the Hohenzollerns' antiquities, from which he removed the Classical sculptures for transfer to the royal gardens at Potsdam and Sans Souci.

In 1777 an unsympathetic visitor wrote in his diary that the Kunstkammer consisted of nothing but "miserable dark rooms way up in the castle. Among the things to be seen there are not many but a few very valuable and worthwhile objects. Still, everything is badly preserved and exhibited."[10] At the turn of the 19th century, following the death of "Old Fritz," as Friedrich the Great had come to be known, the Kunstkammer captured the attention of its owners one last time. The overall collection lost its mathematical and scientific instruments but regained the *naturalia*, the coins and medals, and most of the antiquities from Potsdam and Sans Souci. A guidebook was even issued in 1805.[11] Soon thereafter Napoleon, a brilliant student of Friedrich II's military tactics, entered Berlin as conqueror, bringing along Vivant Denon, Director of the Louvre Museum. Three weeks later the Kunstkammer had been packed up and shipped off to Paris. When returned to Berlin, following the Battle of Waterloo (1815), the booty had been severely damaged.

269

270

Although the collections grew substantially during the 19th century, they would also be decimated by dispersal into specialized museums, beginning in 1831. Only three groups of artifacts were left behind: 1) objets d'art, drawings, furniture, models, arms, and textiles; 2) historic souvenirs; and 3) ethnological items. In 1855, even some of these collections were to be handed over to the Neues Museum. In 1875 the Hohenzollern court closed the Berlin Kunstkammer and had its contents moved to the new Museum of Applied Arts (Kunstgewerbemuseum).

The Kunstkammer of the Landgraves of Hessen/Kassel

At the outset of the Renaissance, the Landgraves of Hessen/Kassel could boast one of the most celebrated Kunstkammern in Germany, although in sheer size, it was not on a par with the collections in Munich and Dresden.[12] Even today some evidence of the medieval treasury survives in a group of exceptional Syrian glasses,[13] a Fatimid bronze lion, and the "Sword of Boabdil," so-called for the last Moorish King of Granada. Very likely all these objects had been brought to Europe by a princely Crusader returning from the Holy Land. A celadon bowl with a Gothic silver-gilt mount of about 1435 may be the earliest known bit of Chinese porcelain to enter a Western collection (fig. 271). This work and the *Katzenelnbogische Willkomm*, a mid-15th-century silver-gilt ewer with a dragon-shaped spout (fig. 270), came to the Hessen family through marriage with the heiress Anna von Katzenelnbogen.

The most famous of Hessen's Landgraves may be Philipp the Magnanimous (r. 1518-1567), who established the Protestant University of Marburg, a move characteristic of his abiding concern for the general welfare of the Hessian people. One of his four sons, Landgrave Wilhelm the Wise (Wilhelm IV; r. 1567-1592), founded the House of Hessen/Kassel. Wilhelm also emerged as a scholar among princes with a developed taste for music, astronomy, mathematics, and the mechanical arts.[15] An accomplished scientist in his own right, he designed and calibrated astronomical clocks and instruments, among them a celebrated planetarium. created in collaboration with his assistants.[16] Thanks to Wilhelm the Wise, Germany acquired its first observatory, which the Landgrave had installed in the palace attic. For his astronomical enterprises, Wilhelm enjoyed the advice of the Danish scientist Tycho Brahe, who arrived in Kassel in 1575.

The reputation of the Hessian court for its scientific interests no doubt prompted the great Swiss clockmaker Jost Bürgi to settle in Kassel in 1579.[17] There he worked for Wilhelm the Wise, who called him "a second Archimedes." Encouraged by Wilhelm's own

271. Celadon cup, *14th-15th century (China)*, European mount 1434-1453. *Porcelain, silver-gilt, and enamel; height (with cover) 8 1/8" (20.6 cm), diameter 6 5/8" (16.8 cm). Landesmuseum, Kassel. Tradition holds that the cup, generally dated to the Ming period, was acquired by Count Philipp von Katzenelnbogen during his pilgrimage to the Holy Land in 1433-1434. The mount can be dated by the coat-of-arms engraved upon it.*

271

work, Bürgi carried clockmaking to new heights of craftsmanship and innovation, an achievement that would never have been possible in, for example, the free Imperial cities of Augsburg and Nuremberg, where strict guild regulations still prevailed. His breakthroughs included a system of logarithms, developed in 1588 independently of John Napier, the Scottish mathematician generally credited with their invention. It was, however, a series of very complex celestial spheres, designed to operate automatically, that brought Bürgi his early and lasting international fame (fig. 272), as well as the attention of Emperor Rudolf II in Prague (see Chaper 7).

Like other Renaissance princes, Landgrave Wilhelm engaged in artistic activities at the same time that he delved deeply into the sciences. He actually excelled at ivory turning, as did Elector Augustus of Saxony, Duke Albrecht V of Bavaria, and more than

272

one Habsburg. Wilhelm also opened a glass manufacture in Kassel, some ten years after the precedent set by Archduke Ferdinand at Innsbruck. The Landgrave's museum possessed as well a number of outstanding art works by such celebrated figures as Barthel Jamnitzer and Elias Lencker, both goldsmiths from Nuremberg. Almost as important was an exquisite Antwerp nautilus-shell cup made in the late 16th century (fig. 273).[18] Wilhelm, a year before he died, began construction on a separate building meant to house his collections, which remained in the old palace.

Landgrave Moritz the Learned (1592-1627), as his name implies, was almost as gifted as his father, Wilhelm the Wise, whom he succeeded in 1592. Moritz spoke ten languages, played several instruments, composed music, wrote a drama, and even performed in it. Almost immediately after his accession, Moritz installed a large armory; he also set about indulging a passion for alchemy and dabbling in both astronomy and architecture. By 1593 the court architects, Hans and Hieronymus Müller, had completed the building planned by Wilhelm the Wise. As in Munich, this was a quadrangular structure with an interior courtyard and a ground floor given over to the royal stables. A nobleman, Lupold von Wedel, who visited the collections displayed upstairs wrote of having viewed "many excellent things... which would take a long time to enumerate... many unicorns... a gun barrel made of wood, which shoots leaden bullets without powder... [and] a sheepskin from India" soft as silk to the touch.[19] Landgrave Moritz also collected Roman antiquities, as we know from a collection he acquired in France in 1603. In 1697 the chronicler Johann Just Winckelmann published a description of the Kassel Kunstkammer, providing a fairly accurate picture of the contents at that time.[20] In other words, the holdings overall were comparable to those in many other princely accumulations of the 16th and 17th centuries. More important, they had survived the Thirty Years War largely unscathed.

At the end of the 17th century the gifts so evident in Wilhelm and Moritz reappeared, after a hiatus of three generations, in the person of Landgrave Karl (r. 1675-1730). Until he came of age, the landgraviate functioned under the regency of his mother, Landgravine Hedwig Sophia, a sister of the art-loving "Great Elector" Friedrich Wilhelm of Brandenburg. Karl, a true contemporary of Louis XIV, loved building – building in the grand Baroque style – an obsession that would leave Kassel blessed with some of its finest edifices, among them the *Schloss* with its cascading fountains, the Orangerie, and the Menagerie. He also transformed the Ottoneum, a theatre built by his great grandfather Moritz, into a giant Kunstkammer known as the

273

272. *Jost Bürgi. Clockwork celestial globe, c. 1582-1586 (Kassel). Brass fire-gilt, bronze, and iron; height 18 5/8" (48 cm). Astronomisch-Physikalisches Kabinett, Kassel. Bürgi, a Swiss horologist, worked for the Landgraves of Hessen/Kassel from 1579 until 1603. He is best known for a series of celestial globes made while in service to Landgrave Wilhelm IV (Wilhelm the Wise), including the present example with stars engraved by Anton Eisenhoit of Warburg.*

273. *Nautilus cup, c. 1560 (Antwerp). Silver-gilt, nautilus shell, shells, and wax; height 9 3/4" (24.7 cm). Landesmuseum, Kassel. The Landgraves of Hessen/Kassel, powerful Renaissance lords, possessed a treasury with exceptional medieval objects and a well-stocked silver vault. A remarkable piece from their collection is this mounted nautilus-shell cup, which must have been in the original Silberkammer, even though it appears first only in the Fridericianum of c. 1780. The décor of shells and swags molded of wax was applied in the 18th century. As combinations of naturalia and artificialia, such cups were ideal Kunstkammer items.*

274. *Philipp Hainhofer.* The Pommersche
Kunstschrank, *1611-1615 (Augsburg).
Ebony, palissandre, rosewood, silver
parcel-gilt, enamel, and precious
stones; height 53 ¹/₂" (136 cm) width
45 ¹/₄" (115 cm). Formerly
Kunstgewerbemuseum, Berlin. The
cabinet of this most famous of
Kunstschränke,* those miniature
Kunstkammern created by the
Augsburg patrician/dealer/collector
Philipp Hainhofer, disappeared during
World War II, although its eclectic
collection of silver wares, paintings,
games, instruments, tools, and
pharmaceutical items survived.
Hainhofer depended on the talents of
the cabinetmaker Ulrich Baumgarten
and the goldsmith Matthias Walbaum,
while he assumed the all-important
task of organizing the decoration and
assembling the contents. The
Pommersche Kunstschrank, made for
Duke Philipp II von Pommern
(Pomerania), cost 20,000 thalers and
stood in the castle at Stettin. In 1660
Duchess Anna von Pommern left it to
Electress Dorothea von Brandenburg.
The treasure burned in 1944, along
with the Kunstgewerbemuseum in
which it was housed.*

Kunsthaus, inaugurated in 1709.[21] Here Landgrave Karl took the innovative step of displaying art – perhaps as many as 100 paintings – along with the contents of a highly systematic *Kunst- und Wunder-Kammer*. The museum also contained an "anatomical room" reserved for "abnormalities," as well as a third-floor *Drehkammer*, in which the Landgrave could enjoy his favorite pastime, ivory turning. His taste for ivory found further outlet in the Kunstkammer's collection of fine carvings by Leonhard Kern and Ignaz Elhafen. Alongside them was an ivory carving by Peter the Great, presented, through an emissary, by the carver himself to Landgrave Karl, who thereby affirmed the amicable relations among the artist/princes of the period. Crowning the Kunstkammer was an observatory raised on a platform supported by the roof.

Two generations later, Landgrave Friedrich II (r. 1760-1785) commissioned the Fridericianum, a Palladian-style building designed by the architect Simon Louis du Ry and erected between 1769 and 1779.[22] It was the purest expression of the Kunstkammer and the last of the genre, as well as the first purpose-built modern museum, an institution freely open to the public. The layout of the collections followed that of the old Kunstkammer, except for the paintings, which would now hang in a gallery of their own.

Philipp Hainhofer
and the Augsburg Kunstschrank

So frequently has Philipp Hainhofer been cited and quoted in this book that his very name becomes a kind of leitmotif or thread running through and linking many of the great German Kunstkammer collections of the 17th century.[23] Indeed, Hainhofer is the indispensable witness to the Kunstkammer phenomenon, given that his passion for such collecting drove him to visit every princely accumulation he could find a means of entering. In most instances he succeeded, thanks in large part to his being an Augsburg patrician and a collector in his own right, as well as a dealer, a traveler, and a compulsive chronicler. In diaries and letters Hainhofer left invaluable, often picturesque, and tantalizing descriptions of what were Europe's earliest museums, nearly all of which disappeared long ago. Between 1603 and 1611, he visited the Wittelsbachs' Munich Kunstkammer, with its 6,000 items, on three different occasions, because, as he explained, "to see everything properly not even two or three days are sufficient, rather as many months or more."[24] Twelve years later he traveled across the mountains to Schloss Ambras, which, of course, housed the great Kunstkammer collection

assembled by Archduke Ferdinand of Tyrol. While waiting for dinner to be announced, the obsessive Hainhofer confessed: "I should much rather have visited the Kunstkammer than eat the finest meal."

Philipp Hainhofer himself, a colorful figure, prompted a few literary observations, one of which came from Wilhelm V of Bavaria in a letter of 1607 to his son, the reigning Duke Maximilian I: "A citizen of Augsburg whom, apart from his [Protestant] religion, I hold to be an honorable and intelligent young man, who is learned as well as being a merchant and in whose house I saw all kinds of foreign and strange things as well as almost an entire Kunstkammer."[25] Also in 1607, Hainhofer had become the trusted political agent in Germany for King Henri IV of France.

Philipp Hainhofer, needless to say, created his own Kunstkammer, which became one of the attractions of Augsburg. His collection of shells was a source of great pride; moreover, he believed it outclassed every other assemblage of its kind. The glory of the Hainhofer achievement, however, lay in the monumental *Mehrzweckmöbel*, that is, multi-purpose, silver-mounted ebony cabinets called *Kunstschränke*. A *Kunstschrank* could also have been characterized as a *Gesamtkunstwerk*, long before Richard Wagner adopted the term in the 19th century to mean a "total work of art." The *Kunstschränke* created by Hainhofer were highly sophisticated products of collaboration between their inventor and perhaps as many as a dozen or more craftsmen, such as a cabinetmaker, one or more painters and sculptors, and several goldsmiths. Each

274

275

277

Kunstschrank had a multitude of drawers filled with myriad implements and objects, both *naturalia* and *artificialia*, all requiring days to discover, examine, and comprehend. As this would suggest, a *Kunstschrank*, with its encyclopedic contents and its intricate program of paintings and sculptures, constituted a Kunstkammer in small. One such assemblage could take years of diligent search merely to gather all the necessary ingredients.

The first of Hainhofer's masterworks was the so-called *Pommersche Kunstschrank*, begun in 1610 for Duke Philipp II of Pomerania. It took seven years to complete and cost the astronomical sum of 20,000 thalers (fig. 274). A painting from the period portrays Hainhofer presenting the *Kunstschrank* to his Pomeranian patron (fig. 275). The contents have been preserved, although the cabinet disappeared during World War II. A comparable cabinet that survives, albeit without its contents, is the *stipo tedesco* in Florence's Museo degli Argenti.[27] Assembled between 1619 and 1626, it was sold to Archduke Leopold V of Tyrol, whose wife, Claudia de' Medici, subsequently presented it to her nephew, Grand Duke Ferdinando II of Tuscany (see Chapter 4). He appears to have received it without the wondrous contents, but an inventory of what Hainhofer planned has been published.[28]

Among extant *Kunstschränke*, the most perfect is the one Hainhofer created in 1626-1631, a masterwork presented in 1632 by the grateful citizens of Augsburg to Gustavus Adolphus, the great warrior King of Sweden (fig. 276).[29] It cost them 6,500 thalers and survives almost intact in the Chancellor's Room at Uppsala University. The only missing contents are the *naturalia*, chiefly minerals, and the huge collection of coins and medals, all now integrated with the University's larger collections. The most striking part of the Uppsala cabinet is its crowning feature: a boat-shaped ewer formed of a Seychelle nut in a parcel-gilt mount chased with

shells, crabs, tortoises, and other sea creatures. It stands in a lush garden of red, white, and black coral branches, shells, and crystals (fig. 277). As for the paintings on the Uppsala *Kunstschrank*, Hainhofer called them "a compendium of all Holy Scripture." Elsewhere the iconography represents the animal, plant, and mineral kingdoms, the four known continents, the four seasons, and all the known epochs of history. The drawers contain finely wrought silver instruments, a medicine cabinet, and a ewer with basin. Also present are silver animals cast from nature in the *style rustique*, as well as an automated scene of Apollo and Cyparissus changing into a cypress tree, a kind of metamorphosis much appreciated at the time. In a lighter vein there are, for the entertainment of the beholder, a deck of cards, a chess set, and other parlor games, along with vexing mirrors and spectacles. Among the practical jokes are two pairs of gloves sewn together so that they cannot be worn, also artificial eggs, "halves of nuts with illusionistic wire insects," and a mug that cannot be drunk from. The most sophisticated component is a set of virginals, an early keyboard instrument; it can be played or made to operate automatically either at pre-set times or whenever the doors of its compartment are opened. Such cabinets, with their miniaturized contents, were practical as well as enchanting. In the Uppsala *Kunstschrank*, for example, the compartment housing the ewer and basin is water-stained, suggesting that it may have been used by none other than Queen Christina of Sweden.[31]

276

275. *Anton Mozart. Philipp Hainhofer Presenting the Pommersche Kunstschrank to Duke Philipp von Pommern, c. 1617 (Augsburg). Kunstgewerbemuseum, Berlin. The Pommersche Kunstschrank took seven years to complete and over three weeks to transport from Augsburg to Stettin, where it arrived on 24 August 1617. The presentation depicted here - a fictitious scene - would have occurred on the 30th of August 1617. Also portrayed are the 26 Augsburg craftsman involved in the project.*

276. *Philipp Hainhofer. The Uppsala Kunstschrank, 1626-1631 (Augsburg). Uppsala University, Sweden. When Gustavus Adolphus of Sweden made his triumphal entry into Lutheran Augsburg at the height of the Thirty Years War, the city's grateful councilmen presented the hero with a Kunstschrank for which Philipp Hainhofer received 6,500 thalers. After the King died on the battlefield at Lützen, the cabinet and its contents were sent to his daughter, Queen Christina, who installed them in the royal castle at Svartsjoe. Presented to Uppsala University in 1694 by King Charles, this Kunstschrank is the most perfect of Hainhofer's extant creations.*

277. *Detail of the crowning feature atop the Uppsala Kunstschrank (fig. 276): a magnificent Seychelle-nut ewer mounted by Johannes I Lencker of Augsburg.*

XII

Two Baltic Collections

The Danish Royal Collections

Little, if anything, is known of whatever cultural interests may have captivated the medieval rulers of Denmark and Sweden, who devoted themselves primarily to war and political rivalry.[1] In 1448, however, the House of Oldenburg began their 400-year reign over Denmark and Norway, Southern Sweden, Schleswig, and Holstein. Yet, from the reign Christian I (1448-1481) only one heirloom of artistic worth has been handed down in the Danish royal family: a large Gothic silver horn dating to around 1465 (fig. 278). Even less survives from the benevolent burgher King, Christian II (1481-1559), despite his marriage to Isabella of Austria, a sister of Emperor Charles V and thus the daughter of the collecting Habsburgs. Then came the Reformation, and with it conditions more favorable to cultural engagement, which emerged after 1536, when Christian III (r. 1534-1559) allowed revenues from seven bishoprics and over seventy monasteries to flow into his own coffers. By the end of the 16th century the royal family owned more than half the land in Denmark, making it easily within the means of King Frederick II to subsidize Tycho Brahe, the most prominent astronomer of the age, whose observatory was on the island of Hven near Copenhagen.

King Christian IV (r. 1588-1648), a leading defender of the Protestant cause during the Thirty Years War, anticipated Louis XIV in his love of building (fig. 279).[2] This extended from Christiana, the future Oslo he founded in Norway, to Frederiksborg Castle in northern Zeeland, a fine brick monument in the Dutch Renaissance style erected in 1599-1609 on a series of islands.[3] The courtyard at Frederiksborg was graced by the *Neptune Fountain*, which boasted a series of bronze figures by Adriaen de Vries, at least until a Swedish army took them as booty in 1659. In the surrounding park Christian built "Sparenpenge," a hunting lodge in which he installed a *Kunstkammers*, a suite of rooms filled with rare and valuable arms.

At picturesque Rosenborg Castle, another of the King's commissioned residences (fig. 280), Christian IV installed "a small cabinet in which were some Japanese swords, knives, and tapestries, also paintings and pictures."[4] In addition to architecture and collecting, Christian IV saw to it that Danish kings would be properly crowned, with a magnificent, richly jeweled diadem executed in 1595-1596 by Dirk Fyring. It remains the greatest of all the treasures in the Danish crown jewels.[5]

When Christian IV's younger son unexpectedly succeeded to the throne as Frederick III (r. 1648-1670), he had spent a decade as Archbishop of Bremen and then two years in Flensburg as

278. *The Oldenburg Horn, c. 1465 (Germany). Silver-gilt and enamel; height 13" (33 cm). Rosenborg Castle, Copenhagen. Legend holds that in 989, while hunting, Count Otto, the first of the Oldenburg nobles, received this horn from a beautiful maiden. According to another tradition, King Christian I donated the horn to the treasury of Cologne Cathedral, whence it would be returned to Protestant Denmark following the Reformation.*

279. *François Dieussart. King Christian IV of Denmark and Norway, 1650 (Glückstadt). Bronze; height 40 ½" (103 cm). Rosenborg Castle, Copenhagen. Here the monarch is portrayed at the age of 66, a year before he lost an eye at the Battle of Kohlberger Heide. Modeled in 1643, the bust was cast in 1650 at the cannon foundry in Glückstadt.*

279

281

280

280. *Rosenborg Castle, Copenhagen. 1606-1758. Built mainly in 1613-1617 as a summer residence for Kirsten Munk, the morganatic wife of Christian IV, Rosenborg Castle has become a royal treasure house, complete with original decorations and numerous items from the royal Kunstkammer.*

281. *Abraham Wuchters. King Frederick III of Denmark and Norway, 1645-1646. Oil on canvas; 93 1/4 x 56 1/2" (237 x 144 cm). Rosenborg Castle, Copenhagen. It was Frederick III who in c. 1650 founded the Danish Royal Library and Kunstkammer, both of which would be transferred in the 1670s to the purpose-built edifice seen here.*

282. *Museum Wormianum (catalogue frontispiece), 1655. Assembled and established by Ole Worm, Professor of Natural Philosophy, as well as Greek, Latin, and Medicine, at the University of Copenhagen, the Museum Wormianum was acquired by Frederick III in 1655 and incorporated into the Danish Royal collections.*

283. *The Royal Arsenal, Library, and Kunstkammer in Copenhagen (1665-1680), as represented in a painting by Johannes Rach and Heinrich Eegberg.*

Governor of the Duchies of Schleswig and Holstein (fig. 281). In the latter capacity he would have come to know the museum at Gottorp formed by his cousin, Duke Frederik, with the help of the mathematician Adam Olearius. Thus stimulated, Frederick began to create a Kunstkammer and a library at Slotsholmen Castle. A brief catalogue of the Kunstkammer, dating from 1674, describes eight separate "apartments" containing the types of objects common to such collections.

Frederick III purchased the renowned art, ethnographic, and natural-history holdings of Ole Worm (fig. 282).[6] A professor of Latin, Greek, and medicine, Dr. Worm was the father of Nordic archaeology and an early debunker of the unicorn myth. In *Museum Wormianum*, he published the collection acquired by his sovereign, classifying the world in four large categories: 1) inanimate objects; 2) plants; 3) animals and human beings; and 4) man-made

objects. Thanks to the Worm collection, the royal Danish Kunstkammer evolved into one of the most important in Europe.

To accommodate his growing collections, King Frederick had an extended oblong building erected in the years 1665-1680 (fig. 283). It housed the arsenal on the ground floor, the library on the first floor, the Kunstkammer on the second floor, and the Chamber of Models under the eaves. A second inventory, dated 1696, was drawn up in conjunction with a catalogue published under the title *Museum Regnium*. An inventory of 1737 accounts for almost 4,000 items, not including coins and medals.[7] Of these, researchers have identified 2,152 pieces, today scattered throughout seventeen Danish and five foreign museums. The later inventory shows the collections organized into categories, each with its own room or gallery. As a result, we know that the Chamber of Medals contained not only modern and antique coins but also a number of paintings, mainly portraits, some of which were copies after Dürer, others drawings by Karel van Mandet (the "Vasari of the North"), and one fine original oil by Gerard Dou. The Chamber of Naturalia held mostly shells and minerals, but also an Egyptian mummy case, skins and bones of mammoths, hippopotami, and rhinoceri, and insects frozen in amber.

A star attraction of the Chamber of Artifacts was a silver-gilt equestrian figure of Christian IV tilting, a prize, it would seem, won by the King at a tournament staged for his coronation (fig. 284).[8] It shared space with other silver and silver-gilt objects, as well as with ivories, bronzes, a magnificent tureen of Icelandic obsidian,[9] *pietre dure* panels mounted on tables, objects fashioned of amber, and glass works, including three "Morra players" from Murano, similar to figures at Schloss Ambras (fig. 138).[10] The Indian Chamber contained a vast collection of artifacts from Brazil, India, China, Japan, and Burma, including a group of colorful paintings of African and South American natives by Albert Eckhout. These were a gift to Frederick III from Prince

282

283

284

285

286

Johann Moritz of Nassau (fig. 285).[11] The Chamber of Antiquities included Nordic as well as Classical works, in addition to choice medieval treasures, such as a rare French enameled silver-gilt ewer,[12] reliquaries from Ireland and Limoges,[13] and the "Oldenburg Horn" (fig. 278).

As in the Munich and Ambras Kunstkammern, there were portraits of royals and celebrities, gathered in the Chamber of Heroes. Also reminiscent of Munich were the Gallery Chamber filled with Old Master paintings and the Chamber of Models housing architectural maquettes. In a genuine innovation, the Danish Kunstkammer offered a Chamber of Perspectives hung with trompe-l'oeil paintings of architecture, still lifes, and other subjects. After this came the equally novel Chamber of Art-Anatomy, a venue for skeletons and "deformities," and finally the Antechamber.

In 1824 the Danish Kunstkammer was broken up and many of its holdings transferred to Rosenborg Castle, which would be opened to the public in 1833. Meanwhile, the collections already housed at Rosenborg – silver, coins and medals, shells and minerals – were integrated with other, more specialized museums in Copenhagen. Since 1975, the crown jewels, consigned to the Rosenborg treasury by King Christian V (r. 1646-1699), have been on view in the safety of the castle's vaulted basement. Today

Rosenborg, with its chronologically ordered collections, evokes the life-style of the Danish royal family during the 17th and 18th centuries. The most elaborate Kunstkammer object displayed here may be the cameo-encrusted gold and turqoise tureen confiscated by Frederick III from Corfitz Ulfeldt, the husband of the daughter Christian IV had with his morganatic wife, Kirsten Munk.[14] Other important Kunstkammer features are wall cabinets crammed with turned ivory and wood cups and covers, some of them dating back to the 16th century (fig. 286).

The Swedish Royal Lyvrustkammer and Treasury

After centuries during which its history was closely interwoven with that of Denmark and Norway, Sweden began life as an independent nation only in the 1520s, when Gustav Vasa (c. 1494-1560) managed to wrest his country free of domination by the Kings of Denmark.[16] As elsewhere in Protestant Europe, the Reformation secured the throne by legitimating the King's expropriation of Church properties. Soon the castles inhabited by Gustav Vasa would be richly furnished with tapestries, paintings, and armor.[17] Apart from music, the King's cultural interests, if any, remain largely unknown, although entries in the Royal Wardrobe make it possible to trace a number of art works to his reign.

Gustav's three sons, Erik, Johan, and Karl, grew up to be genuine Renaissance Princes. The eldest, who would reign as Erik XIV (1560-1568), was literate in both Latin and German, as well as more than eager to emulate the lavishness of European court life. His regalia, which survive in the Swedish Royal Treasury, comprise a crown and orb made by the Flemish goldsmith Cornelius van der Weyden[18] and a sceptre fashioned by Hans Heidenrik.[19] All three brothers would reign in turn, the second and third by force of rebellion, beginning with Johan, who unseated the depressed and temporarily insane Erik. Karl then replaced Johan's Catholic son, Sigismund, who, through his mother, had inherited the crowns of Poland as well as Sweden. All three Vasa brothers patronized the arts, encouraging local talents while inviting foreign craftsmen to Sweden.

The successor to Karl IX was his sixteen-year-old son Gustavus Adolphus (1594-1632), generally regarded as the greatest of all Swedish sovereigns. Fluent in five languages, and literate in both Latin and Greek, Gustavus Adolphus excelled in oratory as well as in leadership and military strategy. Having successfully concluded a war with Denmark and Russia begun by his father, Gustavus Adolphus took up the Protestant cause in the Thirty Years War and mostly prevailed on the Continent against the Habsburg Emperor and the Catholic League. Throughout the long years of conflict, the grateful cities of Protestant Europe kept the King and his armies propitiated with gifts of exceptional works, most of which, along with a great wealth of booty, would be taken home for the cultural enrichment of Sweden. The free Imperial city of Augsburg, for instance, presented Gustavus Adolphus with a famous *Kunstschrank*, or art cabinet, created by Philip Hainhofer (fig. 276). The neighboring city of Nuremberg offered a magnificent pair of parcel-gilt wine cups and covers cast by Christoph Jamnitzer, engraved by Johann Hauer, and completed by Jeremias Ritter (fig. 289).

Within the same year, 1632, Gustavus Adolphus perished at the Battle of Lützen, after which the blood-stained garments worn by him in various encounters were placed on display at the *Lyvrustkammer*, or "Royal Armory," which thereupon became a national "memorial museum." The King had been fond of music and the arts in general; moreover, it is during his reign that we find the first mention of an "Art and Curio Chamber," situated in Tre Kronor Castle.

Christina (1626-1689), the only surviving child of Gustavus Adolphus, was not quite six years old when her father died in Saxony.[20] Educated under the guidance of the Regent, Axel Oxenstierna, Christina grew up knowing French, German, Italian, Dutch, and Latin, as well as a smattering of Greek, Hebrew, and Arabic. This most erudite of Queens studied Classical philology, philosophy, theology, mathematics, astronomy, art, and music (fig. 287). She also corresponded with Pascal and brought Descartes to Stockholm, where the elderly French philosopher caught cold and died. He survived long enough, however, to plan an academy for his patroness, who promptly made it a place to which renowned scholars, poets, physicians, diplomats, and statesmen were pleased to come. Christina also gave the Vasas their first true collector. She vastly enlarged the royal library, acquiring books from the estates of Cardinal Mazarin and Hugo Grotius, among many others. For her museum of antique sculpture in Ultima Thule, the Queen had agents scouting throughout Greece and Asia Minor. In Amsterdam, Michel le Blon served as her agent (and spy), a fact known from an inventory of 1652-1653, which lists about a hundred items acquired from "Sieur Blom." Christina's collection of more than 5,000 silver coins was enriched by the coin cabinet of Elector Maximilian I of Bavaria, seized by Gustavus Adolphus during the plunder of Munich in 1632.

287

287. *Sébastien Bourdon. Queen Christina of Sweden, 1653. Oil on canvas; 28 1/4 x 22 7/8" (72 x 58 cm). Royal Collection, Stockholm.*

288. *Tureen with cameos, c. 1700 (Holland?). Silver-gilt, enamel, and cameos; height 6 3/4". Royal Collection, Stockholm. This is the finest objet d'art acquired by Queen Hedvig Eleonora (1636-1715), daughter of Frederick III, Duke of Holstein-Gottorp, and wife of King Charles X.*

288

289. Christoph Jamnitzer, Johann Hauer, and Jeremias Ritter. *Hercules with Terrestrial Globe (or Atlas with Celestial Globe)*, c. 1618-1632 (Nuremberg). Silver parcel-gilt; height 22 ³/₄" (57.8 cm). Kungl. Husgeraedskammaren, Stockholm. One of a pair of wine cups presented by the City of Nuremberg to King Gustavus Adolphus at his victorious entry into the city on 31 March 1632. The goldsmith Jeremias Ritter finished the pieces from their unfinished state left by Jamnitzer at his death in 1618 and offered by his widow. In Sweden the treasures would be treated as part of the royal regalia used at coronations.

290. Georg Petel and Ian Herck. *Saltcellar*, 1627-1628 (Antwerp?). Ivory and silver-gilt; height 17 ³/₈" (44 cm). Kungl. Husgeraedskammaren, Stockholm. Petel took his design from drawings by Rubens, whose estate sold the saltcellar to Queen Christina. Ian Herck mounted the ivory in silver-gilt.

289

Thanks partly to the influence of her favorite, Magnus Gabriel de la Gardie, Christina conceived a passion for everything French. Not only was her court painter Sébastien Bourdon, but everything made for her coronation – coach, robe, throne canopy, vestments, and saddles – had been commissioned in Paris. Exceptions were tapestries obtained from weavers in Delft by Ambassador Spiering, who also acquired an ivory saltcellar crafted by Georg Petel for Peter Paul Rubens (fig. 290).

Christina's greatest coup came in 1648, when, at the end of the Thirty Years War, the Swedish army looted Prague, including the Hradschin crammed with the collection of Rudolf II. The military had been egged on by the Queen herself: "And be sure, I entreat you, to preserve and send me the library and the curiosities found in Prag; you know they are the only things I value."[21] By May 1649 she was unpacking the immense booty including 600 hardostone vessels and paintings by Titian, Veronese, and Correggio.[23]

By mid-century Christina found herself increasingly attracted to Catholicism. Four years later she abdicated in favor of her cousin Charles and departed for the Continent, where she would be formally received into the Church at Innsbruck. Needless to say, the Queen visited the collection at Schloss Ambras (see Chapter 6). Once settled in the Palazzo Riario in Rome, she lived for the last three decades of her life surrounded by favorite treasures shipped from Sweden: 19 bronzes, 72 tapestries, some 50 scientific instruments and objets d'art, at least as many drawings, and 103 paintings,[24] almost all of them Italian masterpieces and about half of these from the Habsburg collection in Prague.

Charles X (1654-1660), Christina's successor, was another warrior King, whose first exploit was to invade Poland and then cross the frozen straits to threaten an unprepared Copenhagen. His most eminent cultural feat may have been the forceful transfer of Adriaen de Vries's bronze fountain sculptures from Frederiksborg Castle to Drottningholm in Sweden. Queen Hedvig Eleonora, however, was a collector, with a particular eye for treasures of Dutch and Italian origin. She also commissioned works from Swedish craftsmen and employed both an ebony turner and a rock-crystal cutter at her court. At Ulriksdal Castle she installed most of her valuable objects in a sort of Kunstkammer, where the *pièce de résistance* was a 17th-century silver-gilt cup and cover embellished with enamel and a multitude of cameos (fig. 288). A 1719 inventory of her property at Drottningholm lists 350 articles of porcelain, pottery, ivory, rock crystal, and semiprecious stones mounted in silver-gilt and enamel. Most of them are now exhibited either in a gallery at the Royal Castle or in the Royal Armory.

290

Bibliography

The sources for the text are cited in the numbered notes. The following is a recommended reading list organized by subject.

General
Asch, R., and A. Birke. *Princes, Patronage, and the Nobility: The Court at the Beginning of the Modern Age.* Oxford, 1991.
Arte e Scienza: Wunderkammer (exh cat). Venice, 1986.
Balsinger, B.J. *The Kunst- und Wunderkammern: A Catalogue Raisonné of Collecting in Germany, France, and England: 1565-1750* (PhD thesis). Pittsburg, 1970.
Elam, C. *Studioli and Renaissance Court Patronage* (unpub MA report). London, 1970.
Fleming, J., and H. Honour. *The Penguin Dictionary of Decorative Arts.* London/NY, 1989.
Händler, U. *Fürstliche Mäzene und Sammler in Deutschland von 1500-1620.* Halm und Berliner, 1931.
Holst, N. von. *Creators, Collectors, and Connoisseurs: The Anatomy of Artistic Taste from Antiquity to the Present Day.* NY, 1967.
Impey, O., and A. MacGregor. *The Origins of Museums: The Cabinets of Curiosities in Sixteenth- and Seventeenth-Century Europe.* Oxford, 1985.
Liebenwein, W. *Studiolo: Die Entstehung eines Raumtyps und seine Entwicklung bis um 1600,* in Frankfurther Forschungen zur Kunst (6), Berlin, 1977.
___. *Studiolo: Storia e tipologia di uno spazio culturale.* Modena, 1992.
Münsterberger, W. *Collecting: An Unruly Passion: Psychological Perspectives.* Princeton, NJ, 1994.
Princely Taste: Treasures from Great Private Collections (exh cat). Jerusalem, 1995.
Sandrart, J. von. *Teutsche Academie der Edlen Bau-, Bild- und Mahlerey-Künste.* Nuremberg, 1679 (Part II); Munich, 1925, pp. 305-334.
Schlosser, J. von. *Kunst und Wunderkammern der Spätrenaissance. Monographien des Kunstgewerbes* (XI, NF). Leipzig, 1908 (2nd enlarged ed., 1978).
Steingräber, E. *Royal Treasures.* NY, 1969.
Weiss, R. *The Renaissance Discovery of Classical Antiquity.* Oxford, 1969.

Aspects of Kunstkammer Collecting
Bertele, H. von. *Globes and Spheres.* Lausanne, 1961.
David, S. *Ziervasen der Renaissance bis zum Klassizismus* (PhD thesis). Kiel, 1964.
Fritz, R. *Die Gefäße aus Kokosnuss in Mitteleuropa: 1250-1880.* Mainz, 1983.
Hackenbroch, Y. *Renaissance Jewellery.* London, 1979.
Haspels, J.J.L. *Automatic Musical Instruments: Their Mechanics and Music: 1520-1820.* Zwolle, 1987.
Hayward, J.F. *Virtuoso Goldsmiths: 1540-1620.* NY, 1976.
Hernmarck, C. *The Art of the European Silversmith: 1430-1830* (2 vols). NY, 1977.
Kohlhausen, H. *Nürnberger Goldschmiedekunst des Mittelalters und der Dürerzeit: 1240-1540.* Berlin, 1968.
Kris, E. *Meister und Meisterwerke der Steinschneidekunst.* Vienna, 1929.
___. *Goldschmiedearbeiten der Gotik, Renaissance, und des Barock.* Vienna, 1932.
Laloux, V., and P. Cruysmans. *L'Oeil de l'hibou: Le Bestiaire des orfèvres.* Lausanne/Paris, 1994.
Maurice, K. *Der drechselnde Souverän: Materialien zu einer fürstlichen Maschinenkunst.* Zurich, 1985.
___, and O. Mayr (eds). *The Clockwork Universe: German Clocks and Automata: 1550-1650.* Washington, DC, 1980.
Mette, H.-U. *Der Nautiluspokal: Wie Kunst und Natur miteinander spielen.* Munich, 1995.
Philippovich, E. von. *Elfenbein* (2nd ed). Munich, 1982.
Princely Magnificence: Court Jewels of the Renaissance: 1500-1630 (exh cat). London, 1981.
Seelig, L., et al. *Silber und Gold: Augsburger Goldschmiedekunst für die Höfe Europas* (exh cat, 2 vols). Munich, 1994.
Seling, H. *Die Kunst der Augsburger Goldschmiede: 1529-1868* (3 vols). Munich, 1980.
Wenzel Jamnitzer und die Nürnberger Goldschmiedekunst: 1500-1700 (exh cat). Nuremberg, 1985.

The French Royal Collections
Aumale, Duc d'. *Inventaire de tous les meubles du Cardinal Mazarin dressé en 1653 et publié d'après l'original conservé dans les Archives de Condé.* London, 1861.
Barbet de Jouy, H. *Galerie d'Apollon: Notice des Gemmes et Joyaux,* Paris, 1867.
Béguin, S. *L'École de Fontainebleau: Le Maniérisme à la cour de France.* Paris, 1960.
Bimbenet-Privat, M. *Les Orfèvres parisiens de la Renaissance.* Paris, 1992.
___, et al. *L'Orfèvrerie parisienne de la Renaissance: Trésors dispersés.* Paris, 1995.
Bonaffé, E. *Recherches sur les collections de Richelieu.* Paris, 1883.
Carlier, Y. «Les Cabinets du Grand Dauphin au château de Versailles,» *Bulletin de la Société de l'Histoire de l'Art Francais,* 1987, pp. 45-90.
Cox-Rearick, J. *Royal Treasures: The Collection of François I.* Antwerp/NY, 1995.
Das Goldene Rössl: Ein Meisterwerk der Pariser Hofkunst um 1400 (exh cat). Munich, 1995.
Durand, J. *The Louvre: Objets d'art.* Paris, 1995.
Fardoulis-Vitart, A. *Le Cabinet du Roi et les anciens Cabinets de Curiosités dans les collections du Musée de l'Homme* (diplôme). Paris, 1979.
Guiffrey, J.J. *Inventaire général du mobilier de la Couronne sous Louis XIV: 1683-1715* (2 vols). Paris, 1885.
___ (ed). *Inventaires de Jean, duc de Berry: 1401-1416* (2 vols). Paris, 1894-1896.
Iñiguez, D. *Catalogo de las Alhajas del Delfin* (2nd rev ed). Madrid, 1989.
Labartes, J. *Inventaires du mobilier de Charles V, roi de France.* Paris, 1879.
Lightbown, R.W. *Secular Goldsmiths' Work in Medieval France: A History,* in Reports of the Research Committee of the Society of Antiquaries of London (XXXVI). London, 1978.
Marquet de Vasselot, J.J. *Catalogue sommaire de l'orfèvrerie, de l'émaillerie et des gemmes du moyen age au XVIIe siècle.* Paris, 1914.
Scaillerez, C. *François Ier et ses artistes dans les collections du Louvre* (exh cat). Paris, 1992.
Schnapper, A. *Curieux du Grand Siècle: Collections et collectionneurs dans la France du XVIIe siècle.* Paris, 1994.
Zerner, H. *The School of Fontainebleau.* NY, 1969.

The Medici Collections
Aschengreen-Piacenti, K. *Il Museo degli Argenti a Firenze.* Milan, 1968.
Avery, C. *Giambologna: The Complete Sculpture.* Oxford, 1987.
Berti, L. *Il principe dello studiolo: Francesco I dei Medici e la fine del Rinascimento Fiorentino.* Florence, 1967.
Chastel, A. *Art et Humanisme à Florence au temps de Laurent le Magnifique.* Paris, 1959.
Chiarini, A., and K. Aschengreen-Piacenti. *Artisti alla Corte granducale* (exh cat). Florence, 1969.
Curiosità di una reggia: Vicende della guardaroba di Palazzo Pitti (exh cat). Florence, 1979.
Dacos, N., A. Guliano, and U. Pannuti. *Il tesoro di Lorenzo il Magnifico: Le Gemme.* Florence, 1972.
___, et al. *Il tesoro di Lorenzo il Magnifico: Repertorio delle gemme e dei vasi.* Florence, 1980.
Gasparri, C., (ed). *Le gemme Farnese.* Naples, 1994.
Giuliano, A., and M.E. Micheli. *I cammei della collezione medicea del Museo Archeologico di Firenze.* Milan, 1978.
Giusti, A., (ed). *Splendori di Pietre Dure: L'Arte di Corte nella Firenze dei Granduchi* (exh cat). Florence, 1988-89.
Hackenbroch, Y., and M. Sframeli (eds). *I gioielli dell'Elettrice Palatina al Museo degli Argenti* (exh cat). Florence, 1972.
Lorenzo il Magnifico e le arti (exh cat). Florence, 1949.
Massinelli, A.M., and F. Tuena. *Treasures of the Medici.* NY, 1992.
Morassi, A. *Il Tesoro dei Medici.* Milan, 1963.
Rossacher, K. *Der Schatz des Erzstiftes Salzburg.* Salzburg, 1966.

The Habsburg Collections
GENERAL
Eichler, F., and E. Kris. *Die Kameen im Kunsthistorischen Museum.* Vienna, 1927.
Kunsthistorisches Museum Wien: Weltliche und Geistliche Schatzkammer: Bildführer. Vienna, 1987.
Leithe-Jasper, M., and R. Distelberger. *The Kunsthistorische Museum, Vienna: The Treasury and the Collection of Sculpture and Decorative Arts.* London, 1982.
Lhotzky, A. *Festchrift des Kunsthistorischen Museums zur Feier des Fünfzigjährigen Bestandes: Die Geschichte der Sammlungen. Zweiter Teil: Erste Hälfte: Von den Anfängen bis zum Tode Kaiser Karls VI.* Vienna, 1941-45.
Scheicher, E. *Die Kunst- und Wunderkammern der Habsburger.* Vienna, 1979.
Strohmer, E. von. *Prunkgefässe aus Bergkristall.* Vienna, 1947.
Trevor-Roper, H. *Princes and Artists: Patronage and Ideology at Four Habsburg Courts.* London, 1976.

The Early Habsburgs
Carlos V y su Ambiente (exh cat). Toledo, 1958.
Friedrich III: Kaiserresidenz Wiener Neustadt (exh cat). Wiener Neustadt, 1966.
Inventario de la alhajas, relicarios, estatuas, pinturas, tapices y otros objetos de valor y curiosidad, donados por el rey Don Felipe II al Monasterio de El Escorial Anos 1571-1598. Madrid, 1929.
Kaiser Karl V (exh cat). Vienna, 1958.
Laborde, Comte M.L. de. "Inventaire des tableaux, livres, joyaux et meubles de Marguerite d'Autriche, fille de Marie de Bourgogne et de Maximilien empereur d'Allemagne, fait et conclus en la ville d'Anvers le XVII avril MCXXIII," *Rev. Arch.,* 1850.
Maximilian I (exh cat). Innsbruck, 1959.
Oberhammer, V. *Die Bronzestandbilder des Maximiliangrabes in der Hofkirche zu Innsbruck.* Innsbruck, 1935.
Plon, E. *Les maîtres italiens au service de la Maison d'Autriche: Leone Leoni et Pompeo Leoni.* Paris, 1887.

Archduke Ferdinand II of Tyrol
Ambraser Kunst und Wunderkammer: Die Bibliothek (exh cat). Vienna, 1965.
Auer, A., and E. Irblich. *Natur und Kunst: Handschriften und Alben aus der Ambraser Sammlung Erzherzog Ferdinands II: 1529-1595* (exh cat). Vienna, 1995.
Garner, H. *Chinese Export Art in Schloss Ambras.* London, 1975.
Hirn, J. *Erzherzog Ferdinand II von Tirol: Geschichte seiner Regierung und seiner Länder* (2 vols.), Innsbruck, 1885-88.
Kunsthistorisches Museum: Sammlungen Schloss Ambras: Die Kunstkammer. Innsbruck, 1977.
Luchner, L. *Denkmal eines Renaissancefürsten: Versuch einer Rekonstruktion des Ambraser Museums von 1583.* Vienna, 1958.
Primisser, A.. *Die Kaiserlich-Königliche Ambraser Sammlung.* Vienna, 1819; Graz, 1972.
Sammlungen Schloss Ambras: Die Rüstkammer (Führer durch das Kunsthistorische Museum). Vienna, 1981

Emperor Rudolf II
Eros und Mythos: Kunst am Hof Rudolfs II (exh cat). Vienna, 1995.
Evans, R.J.W. *Rudolf II and His World: A Study in Intellectual History: 1576-1612.* Oxford, 1984.
Fucikova, E., et al. *Die Kunst am Hofe Rudolfs II.* Prague, 1988.
Kaufmann, T. da Costa. *The School of Prague: Painting at the Court of Rudolf II.* Chicago/London, 1988.
___. *L'École de Prague.* Paris, 1985.
Larsson, L.O. *Adriaen de Vries: Adrianus Fries Hagiensis Batavus: 1545-1626.* Vienna/Munich, 1967.
Prag um 1600: Kunst und Kultur am Hofe Rudolfs II (exh cat, 2 vols). Vienna, 1988.

The Later Habsburgs
Garas, K. "Die Entstehung der Galerie des Erzherzogs Leopold Wilhelm," *Jb. d. kh. Slgen. in Wien* (63), 1967, pp. 39-80.
___. "Das Schicksal der Sammlung des Erzherzogs Leopold Wilhelm," *Jb. d. kh. Slgen. in Wien* (64), 1968, pp. 181-278.
"Inventar der Kunstkammer von 1659," *Jb. d. kh. Slgen. des AHK* (1), 1883 (Reg. 495).
"Inventar des Nachlasses von Kaiser Matthias vom 5. Mai 1619," *Jb. d. kh. Slg. des AHK* (20), 1899 (Reg. 17408).
Mraz, G., and H. Haupt. "Das Inventar der Kunstkammer und der Bibliothek des Erzherzogs Leopold Wilhelm aus dem Jahr 1647," *Jb. d. kh. Slgen. in Wien* (77), 1981.
Wastler, J. *Das Kunstleben am Hof zu Graz unter den Herzogen von Steiermark, den Herzögen Karl und Ferdinand.* Graz, 1897.

The Wittelsbach Kunstkammer in Munich
Baader, B.P. *Der Bayerische Renaissancehof Herzog Wilhelms V.* Leipzig/Strasbourg, 1943.
Brunner, H. *Die Kunstschätze der Münchner Residenz.* Munich, 1977.
Frankenburger, M. *Die Silberkammer der Münchener Residenz.* Munich, 1923.
Reitzenstein, A. von. *Die alte baierische Stadt in den Modellen des Drechslermeisters Jakob Sandtner.* Munich, 1967.
Stockbauer, J. *Die Kunstbestrebungen am bayerischen Hofe unter Herzog Albrecht V und seinem Nachfolger Wilhelm V: Quellenschriften für Kunstgeschichte des Mittelalters und der Renaissance* (8). Vienna, 1874.
Thoma, H., and H. Brunner. *Schatzkammer der Residenz München* (cat.). Munich, 1958-1570.
Um Glauben und Reich: Kurfürst Maximilian I (exh cat). Munich, 1980.
Zimmermann, M.G. *Die bildenden Künste am*

Hofe unter Albrecht V und seinem Nachfolger Wilhelm V. Vienna, 1874.

The Dresden Kunstkammer and the Green Vaults

Asche, S. *Balthasar Permoser un die Barockskulptur des Dresdener Zwingers.* Frankfurt-am-Main, 1966.

Menzhausen, J. *Dresdener Kunstkammer und Grünes Gewölbe.* Leipzig, 1977.

Sponsel, J.L. *Das Grüne Gewölbe zu Dresden* (4 vols). Leipzig, 1925-1932.

Syndram, D., (ed). *Das Grüne Gewölbe zu Dresden: Führer durch seine Geschichte und seine Sammlungen.* Munich, 1994.

Syndram, D. *Prunkstücke des Grünen Gewölbes zu Dresden.* Munich, 1994.

Watzdorf, E. von. *Johann Melchior Dinglinger* (2 vols). Berlin, 1962.

The Brandenburg Kunstkammer in Berlin

China und Japan in der Kunstkammmer der Brandenburgischen Kurfürsten. Berlin, 1932.

Kugler, F. *Beschreibung der in der Königlichen Kunstkammer zu Berlin vorhandenen Kunst-Samlung.* Berlin, 1838.

Theuerkauff, C., et al. *Die Brandeburgisch-Preussische Kunstkammer: Eine Auswahl aus den alten Beständen* (exh cat). Berlin, 1981.

The Kunstkammer of the Landgraves of Hessen-Kassel

Link, E.M. *Die Landgräfliche Kunstkammer Kassel.* Kassel, 1975.

Mackensen, L. von, (ed.) *Die erste Sternwarte Europas mit ihren Instrumenten und Uhren: 400 Jahre Jost Bürgi in Kassel.* Munich, 1979.

Philipp Hainhofer and the Augsburg Kunstschrank

Böttiger, J. *Philipp Hainhofer und der Kunstschrank Gustav Adolfs in Upsala* (1-4). Stockholm, 1909-10.

Gobiet, R. R., (ed.) *Der Briefwechsel zwischen Philipp Hainhofer und Herzog August d. J. von Braunschweig-Lüneburg.* Munich/Berlin, 1984.

Lessing, J., and A. Brüning. *Der Pommersche Kunstschrank.* Berlin, 1905.

The Danish Royal Kunstkammer and Rosenborg Castle in Copenhagen

Gundestrup, B. *The Royal Danish Kunstkammer, 1737* (2 vols). Copenhagen, 1991.

Sophie Amalie 1628-85 (exh cat). Copenhagen, 1986.

Trésors des rois de Danemark (exh cat). Paris, 1979.

The Swedish Royal Collection in Stockholm

Christina, Queen of Sweden (exh cat). Stockholm, 1966.

Conforti M., and G. Walton (eds). *Sweden: A Royal Treasury: 1550-1700* (exh cat). Washington, DC, 1988.

Granberg, O. *Svenska konstsamlingarnas historia fran Gustav Vasas tid till vara dagar.* Stockholm, 1929.

Other Kunstkammer Collections

Béguin, S., (ed.) *Le Studiolo d'Isabelle d'Este.* Paris, 1975.

Beljaev, O. *Kabinett Petra Velikogo.* St. Petersburg, 1800.

Chambers, D., and J. Martineau (eds). *Splendors of the Gonzaga* (exh cat). London, 1982.

De wered binnen handbereik: Nederlandske kunst- en rariteiten- verzamlingen: 1585-1735 (exh cat). Amsterdam, 1992.

Der Schatz des Deutschen Ordens aus Wien (exh cat). Salzburg, 1994.

Fleischhauer, W. *Geschichte der Kunstkammer der Herzöge von Württemberg in Stuttgart.* Stuttgart, 1976.

Neverov, O. *The Collection of Peter's Kunstkammer* (exh. cat). St. Petersburg, 1992.

Peter der Grosse in Westeuropa: Schätze aus dem Kreml (exh cat). Bremen, 1991.

Peter the Great and Holland (exh cat). Amsterdam, 1996.

Stix, A., and E. von Strohmer. *Die Fürstlich Liechtensteinische Kunstkammer.* Vienna, 1938.

Notes

Abbreviations: BN = Bibliothèque Nationale, Paris; BNM = Bayerisches Nationalmuseum. Munich; GMN = Germanisches Nationalmuseum, Nuremberg; KHM = Kunsthistorisches Museum, Vienna; MMA = Metropolitan Museum of Art, New York; *Jb. d. Slg. in Wien* = *Jahrbuch der Sammlungen in Wien; Jb. d. Slgen. d. AHK* = *Jahrbuch der Sammlungen des Allerhöchsten Kaiserhauses.*

The Valois

1. For the flowering of late Gothic culture around 1400, see *Europäische Kunst um 1400* (exh. cat.), KHM, 1962.
2. *La Librairie de Charles V* (exh. cat.), BN, 1968; J. Labarte, *Inventaire du Mobilier de Charles V, roi de France (Collection de documents inedits sur l'histoire de France),* Paris, 1879.
3. For the early records of secular goldsmith work in France, see R.W. Lightbown, *Secular Goldsmiths' Work in Medieval France: A History,* London, 1978.
4. D. Gaborit-Chopin, "Les Collections d'orfèvrerie des princes français au milieu du XIVe siècle d'après les comptes et inventaires," in *Hommage à Hubert Landais: Objets d'art, Collections (Études sur l'art du Moyen Age et de la Renaissance sur l'histoire du goût et des collections),* Paris, 1987.
5. P. Henwood, "Le Trésor royal sous le règne de Charles VI (1380-1422): Études sur les inventaires, les orfèvres et les principaux artistes du roi," *Ec. Nat. des Chartes: Position des thèses,* 1978, pp. 91-98; P. Henwood, "Administration et vie des collections d'orfèvrerie royales sous le règne de Charles VI (1380-1422)," *Ec. Nat. des Chartes* (138), 1980, pp. 179-215.
6. *Das Goldene Rössl: Ein Meisterwerk der Pariser Hofkunst um 1400* (exh. cat.), BNM, 1995.
7. *Ibid.,* cat. 2 (ill. p. 209) and cat. 3 (ill. p. 215). BNM, inv. MA 2607 and 2608.
8. Moranville, *Inventaire de l'orfèvrerie et des joyaux de Louis I, duc d'Anjou,* Paris, 1903.
9. Champeaux and Gaucherie, *Les Travaux d'art exécutés pour Jean de France, duc de Berry,* Paris, 1894.

10. See M. Thomas, *The Golden Age: Manuscript Painting at the Time of Jean, Duke of Berry,* NY, 1979.
11. J. von Schlosser, *Kunst und Wunderkammern der Spätrenaissance (Monographien des Kunstgewerbes* [NF, 11]), Leipzig, 1908, p. 32.
12. J.J. Guiffrey (ed.), *Inventaires de Jean, duc de Berry: 1401-1416* (2 vols.), Paris, 1894-1896.
13. For Salomon Weininger, see O. Kurz, *Fakes,* 1973. (*Faux et Faussaires,* Paris, 1982, p. 217.)
14. See *Das Goldene Rössl, op. cit.,* n. 7, ill. 56, p. 115.
15. Translated from Schlosser, *op. cit.,* p. 33
16. *The Currency of Fame: Portrait Medals of the Renaissance* (exh cat) NY, 1994, pp. 32-33.
17. W. Liebewein, *Studiolo: Die Entstehung eines Raumtyps und seine Entwicklung bis um 1600,* Berlin, 1977.
18. J. Straford, *The Bedford Inventories: The Worldly Goods of John, Duke of Bedford, Regent of France (1389-1435),* London, 1993.
19. F. Hackett, *Francis the First: First Gentleman of France,* NY, 1934, p. 108.
20. The journal of Antonio de Beatis, 1517, quoted from J. Cox-Rearick, *Royal Treasures: The Collection of François I,* Antwerp/NY, 1995, p. 7.
21. Quoted from Cox-Rearick, *op. cit.,* p. 365.
22. *Ibid.,* cat. VI-2, fig. 210, p. 202; cat. VI-3, fig. 216, p. 208.
23. B. Morel, *Les Joyaux de la Couronne de France,* Paris, 1988, pp. 93-95.
24. Cox-Rearick, *op. cit.,* p. 141, fig. 138, figs. 60, 67-73.
25. *Ibid.,* cat. IV-2, 145-146.
26. *Ibid.,* cat. V-11, pp. 179-181, fig. 183.
27. *Ibid.,* p. 364, fig. 399.
28. *Ibid.,* p. 103.
29. M. Bimbenet-Privat, "La Vérité sur l'origine de la 'Coupe de St.-Michel'," *Jb. d. kh. Slgen. in Wien,* vol. 87 (NF, 51), 1992, pp. 127-135.
30. *Ibid.,* pp. 127-135.
31. Cox-Rearick, *op. cit.,* p. 373.
32. M. Bimbenet-Privat, *L'Orfèvrerie parisienne de la Renaissance: Trésors dispersés* (exh cat), Paris, 1995, p. 46.

33. See also *Das Goldene Rössl, op. cit.,* chap. 1, n. 6, p. 114.
34. See also Cox-Rearick, *op. cit.,* pp. 373ff.
35. Père Dan, 1642. See *Ibid.,* p. 373.
36. E. Kris, "Die Verwendung des Naturabgusses bei Wenzel Jamnitzer und Bernard Palissy," *Jb. d. kh. Slgen. in Wien* (NF, 1), 1926, pp. 137ff.
37. R. Distelberger, "Beobachtungen zu den Steinschneide- werkstätten der Miseroni in Mailand und Prag," *Jb. d. kh. Slgen. in Wien,* 74 (NF, 38), 1978, pp. 79-152.
38. P. Lacroix, "L'Inventaire des joyaux de la couronne de France en 1560," *Revue universelle des arts,* 1856.
39. J. Durand, *The Louvre: Objets d'art,* Paris, 1995, p. 71.
40. J.-J. Marquet de Vasselot, "La Vaisselle d'argent de l'ordre du St.-Esprit," *Bull. de la Soc. de l'hist. de l'art français,* 1911, pp. 344-347.
41. D. Alcouffe, "À propos de l'orfèvrerie commandée par Henri III pour l'ordre du St.-Esprit," *Hommage à Hubert Landais, op. cit.,* pp. 135-142.
42. *Ibid.,* fig. 4.
43. *Ibid.,* figs. 8-11.
44. Durand, *op. cit.,* p. 71.

The Bourbons

1. L. Bruel, "Deux inventaires de bagues, joyaux, pierreries et dorures de la reine Marie de Médicis (1609 ou 1610)," *Arch. de l'art francais* (NS, 2), 1908, pp. 186-215.
2. D. Alcouffe, "The Collection of Cardinal Mazarin," *Burl. Mag.,* CXVI, 858 (1974), pp. 514-526.
3. C. Blair (ed) *The History of Silver,* NY, 1987, p. 103.
4. *Ibid.,* p. 99.
5. J.J. Guiffrey, *Inventaire général du mobilier de la Couronne sous Louis XIV: 1683-1715,* Paris, 1885, pp. 171-220 ("Agates et autres pierres de couleur"); pp. 221-268 ("Cristaux de roche").
6. D. Alcouffe, "La Collection de Gemmes de Louis XIV: Identification de quelques pièces aliénées," *Bull. de la Soc. de l'art Francais,* 1977, pp. 109-125.
7. Alcouffe, *op. cit.* (1977, see n. 2).
8. D.A. Iñiguez, *Catalogo de las Alhajas del Delfin,* Madrid, 1954; see also Iñiguez,

Catalogo de las Alhajas del Delfin (2nd rev ed), Madrid, 1989.
9. P. Verlet, "Les gemmes du Dauphin," *Art de France,* III, 1963, pp. 136-153.
10. Iñiguez, *op. cit.,* cat. 2.
11. *Ibid.,* cat. 19.
12. *Ibid.,* cat. 32.
13. *Ibid.,* cat. 67.
14. *Ibid.,* cat. 69.
15. *Ibid.,* cat. 73.
16. *Ibid.*
17. M. Bimbenet-Privat, "L'Orfèvrerie parisienne au XVIe siècle: Nouvelles identifications: L'Oeuvre des Toutain," *Rev. de l'Art,* 61, 1983, pp. 53-60.
18. Iñiguez, *op. cit.* (1989), cat. 74.
19. R. Distelberger, "Die Sarachi Werkstatt und Annibale Fontana," *Jb. d. kh. Slgen.,* 71 (NF, 35), 1975, pp. 95-164.
20. R. Distelberger, "Beobachtungen zu den Steinschneidewerkstätten der Miseroni in Mailand un Prag," *Jb. d. kh. Slgen.,* 74 (NF, 38), 1978, pp. 79-152; 21. R. Distelberger, "Dionysio und Ferdinand Eusebio Miseroni," *Jb. d. kh. Slgen.,* 75 (NF, 39), 1979, pp. 109-187.

Cosimo, Piero, and Lorenzo de' Medici

1. See A. Morassi, *Il tesoro dei Medici,* Milan, 1963; K. Aschengreen-Piacenti, *Il Museo degli Argenti a Firenze,* Milan, 1967; N. Dacos, et al., *Il tesoro di Lorenzo il Magnifico,* Florence, 1980; A.M. Massinelli and F. Tuena, *Treasures of the Medici,* NY, 1992.
2. See A. Grote, "La formazione e le vicende del tesoro mediceo nel Quattrocento," in Dacos, et al., *op. cit.,* p. 125.
3. Quoted from Massinelli and Tuena, *op. cit.,* p. 20.
4. *Ibid.*
5. A. Filarete, *Trattato dell'Archittetura,* XXV, p. 187.
6. Massinelli and Tuena, *op. cit.,* p. 22.
7. *Ibid.*
8. For a reconstruction of the *studiolo,* see Heikamp and Detlef, "Lo Scrittoio di Piero," in Dacos, et al., *op. cit.,* pp. 169-173. See also S. Béguin, *Le Studiolo d'Isabelle d'Este,* Paris, 1975; O. Raggio and A.M. Wilmering, *The Liberal Arts Studiolo from the Ducal Palace at Gubbio,* MMA, spring

1996; W. Liebenwein, *Studiolo: Storia e tipologia di uno spazio culturale*, Modena, 1992.
9. J. Pope-Hennessy, *Catalogue of Italian Sculpture in the Victoria and Albert Museum*, vol. 1, London, 1964, pp. 104ff; W. Liebewein, *Studiolo: Die Entstähung eines Raumtyps und seine Entwicklung bis um 1600*, Berlin 1977, pp. 81ff.
10. E. Scheicher, *Die Kunst- und Wunderkammern der Habsburger*, Vienna, 1979, p. 41.
11. Filarete, *op. cit.*, II, pp. 186ff. Quoted from Massinelli and Tuena, *op. cit.*, p. 23.
12. Translated from Grote, *op. cit.*, p. 170: "There is a large number of ornate books and alabaster and chalcedony vases mounted in gold in silver."
13. U. Pannuti, "Dall'inventario del cardinale Pietro Barbo (1457)," in Dacos, et al., *op. cit.*, pp. 87-118.
14. Quoted from L. de' Medici, *Tutte le Opere: Scritto Giocosi*, Milan, 1958, p. 153.
15. See U. Panutti, "Formazione, incremento e vicende dell'antica raccolta glittica medicea," in Dacos, et al., *op. cit.*, p. 4; first pub. by F. Gori, *Prodromo della Toscana Illustrata*, Livorno, 1755, pp. 191-194.
16. Massinelli and Tuena, *op. cit.*, pp. 25.
17. *Ibid.*, p. 27.
18. At Lorenzo's death in 1492 an inventory of his property was established, listing some 4,000 items valued at over 75,000 florins. The contents of his *Scrittoio* were estimated at 53,413.5 florins. These included 33 hardstone vases appraised at 21,318 florins, amounting to almost one-third of the total value of the inventory. Twenty-one vases have survived incised in Roman capitals with Lorenzo's collector's mark. For 42 intaglios and cameos that bear Lorenzo de' Medici's collector's mark, see A. Giuliano in Dacos, et al., *op. cit.*, pp. 39-66. A further 19 items can be attributed with all probabilty to the same source (see Pannuti, *op. cit.*, pp. 69-81).
19. Preserved at the Archivio di Stato, Florence, in a transcript of 1512. Transcripts made for Aby Warbug exist at the German Institute in Florence as well as in the Warburg Institute in London.
20. The same inscription can be found on 42 intaglios and cameos from the collection of Lorenzo the Magnificent. See A. Giuliano, *Catalogo delle gemme che recano l'iscrizione : LAU.R.MED*, in Dacos, et al., *op. cit.*, pp. 39-66. Another 19 items of a similar nature can be attributed with probability to the same source. See U. Pannuti, "Catalogo delle gemme che non recamo l'iscrizione LAU.R.MED. ma provenienti dal tesoro di Lorenzo de' Medici," in Dacos, et al., *op.* cit., pp. 69-81.
21. *A Libro dei disegni dei vasi* whith drawings of the vase/reliquaries is preserved at the Bibliotheca Nazionale Centrale, Florence (Cod. Palatino, C.B. 3, 27 [G.F. 183]). The drawings date mostly from the late 16th century.

The Grand Dukes of Tuscany

1. Massinelli and Tuena, *op. cit.*, p. 27.
2. Vasari, *Vite*, IV, p. 177.
3. See C. Gasparri, *Le Gemme Farnese*, Napoli, 1994, cat. 23-54.
4. Morassi, op. cit., p.210
5. Published by C. Conti, *La Prima reggia di Cosimo I*, 1893.
6. Distelberger, *op. cit.* (1975), pp. 95-164; Distelberger, *op. cit.* (1979), pp. 109-187; E. Kris, *Meisterwerke der Steinschneidekunst in der Italienischen Renaissance*, Vienna, 1929.
7. Massinelli and Tuena, *op. cit.*, p. 59.
8. *Ibid.*, p. 61
9. *Ibid.*
10. *Ibid.*, p. 63.
11. *Ibid.*, p. 64.
12. L. Berti, *Il Principe dello Studiolo: Francesco I dei Medici e la fine del rinascimento fiorentino*, Florence, 1967.
13. Massinelli and Tuena, *op. cit.*, p. 64.
14. M. Bucci, *Lo Studiolo di Francesco I (Forma e Colore* 10), Florence, n.d., p. 1.
15. Manuscript inventory of 1589 at the Sovrintendenza alle Gallerie di Firenze (see Aschengreen-Piacenti, *op. cit.*, p. 14).
16. *Ibid.*
17. An inventory of Marie de' Medici's jewelry was published by F. Bruel, "Deux inventaires de bagues, joyaux, pierreries et dorures de la reine Marie de Médicis (1609 ou 1610)," *Arch de l'art franc* (NS, 2), 1908, pp 186-215.
18. See Massinelli and Tuena, *op. cit.*, p. 233.
19. Massinelli and Tuena, *op. cit.*, p. 151.
20. *I Gioielli dell'Elettrice Palatina al Museo degli Argenti* (exh. cat.), Palazzo Pitti, Florence, 1988.
21. Massinelli and Tuena, *op. cit.*, p. 183.
22. K. Rossacher, *Der Schatz des Erztstiftes Salzburg*, Salzburg, 1966.

Early Habsburg Collectors

1. See A. Wheatcroft, *The Habsburgs*, NY, 1995; A. Lhotzky, *Festchrift des Kunsthistorischen Museums zur Feier des Fünfzigjährigen Bestandes: Die Geschichte der Sammlungen. Zweiter Teil: Erste Hälfte: Von den Anfängen bis zum Tode Kaiser Karls VI.* 1740 (2 vols.), Vienna, 1941-45, pp. 1-178; Scheicher, *op. cit.*, pp. 44-65; H. Trevor-Roper, *Princes and Artists: Patronage and Ideology at Four Habsburg Courts*, London, 1976.
2. E. Maurer, *Das Kloster Königsfelden: Die Kunstdenkmäler des Kantons Aargau*, vol. 3, 1954.
3. *Ibid.*, pp. 251-254; *Königsfelden Chronik*, p. 105.
4. Maurer, *op. cit.*, pp. 255-277 (inv. 301).
5. *Ibid.*, pp. 253-254 (Staatsarchiv Aargau, KU 276a).
6. For Charles IV of Bohemia as patron of the arts, see *Europäische Kunst um 1400* (exh. cat.), KHM, 1962, pp. 47ff.
7. Lhotzky, *op. cit.*, vol. 2 (pl. 4 refers to fig. 99).
8. *Ibid.*, vol. 1, p. 26 (translated from p. 33).
9. *Friedrich III, Kaiserresidenz Wiener Neustadt* (exh. cat.), Wiener Neustadt, 1966.
10. Translated from Lhotzky, *op. cit.*, vol 1, pp. 52-53.
11. Scheicher, *op. cit.*, p. 52.
12. Lhotzky, *op. cit.*, vol. 1, p. 55.
13. *Maximilian I* (exh. cat.), Landesmuseum, Innnsbruck, 1969.
14. Scheicher, *op. cit.*, ill. p. 55.
15. V. Oberhammer, *Die Bronzestandbilder des Maximiliangrabes in der Hofkirche zu Innsbruck*, Innsbruck, 1935.
16. Lhotzky, *op. cit.*, vol. 1, p. 130.
17. *Regalos hechos a la princesa doña Margarita de Austria cuando se caso con el principe don Juan de Castilla ano de 1497 (Memorias de la Real Academia de la historia)*, 6, pp. 388ff.
18. Trevor-Roper, *op. cit.*, p. 14.
19. For an inventory of 1516 see Le Glay, *Correspondence de l'empereur Maximilien I et de Marguerite d'Autriche, sa fille, gouvernante de Pays-Bas de 1507 à 1529*, Paris, 1839, app. pp. 466ff. For the inventory of 1523 see Comte M.L. de Laborde, "Inventaire des tableaux, livres, joyaux et meubles de Marguerite d'Autriche, fille de Marie de Bourgogne et de Maximilien empereur d'Allemagne, fait et conclus en la ville d'Anvers le XVII avril MCXXIII," *Rev. Arch.*, 1850, pp. 336ff. and 80ff. For an inventory of 1524-1530 see *Jb. d. Slgen. d. AKH*, III, 1885, reg. 2979.
20. Translated from Lhotzky, *op. cit.*, vol. 1, p. 145.
21. Translated from Scheicher, *op. cit.*, p. 67.
22. Translated from Lhotzky, *op. cit.*, vol. 1, p. 155.
23. Letter of Juan Michiel Cavalier dated 1571. See Lhotzky, *op. cit.*, vol. 1, p. 157.
24. *Wenzel Jamnitzer und die Nürnberger Goldschmiedekunst 1500-1700* (exh. cat.), GNM, 1985, p. 61, fig. 33.

Archduke Ferdinand II of Tyrol

1. Albeit an old publication, the most complete biography is still J. Hirn, *Erzherzog Ferdinand II von Tirol: Geschichte seiner Regierung und seiner Länder* (2 vols.), Innsbruck, 1888. See also Lhotsky, *op. cit.*, vol. 1, pp. 179-202.
2. Inv. PA 1473/4. See S.M. Grossing, *Kaufmannstochter im Kaiserhaus: Phillipine Welser und ihre Heilkunst*, Vienna, 1992.
3. A lively description of a visit by Prince Karl Friedrich von Cleve to Innsbruck in 1574 contains an entertaining passage about the Bacchic rites at Schloss Ambras. See A. Primisser, *Die Kaiserlich-Königliche Ambraser Sammlung*, Graz, 1972 (Vienna, 1819), pp. 37ff.
4. Pliny, *Historia Naturalis*, XXXIII-XXXVII.
5. Quoted and translated from Lhotzky, *op. cit.*, vol. 1, p. 198.
6. See O. Gamber, "Erzherzog Ferdinand und die Ambraser Rüstkammern," *Kunsthistorisches Museum: Sammlungen Schloss Ambras: Die Rüstkammern*, Vienna, 1981, pp. 23-32.
7. *Verzaichnus der Römischen Kayser/König/Fürsten...*, Innsbruck, 1603.
8. H.W. Janson, *History of Art* (2nd ed.), NY, 1977, p. 453.
9. M. Leithe-Jasper, "Der Bergkristallpokal des Herzog Philipps des Guten von Burgund: Das 'Vierte Stück' der Geschenke König Karls IX von Frankreich an Erzherzog Ferdinand II," *Jb. d. kh. Slgen. in Wien* (NF), 1970, pp. 227-242.
10. Bimbenet-Privat, *op. cit.* (1991), pp. 127-135.
11. *Ibid.* (1983), pp. 53-60; 1995, pp. 102.
12. Kris, *op. cit.* (1926), pp. 137ff.
13. Scheicher, *op. cit.*, ill. p. 100 (above).
14. *Ibid.*, p. 102 (below).
15. *Ibid.*, p. 107.
16. P.W. Parshal, "The Print Collection of Ferdinand, Archduke of Tyrol," *Jb. d. kh. Slgen. in Wien* (NF, 78), 1982, pp. 139-184.
17. F. Anders, "Der Federkasten der Ambraser Kunstkammer," *Jb. d. kh. Slgen. in Wien*, 1965, pp. 119ff.

Emperor Rudolf II

1. See Lhotzky, *op. cit.*, vol. 1, pp. 237-298; Trevor-Roper, *op. cit.*, pp. 85-126; E. Fucikova, "The Collection of Rudolf II at Prague: Cabinet of Curiosities or Scientific Museum?" in O. Impey and A. MacGregor (eds.), *The Origins of Museums: The Cabinets of Curiosities in Sixteenth- and Seventeenth-Century Europe*, Oxford, 1985, pp. 47-53; *Eros und Mythos: Kunst am Hof Rudolfs II* (exh. cat.), KHM, 1995; *Prag um 1600: Kunst und Kultur am Hofe Kaiser Rudolfs II* (exh. cat., 2 vols.), KHM, 1988; E. Fucikova, et al., *Die Kunst am Hofe Rudolfs II*, Prague, 1988; Scheicher, *op. cit.*, pp. 142-178; R.J.W. Evans, *Rudolf II and His World: A Study in Intellectual History: 1576-1612*, Oxford, 1984.
2. 1607-1611 Vaduz, *Bibl. des Reg. Fürsten von Liechtenstein*, in R. Bauer and H. Haupt (eds.), *Das Kunstkammerinventar Kaiser Rudolfs II. 1601-11, Jb. d. h. Slgen. in Wien*, LXXII, 1976. The 1619 inventory in Wolfenbüttel, *Herzog August Bibliothek*, was published by W. Köhler, *Jb. d. kh. Slgen. d. AHK*, XXVI, 1906-1907, III, VI-VIII, reg. no. 19449. The inventory of 1621 was published by H. Zimmerman, *Jb. d. h. Slgen. d. AHK*, XXV, 1905, XX-XL, reg. no. 19421.
3. Active in 1576-1593 at the Rudolfine court as portraitist, organizer of festivities, inventor, and art expert. See F.C. Legrand and F. Sluys, *Arcimboldo et les arcimboldesques*, Paris, 1955.
4. Active in Prague during the years 1602-1608.
5. Evans, *op. cit.*, p. 162.
6. See I. Muchka, "Die Architektur unter Rudolf II., gezeigt am Beispiel der Prager Burg," *Prag um 1600, op. cit.*, pp. 85-93; Fucikova, "The Collections of Rudolf II . . . ," *op. cit.*, p. 48 (here the Summer Palace is dated after 1587).
7. Fucikova, *ibid.*, p. 49.
8. See Lhotzky, *op. cit.*, vol. 1, pp. 297-298.
9. *Ibid.*, pp. 283-284.
10. *Ibid.*, pp. 285ff.
11. Active in Prague in 1581-1611. In 1595 Spranger was ennobled by Rudolf. The inventory of 1621 lists 26 of his paintings. See K. Oberhuber, *Die stilistische Entwicklung im Werk Bartholomäus Sprangers* (PhD thesis), Vienna, 1958.
12. Active as *Kammermaler* in Prague in 1592-1615. With an annual salary of 200 gulden, Hans von Aachen was one of Rudolf's highest paid artists. The 1621 inventory lists 31 of his paintings. See R.A. Peltzer, "Der Hofmaler Hans von Aachen, seine Schule und seine Zeit," *Jb. d. kh. Slgen. des. AHK*, 30, 1911-1912, pp. 59-216.
13. In service to Rudolf as *Kammermaler* during the years 1591-1609. See J. Zimmer, *Joseph Heintz der Ältere als Maler*, Weissenhorn, 1971.
14. See *Eros und Mythos: Kunst am Hofe Rudolfs II.* (exh. cat.), KHM, 1995.
15. *Prag um 1600, op. cit.*, I, cat. 154, 155, 157, 159, 160, 164.
16. *Ibid.*, cat. 47.
17. *Ibid.*, cat. 48.
18. The marriage turned out to be exceedingly unhappy, thanks in part to the Grand Duke's notorious relationship with Bianca Capello. Other Habsburg/Medici marriages were those of Alessandro, Duke of Florence, and Margaret of Austria, an illegitimate daughter of Emperor Charles V; Claudia, a daughter of Ferdinando I, and Leopold, a son of Archduke Charles of Styria (1608); and Claudia's brother Cosimo II and Maria Magdalena (Maria Maddalena), a sister of Archduke Leopold.
19. Active in Prague c. 1593 - c. 1620. See L.O. Larsson, *Adriaen de Vries: Adrianus Fries Hagiensis Batavus 1545-1626*, Vienna/Munich, 1967.
20. *Prag um 1600, op. cit.*, I, cat. 56.
21. D. Syndram (ed.), *Das Grüne Gewölbe zu Dresden: Führer durch seine Geschichte und seine Sammlungen*, Munich, 1994, p. 43, cat. 28.
22. *Prag um 1600, op. cit.*, cat. 354 (a cup and cover); p. 452, ill. 3 (a plaquette); and ill. 5 (a sideboard dish); see also cat. 528-533.

23. *Ibid.*, II, cat. 685.
24. *Ibid.*, I, cat. 425.
25. K. Maurice, "Jost Bürgi, or on Innovation," *The Clockwork Universe: German Clocks and Automata: 1550-1650* (exh. cat.), Smithsonian, Wash., DC, 1980, p. 91.
26. MMA (inv. 17.190.636); *Prag um 1600, op. cit.*, cat. 445.
27. *Prague um 1600, op cit.*, cat. 447; KHM, Vienna (inv. 854).
28. See A. Boetius de Boodt, *Gemmarum et lapidum historia* (1st ed.), Hanau, 1609 (Scheicher, *op. cit.*, p. 160).
29. *Prag um 1600, op. cit.*, I, cat. 357; II, cat. 690 and 689.
30. Trevor-Roper, *op. cit.*, p. 123

Later Habsburgs
1. Translated from Lhotzky, *op. cit.*, p. 300.
2. *Ibid.*, p. 302.
3. *Ibid.*, p. 311 for Latin and a German translation.
4. *Ibid.*, pp. 308ff.
5. *Ibid.*, p. 329.
6. Schlosser, *op. cit.*, ill. 113.
7. Lhotzky, *op. cit.*, p. 329.
8. *Ibid.*, pp. 323ff.
9. *Katalog*, Kunsthistorisches Museum, Vienna, 1988, p. 228.
10. Lhotzky, *op. cit.*, p. 329.
11. K. Garas, "Die Entstehung der Galerie des Erzherzogs Leopold Wilhelm," *Jb. d. kh. Slgen. in Wien*, 63, 1967; K. Garas, "Das Schicksal der Sammlung des Erzherzogs Leopold Wilhelm," *Jd. d. kh. Slgen. in Wien*, 64, 1968.
12. For the treasury of the Order of the Teutonic Knights in Vienna, see *Der Schatz des Deutschen Ordens aus Wien: Katalog der XVII. Sonderschau im Dommuseum zu Salzburg*, 1994.
13. *Ibid.*, cat. 26, cat 8.
14. *Ibid.*, cat. 25.
15. *Ibid.*, cat. 7.

The Wittelsbachs
1. Wed in 1546. Their daughter, Maria, was married to her uncle, Archduke Charles of Styria. Children of this union include Emperor Ferdinand II; Margarete, wife of King Philip III of Spain; Anna and Constanza, successive wives of King Sigismund III of Poland; Count Leopold V of Tyrol, married to Claudia de' Medici; and Maria Magdalena, who married Cosimo II de' Medici.
2. H. Brunner, *Die Kunstschätze der Münchner Residenz*, Munich, 1977, p. 18. (See also S. Riezler, *Die Geschichte Bayerns*, Gotha, 1878-1903, vol. 4, p. 487.)
3. *Ibid.*, p. 18 (Riezler, *op. cit.*, p. 493).
4. O. Hartig, "Die Kunsttätigkeit in München unter Wilhelm IV. und Albrecht V. 1520-1579," *Münch. Jb. d. bild. Kunst* (NF, 10), 1933, pp. 200-211.
5. See Brunner, *op. cit.*, pp. 127-175 ("Die Schatzkammer").
6. L. Seelig, "Die Münchner Kunstkammer: Geschichte, Anlage, Ausstattung," *Jb. d. Bayer. Denkmalpflege*, vol. 40, 1989, pp. 101-138. This fundamental article, heavily annotated, is the main source of information on the Munich Kunstkammer.
7. This museum, housed in a building with a large tunnel vault, was the earliest of its kind north of the Alps. See E. Weski, et al., *Das Antiquarium der Münchner Residenz: Katalog der Skulpturen*, Munich, 1987; Brunner, *op. cit.*, pp. 25-32 ("Das Antiquarium").
8. O. Hartig, "Die Gründung der Münchener Hofbibliothek durch Albrecht V. und Johann

Jakob Fugger," *Abhandlungen der königlichen bayerischen Akademie der Wissenschaften*, Munich, 1917, pp. 49, 93-96.
9. M. Frankenburger, *Die Silberkammer der Münchener Residenz*, Munich, 1923; Brunner, *op. cit.*, pp. 195-210 ("Die Silberkammer").
10. Translated from Brunner, *op. cit.*, p. 195.
11. D.J. Jansen, "Jacopo Strada et le commerce d'art," *Revue de l'art*, 77, 1987, pp. 11-21.
12. Quoted and translated from Brunner, *op. cit.*, p. 127.
13. H. Thoma and H. Brunner, *Schatzkammer der Residenz München* (cat.), Munich, 1958-1570, cat. 636, ill. 64b.
14. *Ibid.*, cat. 637.
15. *Ibid.*, cat. 47.
16. *Ibid.*, cat. 4, ill. 1.
17. Brunner, *op. cit.*, pp. 177-188 ("Die Reiche Kapelle: Der Heiltumsschatz").
18. *Ibid.*, p. 35, ill. 17.
19. *Ibid.*, p. 37, ill. 18.
20. "*Un grandissimo vaso, e maggiore di quanti ne siano stati fabricati nel Cristallo, et era di forma di un ovo, col suo manico et tutto intagliato a figure di cavo*," quoted from Thoma and Brunner, *op. cit.*, cat. 328, p. 162.
21. *Ibid.*, cat. 329, p. 163, ill. 41a/b.
22. L. Seelig, "The Munich *Kunstkammer* 1565-1807," in Impey and MacGregor, *op. cit.*, pp. 76-89; Brunner, *op. cit.*, pp. 17-23; Seelig, *op. cit.* (1989), pp. 101-138. Here a convincing attempt is made to reconstruct the Kunstkammer and its internal disposition.
23. Translated from Brunner, *op. cit.*, p. 20.
24. *Ibid.*, p. 19.
25. Bayerische Staatsbibliothek, inv. 2133/34.
26. C. Häutle, "Die Reisen des Augsburger Philipp Hainhofer nach Eichstädt, München und Regensburg in den Jahren 1611, 1612 und 1613," *Zft. d. Hist. Vereins f. Schwaben und Neuburg*, 8, 1881, p. 1-316.
27. L. Seelig, "Das Gebetbuch des Lorenzo de' Medici," *Weltkunst*, 2, 15 Jan. 1993, pp. 92-93.
28. L. Seelig, "Das Gebetbuch Kurfürst Maximilians I. von Bayern," *Weltkunst*, 2, 15 Jan. 1987, pp. 126-127.
29. Thoma and Brunner, *op. cit.*, cat. 12a, ill. 9.
30. Seelig, *op. cit.* (1987), p. 125, ill. 25.
31. *Ibid.*, p. 126, ill. 26.
32. Brunner. *op. cit.*, pp. 211-214, figs. 223-236.

The Electors of Saxony
1. J. Menzhausen, *Dresdener Kunstkammer und Grünes Gewölbe*, Leipzig, 1977; J. Menzhausen, "Elector Augustus' *Kunstkammer*: an Analysis of the Inventory of 1587," in Impey and MacGregor, *op. cit.*, pp. 69-75. For early descriptions of the contents of the Green Vaults, see T. Beutel, *Chur-Fürstlicher Sächsischer stets grünender hoher Cedern-Wald* (Dresden, 1671), reprinted in 1975 (Leipzig); *Beschreibung des Grünen Gewölbes in Dressden, dem noch beygefüget einige kurze Zusätze zu Herrn Heckels Beschreibung des Königsteins, Franckfurt und Leipzig*, 1737; J.L. Sponsel, *Das Grüne Gewölbe zu Dresden* (4 vols.), Leipzig, 1925-1932.
2. *Dresdner Rüstkammer: Historisches Museum: Meisterwerke aus vier Jahrhunderten*, 1992, p. 45, pl. 14.
3. Menzhausen, *op. cit.* (1977), p. 74.
4. *Ibid.*, p. 74.
5. D. Syndram, *Prunkstücke des Grünen

Gewölbes zu Dresden*, Munich, 1994, p. 92.
6. *Ibid.*, p. 49, p. 84.
7. See *Wiedergewonnen: Elfenbeinstücke aus Dresden* (exh. cat.), Deutsches Elfenbeinmuseum, Erbach, 1995.
8. See K. Maurice, *Der drechselnde Souverän: Materialien zu einer fürstlichen Maschinenkunst*, Zurich, 1985.
9. *Ibid.*, p. 33.
10. See L. Seelig, "'Silberzimmer' und 'Grünes Gewölbe'. Augsburger Goldschmiedekunst am Dresdner Hof Augusts des Starken," *Silber und Gold II: Augsburger Goldschmiedekunst für die Höfe Europas* (exh. cat.), BNM, 1994, pp. 472-493.
11. For the Green Vaults of 1723-1733 see J. Menzhausen, *Das Grüne Gewölbe*, Leipzig, 1968; Syndram, *Das Grüne Gewölbe . . . Führer, op. cit.*
12. *Lettres et mémoires de Charles Louis, Baron von Pöllnitz* (3rd ed.), 1734, p. 142 (1st ed., Amsterdam, 1727).
13. Syndram, *Prunkstücke, op. cit.*, p. 8.
14. W. Holzhausen, "Die Bronzen der kurfürstlich sächsischen Kunstkammer zu Dresden," *Jb. d. Preuss. Kstlgen.*, 54, 1934, pp. 86-118; "Die Bronzen Augusts des Starken in Dresden," *op. cit.*, 60, 1939, pp. 157-185.
15. Menzhausen, *op. cit.* (1977), p. 23.
16. E. von Watzdorf, *Johann Melchior Dinglinger* (2 vols.), Berlin, 1962.
17. *Ibid.*

The Brandenburg Kunstkammern, Berlin
1. See C. Theuerkauff, "The Brandenburg Kunstkammer in Berlin," in Impey and MacGregor, *op. cit.*, pp. 110-114; L. von Ledebur, "Geschichte der königlichen Kunstkammer in Berlin," *Allgemeines Archiv für die Geschichtskunde des Preussischen Staates*, 6, 1831.
2. C. Theuerkauff, et al., *Die Brandenburgisch-Preussische Kunstkammer: Eine Auswahl aus den alten Beständen* (exh. cat.), Staatliche Museen Preussischer Kulturbesitz, Berlin, 1981.
3. *Ibid.*, cat. 42.
4. Prinz Johann Georg von Hohenzollern, "Fürstliches Sammeln," *Friedrich der Grosse: Sammler und Mäzen* (exh. cat.), Kunsthalle der Hypo-Kulturstiftung, Munich, 1993, p. 29, cat. 49-52, 55-57, 66, 82-85, 87-139.
5. W. Baer, "Berliner Golddosen des Königs," *Friedrich der Grosse, op. cit.*, pp. 29ff., cat. 210-283.
6. For the visit of the merchant Henrich Carstens of Bremen, see Theuerkauff, et al., *op. cit*, p. 30.
7. J. Henry, *Allgemeines Verzeichnis des königlichen Kunst-, Naturhistorischen und Antiken-Museums*, Berlin, 1805; *Ibid*, p. 31.

The Kunstkammer of the Landgraves of Hessen/Kassel
8. F.A. Dreier, "Zur Geschichte der Kasseler Kunstkammer," *Zft. d. Ver. f. Hess. Gesch. u. Landeskunde*, 72, 1961; E.M. Link, *Die landgräfliche Kunstkammer Kassel*, 1975; F.A. Dreier, "The Kunstkammer of the Hessian Landgraves in Kassel," in Impey and MacGregor, *op. cit.*, pp. 102-109; see also Scheicher, *op. cit.*, pp. 198-199.
9. Schlosser, *op. cit.*, pp. 155-160, ill. 109; K.E. Demiandt, "Der spätmittelalterliche Silberschatz des hessischen Fürstenhauses," *Hessenland*, 50, 1939, pp. 21-31.
10. B. Stricker, "Die Wissenschaftlichen Bestrebungen des Landgrafen Wilhelm IV.," *Zft. d. Ver. f. Hess. Gesch. u. Landeskunde*,

67, 1956.
11. H.A. Lloyd,. *Some Outstanding Clocks over 700 Years*, London, 1958, pls. 52-57.
12. Maurice, *op. cit.* (1980), pp. 87-113.
13. *Ibid.*, p. 105.
14. J.J. Winckelmann, *Gründliche und wahrhafte Beschreibung der Fürstentuemer Hessen und Hersfeld*, Bremen, 1697, p. 281.
15. Dreier, "The Kunstkammer . . . ," *op cit.*, pl. 40
16. *Ibid.*, pl. 41.

Philipp Hainhofer and the Augsburg Kunstschrank
17. F. Blendinger, "Hainhofer (Ainhofer), Philipp," *Neue deutsche Biographie*, 7, Berlin, 1966, pp. 424-425; see also O. Döring, *Des Augsburger Patriziers Beziehungen zum Herzog Philipp II von Pommern-Stettin*, Vienna, 1894; R. Gobiet (ed.), *Der Briefwechsel zwischen Philipp Hainhofer und Herzog August d. J. von Braunschweig-Lüneburg* (*Forschungshefte, Bayer. Nat. Mus. Münch.*, 8), Munich/Berlin, 1984; C. Häutle, "Die Reisen des Augsburgers Philipp Hainhofer nach Eichstädt, München und Regensburg in den Jahren 1611, 1612, und 1613," *Zft. d. hist. Ver. f. Schwaben und Neuburg*, 1881, 8, pp. 55-148; Schlosser, *op. cit.*, pp. 187-190; D. Heikamp, "Reisemöbel aus dem Umkreis Phillip Hainhofers," *Anz. d. Germ. Nat. Mus. Nuernbg.*, 1966, pp. 91-102.
18. Quoted from H.-O. Boström, «Philipp Hainhofer and Gustavus Adolphus's *Kunstschrank* in Uppsala,» in Impey and MacGregor, *op. cit.*, p. 92
19. B. Volk-Knüttel, "Maximilian I. von Bayern als Sammler und Auftraggeber: Seine Korrespondenz mit Philipp Hainhofer 1611-1615," *Quell. u. Stud. z. Kunstpolitik der Wittelsbacher vom 16. bis zum 18. Jahrhundert* (*Mitt. des Hauses der Bayer. Gesch. I*), Munich/Zurich, 1980, pp. 83-98, 91. Quoted from Boström, *op. cit.*, p. 91.
20. D. Heikamp, "Zur Geschichte der Uffizien Tribuna und der Kunstschränke in Florenz und Deutschland," *Zft. f. Kg.*, 26, 1963, pp. 193-268.
21. O. Döring, "Des Augsburger Patriziers Philipp Hainhofer Reise nach Innsbruck und Dresden," *Quell. zur Kg.* (NF, 10), 1901, pp. 131-138.
22. J. Böttiger, *Philipp Hainhofer und der Kunstschrank Gustav Adolfs in Uppsala*, Stockholm, 1908; Boström, *op.cit.*, pp. 90-101.

The Royal Danish Collection
1. For an introduction see *Trésors des rois de Danemark* (exh. cat.), Petit Palais, Paris, 1979.
2. See S. Heiberg (ed.), *Christian IV and Europe* (exh. cat.), 19th Council of Europe, Denmark, 1988.
3. O. Eller, *Frederiksborg Museum*, Copenhagen, 1986.
4. See M. Bencard and J. Hein, *Rosenborg: De Danske Kongers Kronologiske Samling*, Copenhagen, 1982; M. Bencard, "A Note on the Rosenborg Collection in Copenhagen," in Impey and MacGregor, *op. cit.*, pp. 134-135; *Rosenborg Castle: A Guide to the Chronological Collection of the Danish Kings*, Copenhagen, 1981.
5. See *Rosenborg: De Danske Kongers Kronologiske Samling*, n.d., p. 67.
6. See H.D. Schepelern, "Natural Philosophers and Princely Collectors: Worm, Paludanus, and the Gottorp and Copenhagen Collections," in Impey and MacGregor, *op.*

cit., pp. 121-127.

7. See B. Gundestrup, *The Royal Danish Kunstkammer, 1737* (2 vols.), Nationalmuseet, Copenhagen, 1991; see also B. Gundestrup, "From the Royal Kunstkammer to the Modern Museums of Copenhagen," in Impey and MacGregor, *op. cit.*, pp. 128-133.
8. For another figure, this one of King Frederik III tilting at the ring (Copenhagen, 1654), see Gundestrup, *op. cit.* (1991), vol. 1, cat. 5.8, p. 214.
9. *Ibid.*, cat. 10.188, p. 232.
10. *Rosenborg*, n.d., p. 30. These Morra players once belonged to Karel van Mander, Danish court painter.

11. For 8 large portraits of East and West Indian natives painted by Albert Eckhout in 1641 and 1643, see Grundestrup, *op. cit.* (1991), vol. 2, pp. 125-133; see also vol. 1, pp. 84-85 for paintings of Eskimos dating from 1724.
12. *Ibid.*, vol. 2, cat. 10710, p. 166.
13. *Ibid.*, cat. 9084, p. 179; also vol. 1, cat. 9111, p. 174; cat. 9110 and 9112, p. 178
14. See *Trésors*, cat. 111.
15. See *Trésors*, *op. cit.*, cat. 71.

The Royal Swedish Lyvrustkammer and Treasury
16. See M. Robert, *The Early Vasas: A History of Sweden 1523-1617*, Cambridge, 1968.

17. S. Fogelmarck, *The Treasury* (exh. cat.), Royal Palace, Strangnas, 1970; E. Steingraeber (ed.), *Royal Treasures*, NY, 1969; M. Conforti and G. Walton (eds.), *Sweden: A Royal Treasury: 1550-1700* (exh. cat.), National Gallery, Wash., 1988-1989; O. Granberg, *Svenska konstsamlingarnas historia fran Gustav Vasas tid till vara dagar: 1: Gustav Vasa - Kristina*, Stockholm, 1930.
18. S. Fogelmark, *Die Schatzkammer: Reichskleinodien und Kostbarkeiten: Das Stockholmer Schloss*, 1974, cat. 3, 5.
19. *Ibid.*, cat. 4.
20. G. Masson, *Queen Christina*, London, 1968; S. Stolpe, *Christina of Sweden*, London, 1966; *Christina, Queen of Sweden* (exh.

cat.), Nationalmuseum, Stockholm, 1966.
21. Quoted from Fogelmarck, *op. cit.* (1974), p. 32: "*Songe aussi, ie vous prie, de me conserver et m'envoyer la bibliothèque et les raretés qui se trouvent à Prag; vous savez que ce sont les seules choses dont ie fais estime.*"
22. See *Christina, Queen of Sweden*, cat. 1037.
23. See O. Granberg, *La galerie de tableaux de la reine Christine de Suède ayant apartenu auparavant à l'Empereur Rodolphe II...* (abbr. French ed.), Stockholm, 1897.
24. *Christina, Queen of Sweden*, *op. cit.*, cat. 1043

Index

Photo Credits